Creative Meditation and Multi-Dimensional Consciousness

Creative Meditation and Multi-Dimensional Consciousness

by

Lama Anagarika Govinda
(Anangavajra Knamsum Wangchuk)

Published by Echo Point Books & Media
Brattleboro, Vermont
www.EchoPointBooks.com

All rights reserved.
Neither this work nor any portions thereof may be reproduced, stored in a retrieval system, or transmitted in any capacity without written permission from the publisher.

Copyright © 1976, 2024 by Lama Anagarika Govinda and
Li Gotami Govinda Stiftung

Creative Meditation and Multi-Dimensional Consciousness
ISBN: 978-1-64837-329-9 (casebound)
978-1-64837-330-5 (paperback)

Cover design by Kaitlyn Whitaker

CONTENTS

Foreword ix
Preface xvii
Pronunciation of Sanskrit Words xix

PART I

THE SPIRITUAL UNFOLDMENT OF BUDDHISM:

THE WAY FROM ITS DOCTRINAL FORMULATION TO ITS MEDITATIONAL INTEGRATION

1. The River of Living Tradition 2
2. The Dharma Theory 5
3. The Doctrine of Nonsubstantiality 8
4. The Way of Intuition and Universality 12
5. The Message of the Sixth Patriarch 17
6. Masters of the Mystic Path 22
7. Tantric Experience 28
8. Reason and Intuition 32
9. Concept and Actuality 37
10. The Transforming Power of Creative Imagination 41

PART II

THE BASIC ELEMENTS OF VAJRĀYANA MEDITATION

1. The Transformation of the Constituents of the Human Personality 46
2. The Four Symphonic Movements of Meditation 49
3. The Meaning of Gestures 54
4. Orientation, Color, and Time-Sequence in the Mandala 60
5. Mantras as Seals of Initiation and Symbols of Meditative Experience 66
6. Mantra as Primordial Sound and as Archetypal Word Symbol 70

7. Meaning of the Mantric Seed-Syllable "HRĪH" 76
8. Multidimensionality of Seed-Syllables (Bīja) 82
9. Multidimensionality of Mantric Formulas and
   Their Relationship to the Higher Psychic Centers   88
10. The Two Phases of Meditation and the Cakras
    of the Body-Mandala 94

PART III
MEDITATION AS DIRECT EXPERIENCE AND SPIRITUAL ATTITUDE

1. Polarity and Integration 100
2. The Inward Way 106
3. Body Consciousness 112
4. The Contemplation of Breath and the
   Meaning of Prāna 118
5. The Foundations of Mindfulness 125
6. The Fundamental Principles of Meditation 131
7. The Devotional Attitude in Meditation and Prayer .. 137

PART IV
ART AND MEDITATION

1. The Well of Life 150
2. Parallelism between Art and Meditation 151
3. The Problem of Subject and Object 156
4. Abstract Art 159
5. Symbolism of Elementary Forms and Colors 162
6. Cosmic Meditation 172

PART V
CONTEMPLATIVE THOUGHTS

1. Impermanence and Immortality 182
2. The Conquest of Death 187
3. The Mystery of Life 190
4. The Danger of Words 194
5. Eternity and Infinity 197
6. Analysis and Synthesis 200
7. Individuality and Universality 204

8. The Experience of Awe and the Sense of Wonder 208
9. Contemplative Zen Meditation and the
 Intellectual Attitude of Our Time 214
10. Religion and Science 218
11. The Creative Power of the Mind 221
12. Relativity of Perfection 225

PART VI

DIMENSIONS OF CONSCIOUSNESS

1. Logic and Symbol in the Multidimensional
 Conception of the Universe 230
2. The Conception of Space in Ancient Buddhist
 Art and Thought 236
3. Time and Space and the Problem of Free Will 248
4. The Mystery of Time 256
5. The Problem of Past and Future 267
6. The Two Aspects of Reality 278
 Index 291

DIAGRAMS AND ILLUSTRATIONS

Mudras	57
Mandala of Amitabha	80
The Four Movements of Mantric Sound	82
Basic Structure of the Mandala of the Five Dhyani-Buddhas	83
The Colors of the Five Wisdoms and Their Dhyani-Buddhas	88
Chief Mantras of the Tibetan Nyingma School	93
The Three Zones of the Psychic Centers of the Human Body	97
Figure in Meditation	123
Factors in Meditation	136
Becoming	172
Being	173
Dissolving	174
Turning Inwards	175
Unification	176
Birth of Happiness	177
Samadhi	178
Mandala (*The Sacred Circle*)	179

FOREWORD

When Lama Anagarika Govinda presented the work Creative Meditation and Multi-Dimensional Consciousness in 1976, it was enthusiastically received in Western Buddhist circles. John Blofeld, a well-known interpreter of Chinese spirituality, wrote: "This unique work is undoubtedly one of the most important books on Mahayana doctrine and its application to meditation ever to appear in the English language!"

Blofeld was particularly impressed by Govinda's ability of finding words for things that could hardly be said, such as the doctrine of identity of form and emptiness: "It presents with the utmost possible lucidity, not just the stages of meditative practice, but the underlying principles which have given rise to them; and, in so doing, clarifies concepts which have given rise to them; and, in so doing, clarifies concepts which I had previously thought just could not be made clear to people who have not as yet had those illuminating intuitive experiences that carry the mind beyond the realm of logic and intellectual thought."[1]

Many Western readers have felt that Govinda's texts lead them into the depths of Buddhist teachings and practices. The author's work leaves a significant impact on its audience due to various reasons. Firstly, it is evident that although the writer lived most of his life in Asia and became an Indian citizen, he was of Western descent. His concerns and questions about Buddhism were similar to those of a European. Secondly, he did not confine his thinking and meditation to one of the classical schools of Buddhism.

Buddhism has numerous schools with contradicting themes of teaching and practice. There are mutually exclusive definitions of the goal of Nirvāṇa. The Theravāda, widespread in South Asia, teaches that a person can only find liberation through his own efforts, while the Pure Land schools of China and Japan consider the help of a transcendent Buddha to be indispensable. In Zen, the beginner in meditation is told to sit with an empty mind; whereas in Vajrayāna, which is prevalent in Tibet, it is taught to visualize the images of Buddhas.

Govinda studied and practiced Theravāda for many years, then undertook an intensive practice of Vajrayāna. Later, he experienced Buddhism and the culture of China. He concluded that Buddhism reveals its deepest dimensions when viewed as a whole, and what originally

---

1 John Blofeld: "Creative Meditation and Multi-Dimensional Consciousness (Review)." In: *The International Buddhist Forum Quarterly* (September 1977), p. 77-81.

initiated the experience and teachings of the historical Buddha, cannot be reconstructed. According to him, one can get closer to the origin by taking everything that has developed from it over two and a half millennia seriously. Each school of Buddhism "has an equal claim to represent a true aspect of the teachings of Buddha and to having made a sincere effort to preserve as much as possible of the original words and thoughts of the Enlightened One."[2] The openness to all schools makes the meaning of each one clearer and allows the common origin to emerge beyond contradictory formulations and divergent cultural approaches.

This book expresses Govinda's inclusive attitude. He draws on motifs from Theravāda, Zen, and other Buddhist schools to represent meditation in Tantric Buddhism or Vajrayāna. Moreover, Govinda cites Western philosophers and scientists, and utilizes their beliefs to clarify his own perception. This method does not describe orthodox teachings of any scholastic tradition of Buddhism. It reflects insights gained by the author through his repeated spiritual journeys from West to East and vice versa. Therefore, he perceives the book as a bridge-building between cultures and "an incentive for others to cross the bridge in both directions," as he says in the foreword.

Govinda regards the book as "the fruit of a lifelong study and practice of contemplation and action in the spirit of Buddhism." This does not mean that he wrote it retrospectively in old age, in fact, the book came about over a course of half a century. He published the segments before and alongside his internationally acclaimed books, such as Fundamentals of Tibetan Mysticism and The Way of the White Clouds. They appeared in booklets or magazines; hence, the limited reach. About a decade before his death, he collated the material and enriched it with some new ideas. The result was not a usual non-fiction book, but a testimony based on his personal experience. In addition to essays, the author also uses poems and pictures to convey meditative experiences that cannot be expressed in abstract terms.

Even though the author worked on this book most of his life, he has barely mentioned his personal life in it. During his lifetime, he wanted to put the content in the foreground. From today's point of view, a few hints about the origin of the content in connection with Govinda's life can give an understanding of the book and its concerns.

The core and oldest part of the book consists of seven abstract paintings and poems entitled Cosmic Meditation,[3] that were created in Capri in the 1920s, when Govinda's name was Ernst Lothar Hoffmann. It was the tragic events of that era that brought the 22-year-old to this Italian island.

---

2 Part I, 1.
3 Part IV, 6.

FOREWORD

Hoffmann, born in 1898, had to serve as a soldier in World War I immediately after finishing school. He returned from frontline as he contracted tuberculosis in 1918. In the spring of 1919, he began studying mineralogy at the University of Freiburg in the Black Forest. His dream was to work in South America where his maternal family owned mines, but his health deteriorated and hampered his education. He had to move to a sanatorium in the Swiss mountains for therapy and care. As much as he could, he devoted himself to philosophy and religion, that interested him since school days.

At the age of fifteen, he had read Plato and Goethe excitedly. Through the works of Schopenhauer, he became aware of Buddhism. In 1916, at the age of 18, he started a manuscript comparing Christianity and Buddhism to reconcile Buddhist Nirvāṇa with the Christian concept of god in a pantheistic sense. The work, completed in the infirmary in autumn 1919, was published the following year as his first book. All this while, he turned away from his family's Protestantism and became inclined towards Buddhism.

He settled down in Capri after leaving sanatorium in 1902, like many Germans suffering from tuberculosis did as its climate promised healing. The 22-year-old was soon part of a colorful, artistic and spiritual scene on the Mediterranean island. He became friends with an American painter, Earl Brewster, through whom, he acquainted with writer D. H. Lawrence. Like Ernst Hoffmann, Brewster was deeply drawn to Buddhism. Inspired by conversations with his friend, who was twenty years senior to him, Hoffmann began rigorous meditation following instructions he found in the translated Pāli discourses of Buddha.

During this time, Hoffmann painted faithfully, which was synonymous with meditation for him: art tries "to reveal a higher reality by omitting all accidentals, thus raising the visible form to the value of a symbol, expressing a direct experience of life."[4] The abstract images in this book belonged to a trend that was two decades old. Since the turn of the century, Piet Mondrian, Wassily Kandinsky, Kasimir Malewitsch and František Kupka found their way to this style of art through spiritual impulses. Perhaps, Hoffmann got his inspiration for the abstract depiction of inner experiences from Joseph Anton Schneiderfranken, a painter who called himself Bô Yin Râ and met Govinda in Capri in 1922.

Hoffmann dedicates the first three pictures and poems[5] in this book to the Trimūrti idea of India's theistic tradition. Brahma, Vishnu and Shiva as creator, preserver and destroyer are depicted in Buddhist style in the poems: Brahma's creation appears as an urge to exist. Vishnu

---

4　Part IV, 2.
5　The three poems are first published in Ernst L. Hoffmann: *Rhythmische Aphorismen*. Dresden: Pandora-Verlag 1927.

does not maintain perfect existence, for being is always incomplete and incomprehensible. The third poem addresses Shiva in a prayer to liberate from fixed forms. Destruction is not threatening, but transience becomes an opportunity for change. The following four pictures and poems illustrate the stages of progressive deepening, which are also presented theoretically in this book.[6]

Meditating, painting, and the climate of Capri contributed to the fact that Ernst Hoffmann's illness gradually disappeared. He attended the University of Naples, engaged in archeology and with the Pāli language, in which the teachings of the Buddha are handed down. Eventually, he traveled all over the Mediterranean for a research project on prehistoric architecture, for which he received a grant from the German Archaeological Institute.

After eight years in Capri, his health improved. To devote himself entirely to the teaching and practice of Buddhism, he settled in Ceylon (today's Sri Lanka) in 1928. He studied Theravāda Abhidhamma philosophy. He soon gave up the idea of becoming a Buddhist monk because he felt the associated rules and prohibitions were restrictive. Later, he became an Anagārika, a "homeless person" living without ties and property. He liked the idea of freedom that this term expresses; hence, he adopted it as his first name when he naturalized in India a decade later. Upon ordination as Anagarika, he received the Buddhist name—Govinda.

In 1931, Govinda traveled to northern India, where encounters with Rabindranath Tagore and Tibetan Ngawang Kalsang had decisive influence on his career. Govinda found Tagore's personality close to his ideal version of creative versatility. The 1913 Nobel Prize winner for literature built a spiritual bridge between East and West as a poet, musician and painter. Tagore appointed Govinda as a teacher at the educational institution he founded in Shantiniketan, today's Visva-Bharati University, where he first taught European languages and later, Buddhist culture. His lectures on the symbolism of Buddhist architecture appeared in several book editions with a foreword by Tagore.[7]

Tibetan mystic Ngawang Kalsang (1866-1936), also known as Tomo Geshe, lived as a hermit in wilderness for many years before becoming the head of monasteries in southern Tibet and northern India. This lama of the Gelugpa tradition introduced Govinda to tantric meditation, where colors, forms, sounds (mantra), gestures and movements are important. This corresponded with the attitude of Govinda, who expressed meditative experiences through pictures and poems. The Basic Elements of Vajrayāna Meditation presented in Part II of this book are based on

---

6   Part III, 6.
7   For example *Some Aspects of Stupa Symbolism*. Allahabad & London: Kitabistan 1940.

Govinda's learnings from his time with Ngawang Kalsang and other Tibetan teachers.

Thereafter, Govinda commuted between Tagore's educational center and Darjeeling in the Eastern Himalayas, where a temple of his teacher was located. He also became active elsewhere in India in the 1930s. He taught Buddhist philosophy at Patna University.[8]

Govinda's paintings have been successfully exhibited in several places in India. The Museum of the City of Allahabad, today's Prayāgrāj, opened a Govinda Hall in 1938 with a permanent exhibition of his 90 paintings, Buddhist motifs, landscapes and abstracts. Owing to the controversy surrounding abstract paintings, Govinda gave lectures on art and meditation, which were published as a book in 1936. The corresponding contents form the basis of part IV in this book.

In 1938, after a long process, Govinda eventually became an Indian citizen against the reservations of British colonial authorities. After Hitler came to power in 1933, the opponent of National Socialism no longer wanted to be German. With his naturalization, he became one of the most prominent Indian Buddhists. Therefore, in 1940, he was asked to accompany the influential Chinese master Taixu (1890-1947) on his pilgrimage to the holy places of Buddhism in India.

The relationship with Taixu deepened Govinda's interest in Chinese Buddhism, which is also reflected in this book. In Part I, the section "The Message of the Sixth Patriarch" deserves a special mention: A creative and free life does not require erudition, but above all openness. He was not bothered about dogma or creation of a doctrinal edifice, which he thought were already more than enough. He wanted to inspire people to be open and spontaneous.

In the autumn of 1940, there was a tragic halt in Govinda's life. He was arrested by British military and interned for five years. Despite his British-Indian citizenship, he was treated like a German because of his origins. Petitions and protests being carried out became futile. For Govinda, who loved freedom, years of life in detention camp was the hardest phase of his life. Periods devoted to meditation and writing led to a phase of serious illness and despondency. When he was released at the end of the war, the world and India had changed drastically. Many of the earlier connections could not be resumed.

Govinda, who believed in flexibility and openness, changed his life fundamentally in this situation. In 1947, at the age of 49, he married Rati Petit (1906-1988). This Indian artist, whom he met in Shantiniketan before the war, adopted the name Li Gotami when she converted to Buddhism. Govinda went on expeditions to Tibet with his wife in 1947

---

8 Anagarika Govinda: *The Psychological Attitude of Early Buddhist Philosophy*. Readership Lectures. Patna: Patna University 1936-37.

and 1948. Their pilgrimage to the West Tibet became legendary, where they explored the temples in the deserted capital of Tsaparang and copied Buddhist frescoes to preserve the images for posterity.

In the years following the Tibet Expeditions, Govinda wrote some of the Contemplative Thoughts in Part V of this book. He also published in journals early drafts of the Philosophical Essays (Part VI) on space, time and free will in relation to meditation.

From the 1950s, Govinda and Li Gotami lived in seclusion in Kasar Devi near Almora in northern India, to devote themselves to meditation, work on their research in western Tibet, write and paint. At that time, the work Foundations of Tibetan Mysticism (1956), which was later translated into many languages, was written. It made Govinda famous in spiritual circles beyond India. In 1960, for example, he was invited to an interreligious congress in Venice as a representative of Buddhism, which dealt with the experience of prayer from the perspective of different traditions. Govinda returned to Europe for the first time in three decades. The final section of Part III, "The Devotional Attitude in Meditation and Prayer", is based on the lecture given in Venice. In the decades that followed, Govinda was invited to numerous talks and lectures.

In 1966, Govinda's book The Way of the White Clouds, which revolves around his personal experiences in Tibet, became a bestseller across the globe. In his books, Govinda has inspired many with the method of building bridges between Buddhist experiences and Western thinkers and poets such as Friedrich Nietzsche and Rainer Maria Rilke.

Govinda particularly valued two German thinkers whom he repeatedly quotes in this book. According to Ludwig Klages, reason drives us through soulless technology to the destruction of all life. Oswald Spengler, who saw the emergence of cultures as analogous to plants, thinks that the West withers at the end of a heyday. Here we can see an affinity with a teaching by the Buddha that mankind is in decline.[9]

Govinda saw this downfall as only one side of the coin. According to him, humanity stands at the crossroads "between spiritual freedom and material power, between the wisdom of the heart and the knowledge of the brain, between the dignity of the human individual and the herd-instinct of the mass, between faith in the higher destiny of man through inner development and the belief in material prosperity through an ever-increasing production of goods."[10] Everyone has the free choice between these two paths. Even if humanity took a wrong turn, individuals could still choose the right path.

In the Buddha's discourse mentioned above, minorities reject ethical decay and preserve old values. After the great decline, a new culture is built

---
9 Dīghanikāya 26.
10 Lama Anagarika Govinda: The Way of the White Clouds. London: Hutchinson 1966, p. xi.

based on the values they uphold. This is a millennia-long process that will enable the future appearance of the Buddha Maitreya. So, the other side of the coin is: Despite the downtrend at large, one can participate in an ascent. This does not happen in the fight against unstoppable processes, but in protecting what is valuable, for example, in insisting on being human amid transhumanistic tendencies. Consequently, Govinda valued not only Klages and Spengler, who saw the fall, but also Jean Gebser, Sri Aurobindo and Teilhard de Chardin for their confident visions of the future of mankind.

In the 1970s, when Govinda compiled these texts into the book Creative Meditation and often, only slightly revised them, few who received it enthusiastically suspected that the oldest contents went back to the 1920s. This shows the timelessness of the texts, which illuminate a wide range of insights related to meditation for those who are receptive.

The cosmopolitan Govinda spent the last years of his life in Mill Valley, California, where he died in 1985 after living a creatively rich life. Through his books, he still gives countless people impulses for a spiritual life.

Volker Zotz, the author of this introduction, is a philosopher and religious scholar. He taught and researched as a professor at European and Japanese universities. He was Lama Anagarika Govinda's student until his death in 1985 and is today his heir and administrator of the estate.

PREFACE

This is not a book to teach meditation or to lay down rules and techniques, it is rather the fruit of a lifelong study and practice of contemplation and action in the spirit of Buddhism against the background of contemporary problems of East and West alike.

I have been a citizen of two worlds, nourished by the great traditions of Western culture in my early youth, and sustained by the ancient and sacred traditions of the East, where I spent the greater part of my life.

It is hoped that this book will be a bridge between these two worlds, not a manual or a mere source of information, but an incentive for others to cross the bridge in both directions. It is not to convert anybody to one side of it, but to encourage others to continue the exploration in which I have been engaged—not for the sake of any final solution, but for the joy of knowing that there will be no end to the spiritual adventure of a creative life, which has its own reward in the act of going—not in that of arriving—like a journey that is undertaken in the spirit of a pilgrimage. We may have an aim and a direction, but if it is a true aim, its fulfillment lies in every step toward it. The way itself is the aim!

This reveals the paramount importance of the *way*, and since there is nothing that could be called the *only* way, it means that each human being must find his own way, because if he should imitate any other person's way, he could not be true to his own nature. This is one of the most important things to be kept in mind when we speak about meditation, and therefore a wise teacher is he who helps his pupil find himself and to discover his own way. A Guru who tries to impose his personality, his own way, and his own ideas upon the disciple violates the nature of his disciple. The true task of a Guru is to inspire and not merely to teach. It will then be left to the student to assimilate what is adequate to his nature and his understanding and what is useful to his spiritual growth. Thus his way is forming itself in the act of going. It is this act that carries in itself the aim and the inner direction.

PRONUNCIATION OF SANSKRIT WORDS

Vowels

The pronunciation of vowels corresponds to that of Italian or Spanish, except for the short *a* which sounds somewhat less open. There is also a marked difference between short and long vowels. The latter are marked by a line above the respective letter (ā, ī, ū). *C* and *e* are regarded as long vowels and, therefore, need no diacritical mark. ṛ is a semi-vowel, pronounced like a short *ri* with a rolled *r*.

Consonants

c corresponds to the English *ch*, as in "*ch*ur*ch*," *ch* to *ch-h* in "mat*ch-h*ead." *j* corresponds to the English *j-*, as in "*j*ar." ñ corresponds to the initial sound in "new," or the Spanish ñ, as in "mañana." ṁ nasalizes the preceding vowel, and is pronounced like the English *ng* in "lo*ng*," or as the humming after-sound of *m* in the mantric seed-syllable OM.

In all *aspirates* the *h* following the consonant is audibly pronounced. *th* should never be pronounced like the English *th*, but as two distinct sounds, like *t* and *h* in "ra*t-h*ole."

Similarly: *ph* like in "ta*p-h*ammer,"
dh like in "ma*d-h*ouse,"
kh like in "bloc*k-h*ead,"
jh like in "sle*dge-h*ammer."

The *cerebral* consonants ṭ, ṭh, ḍ, ḍh, ṇ require the tongue to be placed against the roof of the mouth, while in the case of *dentals* (*t, th, d, dh, n*) the tongue touches the teeth.

ś represents a sharp *palatal*, as a forceful pronounced *sh*.
ṣ is a soft *cerebral sh*.
s corresponds to a sharp *s* or *ss*, as in "cro*ss*."

Accent

In Indian languages the accent of a word generally lies on the long vowel (for instance *Ā'nanda, Tathā'gata, nikā'ya*). In words consisting of several syllables and short vowels, the third-last syllable carries the accent (*mȧṇḍala*; not mandála, as often heard). In words of three syllables, in which the first and third (*śȯn'yatā*; not śünyátä). In words of two syllables and short vowels the first syllable is accentuated (*vȧjra, dhȧrma, mȧntra,* in contrast to *vidyȧ, mudrȧ*).

PART I

THE SPIRITUAL UNFOLDMENT OF BUDDHISM:

THE WAY FROM ITS DOCTRINAL FORMULATION TO ITS MEDITATIONAL INTEGRATION

1

THE RIVER OF LIVING TRADITION

IN ORDER TO UNDERSTAND the spirit of Buddhism, as expressed in its sacred scriptures and in its meditational practices, we have to be familiar to some extent with the living stream of Buddhist tradition, as it has come down to us in unbroken continuity from the days of the Buddha, like a mighty river, flowing through many different climes and types of landscapes, in ever changing forms and aspects and ever growing volume;—and yet, the same river! But its sameness does not consist in the identity of its contents, its material elements, its momentary appearance, but in the continuity of its movement and its over-all direction. This sameness, however, can be understood only by those who are able to see the river as a whole, in fact, as an organic whole in constant movement—not as a static unit.

But it is just the latter which most students of Buddhism want to see. They are like a man who sees the river only at a particular point of its course, in a particular setting, or like one who meticulously examines a bucketful of its waters and analyzes its contents. They do not understand that Buddhism is not merely an intellectually formulated doctrine, proclaimed at a certain point in human history, but a movement (in the truest sense of the word) which—though it received its impetus from a single powerful historical personality—revealed its deepest nature in contact with different conditions and circumstances of human life and on ever new levels of human consciousness.

Instead of asking, "What did the Buddha teach?"—a question that can never be answered objectively and with certainty (since the Buddha did not leave any written records), except in the most general and superficial way, by reducing Buddhism to a few standard phrases and dry principles—it would be more fruitful to ask, "What was it that gave Buddhism the impetus to maintain its movement and its spiritual appeal through two-and-a-half milleniums up to the present day?" It is equally important to know under what conditions, under which cultural circumstances, the Buddha taught, and how far his teachings were reflected or modified by his contemporaries as well as by his later followers.

The Buddha's teachings were meant not only for the sixth century B.C.—though they were put into the language of his time and his country—but, according to the Buddha's own declaration, they conveyed a universal meaning, beyond caste, creed, or race, and expressed the laws of a timeless reality. This reality has to be rediscovered from generation to generation, from century to century—nay, from one civilization to another, and every single individual has to realize it by his own experience, in the depths of his own being.

What the Buddha taught did not consist only of what he spoke, but was represented by the totality of what he *was*, by the totality of his personality and his life, which became the deepest symbol of his message to the entire human race. So, the Buddhism that emerged was the gradual unfoldment of a tremendous spiritual impetus, released by the realization of a new dimension of consciousness, far beyond the power of human language and expression, but approachable through a reversal of our inner attitude, from a world of static concepts to the experience of a universe of fluid, interrelated forces and life forms, in which every individual partakes and which is reflected in the depth of human consciousness.

In order to approach this new dimension, old habits of thinking, based on unfounded beliefs and dogmas, had first of all to be overcome. For this reason the Buddha's message had to be formulated in the most convincing and logical language, in order to appeal to a human society just emerging from the age of magic and mythological thought and entering the realm of rational thinking, based on the recognition of the laws of causality and the interconnectedness of all natural and psychic phenomena. This formulation of the Buddha's message on the intellectual plane did not exhaust its meaning; it merely acted as a stimulant and a directive for the unfoldment of all those qualities which the Buddha had demonstrated through his own life and his realization of supreme enlightenment. It was the seed from which the mighty tree of Buddhist tradition grew through the centuries and the millenniums. This growth took ever new forms of expression, as different as the tree is from its seed, or the flower from the root, and yet the same in essence, reproducing the same seed from which it sprang, irrespective of time or place.

Thus, in spite of many differences in conception and formulation, even the comparatively later schools of Buddhism, like the Mahāyāna and the Vajrayāna, are built upon the teachings of the earliest known tradition. Already this was subdivided into many different schools, of which each had its own canonical scriptures. However, only one of these canons has survived and remained intact up to the present day, namely that of the Theravādins, the teachings of the Elders. The reason for their survival was their insular seclusion in Ceylon, on account of which they remained untouched by the spiritual and political revolutions on the mainland of India and the rest of Asia.

Until recently the West was mainly familiar with the texts of this school, so that—even among scholars—the conviction had been formed that Theravāda is the only authentic form of Buddhism, containing the actual words of the Buddha. We must remember, however, that not less than four centuries had passed, before the Pāli Canon was put down in writing. Even if we want to trust the Indian capacity to pass on faithfully the words of great religious leaders orally from Guru to Chela for centuries on end, we must not forget that words are not lifeless objects; they, like all living things, are subject to the law of change and possess many meanings and associations of a spiritual and emotional nature, so that people of different temperaments, different backgrounds, and different mentality —to say nothing of people belonging to different centuries— will associate different meanings, or only a certain aspect of the original meaning, with the same words.

This is evidenced by the fact that at the time the Theravāda Canon was fixed, eighteen different Buddhist schools had already come into existence. No conscientious and unprejudiced scholar can overlook this fact. Therefore we must give to each of the different traditions as much credence as we are willing to give to the Theravādins. Each of them has an equal claim to represent a true aspect of the teachings of the Buddha and to having made a sincere effort to preserve as much as possible of the original words and thoughts of the Enlightened One. Only in this way can we obtain a complete and genuine picture of Buddhist thought and experience which reveals the whole wealth of Buddhist culture and its application in life. Such a complete picture not only enriches our knowledge, but deepens the meaning and the importance of every single phase or school of Buddhism. Such a knowledge is as essential for the understanding of the Pāli scriptures of the Theravādins as for the other contemporary Hīnayāna Schools and the Mahāyāna, which finally took over the main stream of Buddhist tradition and carried it all over Southeast Asia, into the Far East and into Central Asia.

2

THE DHARMA THEORY

ONLY A DETAILED STUDY of the Dharma-theory in the scriptures of the Sarvāstivādins and of the Mahāyāna (Viññānavādins) made it possible to see the teachings of the Theravādins in their true perspective and to arrive at a deeper understanding of their philosophical and metaphysical foundations. The one-sided opinion of earlier scholars, that Buddhism is a purely rationalistic system without any metaphysical background—so to say floating in a kind of spiritual vacuum—represented the teachings of the Buddha as a cold intellectual doctrine, which fitted more into the European "Age of Reason" (which, by the way, coincided with the beginnings of Buddhist research work by Western scholars) than with a religion that inspired one third of humanity with hope and faith.

Helmuth von Glasenapp, who is well-known for his impartial works on the history of Buddhist thought, says:

> The fact that formerly nothing was known about the Dharma-theory, is the cause that many scholars missed a metaphysical foundation in the canonical discourses, and therefore declared the Buddha—according to their respective temperaments—as an agnostic or a mere teacher of ethics; or they deduced from his silence about God, soul and other concepts which contradict the Dharma-theory, a mystic secret doctrine about Ātman, etc.[1]

Even more outspoken is Glasenapp in another essay, in which he explains the Buddhist concept of *"dhammas"* (plural) —the Pāli version of the Sanskrit term *"dharmas"*—whose cooperation, according to their inherent law, brings about what we conceive as personality and the world experienced by it.

This is a concept whose fundamental importance for the Buddhist view of the world and its doctrine of salvation has been revealed only in the course of the last thirty years. Since the word "dhamma" (literally, the supporting element) has already in Pāli several meanings (universal law, righteousness, duty, property, object), one did not realize that besides these meanings, it is used in the Pāli Canon also as a terminal technicus for the ultimate irreducible factors, out of which everything is composed that we believe to perceive within and without ourselves. Since one had not understood this fundamental concept of Buddhist philosophy in its true significance, one could only appreciate the Buddha's ethical principles and his doctrine of liberation; however, one could not realize that the practical side of Buddhism has a theoretical foundation, a "philosophy of becoming," which is unique in the spiritual history of humanity, in so far as it explains everything that exists through the co-operation of only momentary existing forces, arising and disappearing in functional dependence of each other. Due to this Buddhism can renounce the concept of eternal substances (matter, soul, God) which in all other teachings form the supporting basis.[2]

Here we come to the core of the problem. What distinguished the Buddha from his contemporaries and raised him above the general spiritual attitude of his country was his perception of the dynamic nature of reality. The Four Noble Truths (consisting of the truth of suffering, of its origin, of its annihilation, and of the way leading to the annihilation of suffering), as well as the Eightfold Path toward liberation, form the general Indian framework of his teachings, but are not what gives Buddhism its specific character. When the Buddha put the anattā-idea into the center of his teaching, he took the decisive step from a static to a dynamic view of the world, from an emphasis on "being" to an emphasis on "becoming," from the concept of an unchangeable, permanent "I" (ego) to the realization of the interdependence of all forms and aspects of life and the capacity of the individual to grow beyond himself and his self-created limitations. Thus the insurmountable contrast between "I" and "world," "mind" and "matter," "substance" and "appearance," "the eternal" and "the impermanent," etc., was eliminated.

The doctrine of the Buddha is the antithesis of the concept of "substance," which has governed human thought for millenniums. Just as Einstein's theory of relativity influenced and changed the entire mode of modern thinking, in a similar way the anātman-idea of the Buddha caused a revolution in Indian thought. This is not to imply a negation of the religious principles of the past or a skeptical attitude toward metaphysical values; it was more in the nature of a revaluation of these ideas in the light of a profound experience and a new spiritual perspective. The Buddha never doubted the continuity of life beyond death, nor the existence and attainability of higher states of consciousness and existence of a moral law, nor that the universe was governed by equally strict and unalterable laws. Yet, the world in which he lived was for him not merely a material or mechanically determined phenomenon, but a manifestation of living and conscious forces. It was a world which was thoroughly alive with psychic forces in a way which is unimaginable to the people of our times. This becomes all too apparent in the "soulless" and equally uninspiring interpretation of Buddhism by modern Buddhists, who confuse the anātman idea with "soullessness," a term which conveys a totally wrong impression. How can we speak about Buddhist psychology without presupposeing a "psyche"?

The Buddha rejected the idea of an eternal, unchangeable soul-substance, existing as a separate entity or monad, but never denied the existence of consciously directed spiritual and psychic forces which, in spite of their constant flow and change of form and appearance, retained their continuity and organic unity. Man is not a mere mechanism of material elements or physical forces that have been thrown together by blind chance; he is a conscious organism, following its own inherent rules, in which individual tendencies and universal laws are in constant cooperation.

> It appears as if matter and psyche were merely the outer and the inner forms of appearance of the same consciousness-transcending reality, because the ultimate components of matter present themselves to our consciousness in similar form-structures like the ultimate or primordial ground of our innermost being, our universal depth-consciousness, which in Jungian

terminology is represented by (the rather unfortunate expression) "the collective Unconscious."[3]

References and Notes

[1] Helmuth von Glasenapp: *Zur Geschichte der buddhischen Dharmaforschung,* Zeitschrift der Deutschen Morgenlandsichen Gesselschat, Vol. 92 (neue Folge Vol. 17); 1938, p. 414.
[2] *Indische Welt,* Vol. 11, no. 3, 1951, p. 37f.
[3] Marie-Louise von Franz: *Zahl und Zeit,* Ernst Klett Verlag, Stuttgart, 1970, p. 245.

3

THE DOCTRINE OF NONSUBSTANTIALITY

THE BUDDHA FREED THE WORLD from its "thingishness" by opposing a dogmatically hardened and misunderstood "ātmavāda," which originally was born from an experience of inner reality--the living breath of the universe within us—but which in the course of time had frozen into the concept of an unchangeable individual self. The Buddha replaced the idea of an immutable, eternal soul monad incapable of growth and development, with the conception of a spiritual consciousness yearning for freedom and highest enlightenment and capable of attaining this supreme goal in the course of a continuous process of becoming and dissolving.

In this process of transformation we find not only the source of transience and suffering, but also the source of all spiritual life and growth. When the Buddha spoke about this suffering, it was not an outcome of pessimism or "Weltschmerz," but was due to the realization that unless we recognize the nature and cause of our suffering, which is only another word for our imperfection and our wrong attitude, we cannot make use of the tremendous potentialities of our mind and attain a state of perfect enlightenment that will reveal the universality of our innermost being.

This realization was not founded on logical conclusions, but on the Buddha's own experience in the attainment of illumination, in which he transcended the limitations of individuality by overcoming the illusion of egohood. This does not mean that his individuality was annihilated, but only that he did not mistake it any more as the essence of his being. He saw it as a vehicle, a necessary means to become conscious of his universality, the universality of the all-encompassing mind.

Looking back from this experience of highest reality and self-realization, the Enlightened One saw the world in a reversed perspective (reversed from the point of view of the ordinary man), namely in the perspective of the anātman idea: and lo! this apparently inescapable, solid and substantial world dissolved itself into a whirling nebulous mass of insubstantial, eternally rotating elements of continually arising and disintegrating forms. The momentariness of these elements of existence (*dharmas*) which make up the river of life and of all phenomena, make it impossible to apply to them the concepts "being" or "non-being."

> The world, O Kaccāna, is given to dualism, to the "it is" and the "it is not"! He, however, O Kaccāna, who has realized with perfect wisdom how things arise in this world, for him there is no "it is not" in the world. And he, O Kaccāna, who realizes with perfect wisdom how things disappear in this world, for him there is no "it is" in the world. (Pāli Canon: Samyutta Nikāya II, 17)

Being and non-being can be applied only to things or substances existing in themselves, i.e. to absolute units, as represented by our abstract concepts, but never to anything real or actual, because no thing and no being can exist in itself or for itself, but only in relationship to other things or beings, to conscious or unconscious forces of the universe. Concepts such as "identity" and "non-identity," therefore, lose their meaning. It was for this reason that the Sage Nāgasena answered King Milinda's question concerning whether the doer is identical with the reaper of the fruit of his action (be it in this or in a following life): "*Na ca so, na ca añño.*" ("He is neither the same, nor a different one.")

The Buddha, therefore, replaces the concepts of identity and non-identity (which both represent extremes of abstract thought) by the formula of Dependent and Simultaneous Origination (*pratītyasamutpāda*). This was much more than the proclamation of a scientific law of causation, as superficial observers maintained, in order to prove the similarity of the Buddha's idea to their own soulless and mechanistic world-view. Their causality presupposes a purely time-conditioned, unalterable sequence of events, i.e. a necessary and predictable course of action.

The *pratītyasamutpāda*, however, is not confined to a sequence in time, but can also be interpreted as a simultaneous cooperation of all its links, in so far as each of them represents the sum total of all the others, seen under a particular aspect. In other words: from the point of view of time and of the course of individual existence, i.e. from the mundane point of view, the formula of Dependent Origination can be interpreted causally, not however, from the standpoint of highest truth (*paramārtha satyā*).

The causal interpretation is to a certain extent a concession toward a more popular understanding, which requires a concrete example, related to actual life, and not a strictly logical, scientific formula. We, therefore, find even in Pāli texts no uniformity in the presentation of this formula, in which sometimes several links are left out, and where even the reversibility of the sequence of certain links has been pointed out. This is not due to lack of logical thinking, as some critics assume, but it shows that the originators of these different formulations wanted to demonstrate that they were not concerned with a strictly time-conditioned sequence of phenomena following each other with mechanical necessity. What they wanted to point out was the non-substantiality and relativity of all individual phenomena. None of them exists in its own nature, independent of all other factors of life. Therefore they are described as *sūnyam*: empty of self-nature, non-absolute.

But since no first beginning of any individual or of any inner or outer phenomena can be found, it means that each of them has the totality of the universe at its base. Or, if we want to express this from the standpoint of time, we could say that each of these phenomena, and especially every individual, has an infinite past and is, therefore, based on an infinity of relations, which do not and cannot exclude anything that ever existed or is liable to come into existence. All individuals (or rather all that has an individual existence) have, therefore, the whole universe as their common ground, and this universality becomes conscious in the experience of enlightenment, in which the individual awakens into his true all-embracing nature.

In order to become conscious of this all-encompassing nature, we have to empty ourselves from all conceptual thought and

DOCTRINE OF NONSUBSTANTIALITY

discriminating perception. This emptiness (śūnyatā) is not a negative property, but a state of freedom from impediments and limitations, a state of spontaneous receptivity, in which we open ourselves to the all-inclusive reality of a higher dimension. Here we realize the śūnyatā, which forms the central concept of the Prajñā-pāramitā Sūtra. Far from being the expression of a nihilistic philosophy which denies all reality, it is the logical consequence of the anātman doctrine of nonsubstantiality. Śūnyatā is the emptiness of all conceptual designations and at the same time the recognition of a higher, incommensurable and indefinable reality, which can be experienced only in the state of perfect enlightenment.

While we are able to come to an understanding of relativity by way of reasoning, the experience of universality and completeness can be attained only when all conceptual thought (kalpana), all word-thinking, has come to rest. The realization of the teachings of the Prajñā-pāramitā Sūtra can come about only on the path of meditative practice (yogācāra), through a transformation of our consciousness. Meditation in this sense is, therefore, no more a search after intellectual solutions or an analysis of worldly phenomena with worldly means—which would merely be a moving around in circles—but a breaking out from this circle, an abandoning of our thought-habits in order "to reach the other shore" (as it has been said not only in the Prajñā-pāramitā-hridaya, but also in the ancient Sutta Nipāta of the Pāli Canon). This requires a complete reversal of our outlook, a complete spiritual transformation or, as the Lankāvatāra Sūtra expresses it, "a turning about in the deepest seat of our consciousness." This reversal brings about a new spiritual outlook, similar to that which the Buddha experienced when returning from the Tree of Enlightenment. A new dimension of consciousness is being opened by this experience, which transcends the limits of mundane thought.

The exploration of this consciousness, which goes beyond the boundaries of individual existence, is the special merit of the Vijñānavādins or Yogācārins, as they were also called, because they were not content merely with a theoretical exploration but regarded practical experience as the only legitimate way for the acquisition of true knowledge. For them not the thought process but the consciousness itself is the ultimate judge of reality; and the deeper we descend into this reality, the clearer will its true nature reveal itself—a nature before which all words turn back, because only negations such as "infinity," "timelessness," "emptiness," and the like, can hint at the enormity of this experience.

In the universality of this primordial ground of consciousness the *Vijñānavādins* discovered the source of all forms of existence, their dependent origination and transformation, and also their coming to rest in the state of perfect enlightenment.

4

THE WAY OF INTUITION AND UNIVERSALITY

IF WE WANT TO GIVE CREDENCE to the early scriptures of Buddhism which without exception agree in their description of the Buddha's enlightenment, we can have no doubt that here we are confronted with an experience of such all-embracing universality that all limitations of time and space are transcended, and with them the illusion of the substantiality of our empirical world and of our separate egohood.

Recognizing this experience as the real starting point of Buddhism and not only as a distant, more or less theoretical aim or ideal, more and more Buddhists turned from the intellectual, scholastic, or mainly philosophical and epistemological formulations to the universal message conveyed through the very life and figure of the Buddha. He was the embodiment and symbol of one who had awakened to the ultimate reality of his own being, through creative meditation, in which all conceptual thought and ratiocination were swept away in the tremendous vision of the real nature of the Mind that encompasses both the individual and the universe. It became evident that what the Buddha taught was more than the words and concepts of a single period of human history could express, because it was an attitude of heart and mind, a creative direction of thought, and an aspiration toward the highest fulfillment of all faculties of the human being by way of various meditational practices.

Just as the laying down of the first principles of mathematical thought (as in geometry, arithmetic, and algebra) or the principles of scientific thinking contained the seeds of all further exploration and knowledge, without contradicting the vastly more complex discoveries and results of later times, and without being made superfluous by them, the early formulations of Buddhism confined themselves to the principles and methods on which the unfoldment of the human mind could depend, without imprisoning them in dogmatic assertations which would have to be accepted without any chance of verification. Thus word and concept, and all purely doctrinal, ethical, or philosophical formulations, receded behind the language of archetypal symbols, the visions of inner experience, and meditative realization (*dhyāna*).

While in India, and later in Tibet, this resulted (besides the mainstream of the Yogācārins) in the spiritual revolution of the Mahāsiddhas, (the Masters of the Mystic Path, who abandoned the monastic institutions in order to devote themselves entirely to a life of meditation and a new kind of *sādhana* or contemplative practice, from which the Tantras originated). Then an equally powerful meditative movement arose, in the Far Eastern countries of Buddhism, in the form of the Dhyāna School of China, known as *Ch'an,* and its Japanese equivalent, *Zen.*

The followers of *Ch'an* and *Zen,* as well as those of the Siddhas, tried to go back to the very origin of Buddhist tradition by insisting on the spontaneity and the essential qualities of the human mind. Basically this is not different from the teaching of the Buddha, if only we can free it from the cobwebs of habitual thought and prejudice. They maintain that we have to replace book knowledge by direct experience, scholarliness by intuition, and the historical Buddha by the Buddha within us, i.e. by the awakening of the potentialities of our own mind, which will lead to the realization of perfect enlightenment.

This was a courageous attempt. Such an approach requires complete self-dedication and surrender of one's whole being, without reservations, without holding back anything to which the ego can cling. It is like playing "va banque" on the spiritual plane, a game in which one may gain or lose everything; to miss the aim even by a hairsbreadth is equal to being worlds apart from it. The Ch'an practice has, therefore, been compared to a leap into a bottomless abyss, with a letting go of all familiar ideas and prejudices. The precipice is the unfathomable depth of our own consciousness, which yawns beyond the narrow circle of our egocentric world of illusions. In order to find the courage to leap into the depths, we require a certain inner preparation and a spiritual stimulus strong enough to enable us to take the risk. Unless the mind has become mature enough to recognize or to become aware of its own depths, there will be no urge to explore them and no faith in the final result of the daring undertaking. It is here that the faith in the Buddha as one who has gone this way (this is the meaning of the appellation Tathāgata) comes in, a faith that is justified by the result and the example of his life and the lasting effect it had on all who followed him. But unless we are ready to take the risks which the Buddha took, when he set out on his lonely way to enlightenment in the forest of Uruvela, nothing can be gained. Those who feel content in their ignorance or in their limited knowledge will have no inclination to take the risk, either because they have not yet reached the point where the problem begins or because they trust the flimsy superstructure of their logical speculations under which the problem has been buried. The former know nothing of the gaping abyss; the latter believe they can bridge it intellectually.

The follower of Ch'an or Zen, however, knows that all logical and philosophical solutions and definitions are limited and one-sided, because reality lies beyond all contradictory, mutually exclusive pairs of opposites with which our two-dimensional logic operates. He, therefore, uses his thought activity only as a means of becoming conscious of the unthinkable and to realize the problematic character of the world and the mystery of his own existence, without expecting solutions which go beyond the limited nature of his intellect. He, therefore, tries to avoid ready-made mental associations and judgments and endeavors to remain in a state of pure contemplation, seeing things as if he were perceiving for the first time, spontaneously, without prejudice, free from likes or dislikes.

Then everything will turn into a wonder and become a door to the great mystery of life, behind which the wealth of the whole universe is hidden, together with the Great Emptiness (śūnyatā) which makes this plenitude possible. This may frighten us, because it is so inconceivable to our senses and appears so abysmal to our ego-centered consciousness, bent as the latter is on maintaining its own identity. If we could give up this egocentric, discriminating, and dissecting attitude of our intellect even for one moment, the true nature of all things would manifest themselves "like the sun that rises through empty space and illuminates the whole universe unhindered and without limits." In other words, as soon as we succeed in silencing the restless activity of the intellect and give a chance to intuition, the pure all-embracing spirit in us will manifest itself.

We need not shun sense activities or the perception of sense objects, but only our ego-conditioned judgments and attitudes. We must understand that the true spirit (the universal depth-consciousness) expresses itself in these perceptions and sense activities without being dependent on them. One should not form judgments on the ground of such perceptions, nor should one allow one's thoughts to be determined and led by them. And yet one should abstain from imagining the universal consciousness as something separate from them or renouncing them in the pursuance of what one imagines to be religious aims. (This is why asceticism was rejected by the Buddha and replaced by control, not by suppression of the senses.) One should neither cling to them, nor renounce them, neither dwell upon them, nor reject them; but one should remain independent of everything that is either above or below or around us. There is no place in which Ch'an (the way of inner vision—*dhyāna*) cannot be practiced, because it is not concerned with an ascetic negation of the senses or the material world as conceived by the senses, but with the gaining of a deeper, wider, more universal consciousness, which comprises both sides of reality: the finite and the infinite, the material and the immaterial, mind and matter, form and the formless, the impermanent and the eternal, the conditioned and the unconditioned.

The more and the longer we can abstain from seeing things habitually, the more we shall realize their inconceivable, essentially unlimited (because universally conditioned and interrelated) nature. Habit kills intuition, because habit prevents living experience, direct perception. When our thinking has advanced to the point where the existential problem arises, we should not allow ourselves to be satisfied with intellectual solutions or lose ourselves in the pursuance of facts and figures, proofs and abstract truths, which are incontrovertible but have no bearing on life or which—as in the case of science—create more problems than they can solve. Nevertheless, we should have the courage to penetrate to the very limits of thought, where words become paradoxes and logic turns against itself.

In the moment we open our inner eye—instead of looking outward into a world of apparent material reality—illusion disappears and we suddenly become aware of true reality. This is why the Dhyāna School speaks of "sudden enlightenment." It is a reversal of our perspective, a new orientation which leads to a readjustment of all values. Due to this, the world of sense perception loses all its absoluteness and substantiality and takes its rightful place in the order of relative and time-conditioned phenomena. Here begins the path of the Buddha, the path toward realization of Buddhahood within ourselves, as represented by the main meditation schools of Mahāyāna Buddhism.

Meditation was always the main requisite of the Buddhist doctrine of liberation. However, the more the different techniques of meditation, their psychological definitions and their metaphysical and philosophical principles were explained, classified, and fixed in commentaries and subcommentaries, the more the practice of meditation was neglected and suffocated by theoretical discussions, moral rules and regulations, and endless recitations of sacred texts. The reaction was a revolt against scriptures and learnedness and a return to a more spontaneous and direct experience. The pedantry of scholastic thought and intellectual logic was countered by the weapon of the paradox which, like a sharp sword, cut through the knots of artificially created problems with the speed of a flash of lightning which gives us a glimpse of the true nature of things. The paradox, however, is a double-edged sword. As soon as it becomes a matter of routine, it destroys the very thing it has helped to reveal. The force of a paradox, like that of a sword, lies in the unexpectedness and speed with which it is handled; otherwise it is no better than the knife in the hand of a butcher.

A fine example of this is the story of two Chinese monks who had a dispute about a flag moving in the wind. The one maintained that the flag was moving; the other, that it was the wind that moved. Hui-Neng, the Sixth Patriarch in China, who overheard their discussion, said: "Neither the wind nor the flag is moving, your mind moves." But Mummon, a Japanese Patriarch of the thirteenth century, not satisfied with this answer, went one step further and said: "Neither the wind, nor the flag, nor the mind is moving," thus going back to the ultimate principle of *śūnyatā*, in which there is neither going nor coming, but in which both subjective and objective aspects of reality are included.

This reality beyond the opposites, however, is not to be separated or abstracted from its exponents; the momentariness is not to be distinguished from eternity. The most perfect individual self-expression is the most objective description of the world. The greatest artist is he who expresses what is felt by everybody. But how does he do it? By being more subjective than others. The more he expresses *himself*, i.e. his innermost being, the nearer he comes to others. Our real nature is not our imaginary, limited ego; it is vast, all-comprehensive, and intangible as empty space. It is *śūnyatā* in its deepest sense. The secret of art is that it reveals the supra-individual through individuality, the "not-self" through the "self," the object through the subject. Art in itself is a kind of paradox, and that is why all meditative schools of Buddhism in the Far East, as well as in Tibet and its dependencies, give it such great importance.

5

THE MESSAGE OF THE SIXTH PATRIARCH

As AN EXAMPLE for the ideal use of paradoxes, we may mention the Sūtra of the Sixth Patriarch. He succeeded in expressing the spiritual attitude of Ch'an in a way which neither offends our common sense nor attempts to make common sense the measure of all things. The reader of this scripture is introduced at the very beginning into the right atmosphere, which enables him to rise from the plane of his everyday consciousness to spontaneous participation in the reality of a higher level of consciousness. The figure of the Sixth Patriarch impresses one by his natural spontaneity, which should be inherent in every human being and with which the unprejudiced reader can easily identify himself. In this way he is able to participate inwardly in the experiences and teachings of the Sixth Patriarch, whose very life has become the symbol of Ch'an Buddhism at its best.

The novice of Kwang-tung, whose mind was not yet burdened by any philosophical problem, penetrated spontaneously into the center of spiritual life: the experience of Buddahood. This experience does not depend on monastic rules and learnedness, on asceticism and virtuousness, on book knowledge and the recitation of sacred texts, but only on the realization of the living spirit within us.

The Sixth Patriarch attained to a state of spontaneous enlightenment without having had any formal education or book knowledge, though on the other hand it was through listening to the recitation of the Diamond Sūtra that his interest was aroused and his spiritual eye was opened. Spontaneous experience, therefore, can very well be the product of an ancient hallowed tradition, if this tradition contains symbols of a supramental reality (modern psychology would call them "archetypal symbols") or formulations which lead the mind beyond the narrow circle of mundane reasoning. In the unexpected clash between a sensitive mind and such symbols and formulations, the doors of inner perception are suddenly opened and the individual is enabled to identify himself with this supramental reality contained in those mysterious formulations and symbols.

The Sixth Patriarch came from a good but impoverished family in Kwang-tung. One day, while he was selling firewood on the market of Kanton, he listened to the recitation of the Diamond Sūtra, and this aroused such a deep response in him that he decided to enter a monastery of the Ch'an School, whose abbot was the Fifth Patriarch. He became a novice there, and as such he was given the lowliest work in the monastery's stable and kitchen. One day the abbot called up all his disciples in order to choose a successor. As he wanted to be sure to select a worthy successor, one who had not only understood but had realized the message of Ch'an, he asked the assembled monks to write a stanza about the innermost nature of the mind. However, nobody dared to come forward, with the exception of the learned Shin-shau, whom everybody already regarded as the successor of the Fifth Patriarch. He wrote his verse on the wall of the corridor, in order to find out the opinion of the Patriarch and to announce his authorship only if the Patriarch was pleased with the stanza. The Patriarch, however, though he praised the lines, asked Shin-shau to meditate upon them for a few more days and then to write another stanza which showed that its author had passed through the "gate of enlightenment"—in other words, that he had really experienced what he wrote about.

Two days later it happened that a young man, who passed by the room in which the young novice from Kwang-tung was husking rice, recited aloud the stanza of Shin-shau. The novice, thereupon, went into the corridor where Shin-shau had written his stanza and asked a visitor, whom he happened to meet there, to read the verse for him, since he himself could neither read nor write. After the visitor had read out the verse to him, the novice said that he too had composed a stanza, and he asked the visitor to write it under the lines of Shin-shau.

When the other monks saw the new stanza, they were filled with wonder, and when they found out who had composed it, they said to each other: "How was it possible that we allowed such an enlightened person to work for us?" The Patriarch, however, fearing the jealousy of the other monks, who might harm the novice if they knew that he was to become the Patriarch's successor, erased the stanza with one of his straw-sandals and asked the young man to call on him during the night. When everybody in the monastery was deep asleep, he gave the novice the insignia of his future office and made him the Sixth Patriarch. He then bade him to leave the monastery at once and to return only after he, the Fifth Patriarch, had passed away. The novice did as he was told, and when he returned with the robes of office, he was recognized as the Sixth Patriarch under the name of Wei-lang.

Let us now consider the stanzas of Shin-shau and those of the Sixth Patriarch, because they give us a valuable insight into the mental attitude of the Ch'an School. The stanza of Shin-shau ran:

> Our body is like a bodhi-tree,
> Our mind is like a clear mirror;
> From hour to hour it must be cleansed,
> So that no dust can collect upon it.

This verse shows not only a pedantic concern for the preservation of the purity of the "inner mirror," the Original Mind (which is at any rate beyond "purity" and "impurity"), but apart from this it shows that the author of this stanza does not speak from his own experience, but only as a man of letters, because the verse is based on a saying in the Svetasvatara Upanishad:

> Just as a mirror, that was covered with dust,
> Shines forth like fire, if it is cleansed,
> In the same way will he, who has realized the nature
>   of the soul,
> Attain the goal and liberate himself from grief!

Thus Shin-shau was only repeating the standpoint of the Upanishads, without having experienced the reality of the Original Mind, while the young novice, who had grasped the quintessence of the Diamond Sūtra in an act of direct perception, had experienced in that moment the true nature of the mind. This is shown by his stanza, which at the same time rejects that of Shin-shau by revealing the Buddhist point of view as understood by the masters of Ch'an:

> The Bodhi is not a tree at all,
> Nor is the mind a case of mirrors.
> When everything is empty,
> Where could the dust collect?

The Original Mind, realized as the "Buddha Mind" or the principle of *bodhi,* the urge for enlightenment, which is a latent property of every consciousness, is not only a reflection of the universe—something that "mirrors" the universe—but it is the universal reality itself. To the limited intellect it can only appear as a kind of metaphysical emptiness, the absence of all qualities and possibilities of definition. *Bodhi* is, therefore, not something that has originated or grown like a tree; neither is the mind a mere mirror which only reflects reality in a secondary capacity. Since the mind itself is the all-encompassing emptiness (*śūnyatā*), where could dust ever collect? "The essence of the mind it great, we say, because it embraces all things, for all things are of our nature." Thus it is not a question of improving or of cleansing our mind, but of becoming conscious of its universality. What we can improve is our intellect, our limited individual consciousness. This however, can never lead us beyond its own limits, because we remain in the strictly circumscribed circle of its inherent laws (of time and space, of logic and causality). Only the leap across the boundary, the giving up of all those contents which fetter us to those laws, can give us the experience of the totality of the spirit and the realization of its true nature, which is what we call Enlightenment.

The true nature of our mind embraces all that lives. The Bodhisattva-vow to free all living beings is therefore not so presumptuous as it sounds. It is not born from the illusion that a mortal man could set himself up as the savior of all beings or the redeemer of the whole world, but it is an outcome of the realization that only in the state of enlightenment shall we be able to become one with all that lives. In this act of unification we liberate ourselves and all living beings, which are potentially present and take part in the nature of our mind—nay, who are part of our mind in the deepest sense.

This is the reason why, according to the teachings of the Mahāyāna, the liberation from one's own sufferings, the mere extinction of the will to live and of all desires, is regarded as insufficient, and why the striving after perfect enlightenment (*samyak-sambodhi*) is considered the only goal worthy of a follower of the Buddha. As long as we despise the world and merely try to escape from it, we have neither overcome it nor mastered it and are far from having attained liberation. Therefore it is said: "This world is the Buddha-world, within which enlightenment can be found. To search after enlightenment by separating oneself from the world is as foolish as searching for the horn of a hare." For: "He who treads earnestly the path of the world, will not see the faults of the world."

In a similar way we should not imagine that by the suppression of thought or of our intellectual faculties, we can attain enlightenment. "It is a great mistake to suppress all thought," says Wei Lang, the Sixth Patriarch. Ch'an is the way to overcome the limitations of our intellectual attitude. But first we must have developed our intellect, our capacity to think, to reason and to discern, before we are able to appreciate Ch'an. If we had no intellect, i.e. if we had never developed and mastered it, we could not overcome or go beyond it; only what we master is really our own. The intellect is as necessary for the overcoming of mere emotionality and muddleheadedness as intuition is necessary for overcoming the limitations of the intellect and its discriminations.

Reason, the highest property of the intellect, is what guides our purposive thought. Purposes, however, are limited; and therefore reason can operate only in what is limited. Wisdom (*prajña*) alone can accept and intuitively realize the unlimited, the timeless and the infinite, by renouncing explanations and by recognizing the mystery, which can only be felt, experienced, and finally realized in life—and which can never be defined. Wisdom has its roots in experience, in the realization of our innermost being. Reason has its roots in thought. Yet, wisdom will not despise either thought or reason, but will use them where they belong, namely in the realm of purposeful action, as well as for the pursuit of science and for coordinating our sense impressions, perceptions, sensations, feelings, and emotions into a meaningful whole.

Here the creative side of our thought comes into play, converting the raw material of experience into the perception of a reasonable world. How big or how small this world is, depends on the creative faculty of the individual mind. The small mind lives in the world of his ephemeral wants and desires, the great mind in the infinity of the universe and in the constant awareness of that fathomless mystery which gives depth and width to his life and thus prevents him from mistaking his sense world for ultimate reality. He, however, who has penetrated to the limits of thought, dares to take the leap into the Great Emptiness, the primordial ground of his own boundless being.

6

MASTERS OF THE MYSTIC PATH

WHEN RELIGION GROWS OLD, faith turns into dogma, experience is replaced by book knowledge, virtue by adherence to rules, devotion by ritualism, meditation by metaphysical speculation, and wisdom by scholasticism. The time is then ripe for another "existential leap," for a rediscovery of truth and a fresh attempt to give it expression in life.

This is what happened in the sixth century B.C., when the Buddha revived Indian religious experience through the rediscovery of the "ancient Dharma" (as the Buddha himself called his teaching) that ran like an underground stream through the pre-Vedic traditions, Shramanas or wandering ascetics of various kinds, and found expression in the nontheistic teachings of Yoga, Sāmkhya, and Jainism. It was a Dharma, a religious attitude, that was based neither on sacrifices (*yajñā*), nor on caste distinctions (*varṇa*), nor on the worship of powerful gods, but on self-discipline and meditation (*yoga* and *bhāvanā*); it was rooted in ethical values (*śila*), compassion (*karuṇā*) and respect for life (*ahimsa*), the dignity of the individual, irrespective of caste and responsible for his own deeds (*karma*), instead of being dependent on the whims of external powers (*devas*), who had to be placated by bloody sacrifices and priestly rituals. At the same time the Buddha realized that it is not the results of human thinking, the ideas, beliefs, and formulas or the conceptual knowledge that matters, but rather the way, the method that leads to the results, the spiritual attitude behind them.

Again, a millennium later, Buddhism had crystallized into so many philosophical schools and monastic institutions that the individual was in danger of getting lost in them, like a lone seafarer in the immensity of the ocean. Thus, a new urge for the certainty of direct experience sprang up, an urge to come in touch again with the reality of life as well as with its source.

> That is the certainty that the meaning of existence is open and accessible in the actual lived concrete, not above the struggle with reality, but *in* it. That meaning is open and accessible in the actually lived concrete does not mean that it is to be won and possessed through any type of analytical or synthetic investigation or through any type of reflection upon the lived concrete. Meaning is to be experienced in living action and suffering itself, in the unreduced immediacy of the moment.

In search of this certainty and immediacy of experience, monks left their monasteries, laymen their families, kings their palaces, and scholars their teaching chairs. Some became wandering ascetics or forest dwellers, others devoted themselves to a meditative life, while continuing their ordinary occupations. But all of them discarded the distinctions between clergy and laity, monkhood and householders' life; they recognized neither caste nor social positions and devoted themselves wholeheartedly to the exploration of the ultimate ground of reality by taking that "existential leap" into the depth of their own fathomless being. After they had attained realization they became spiritual teachers, inspirers, poets, and singers, who left behind them many pupils as well as written records of their lives and teachings, their songs and sayings. They were masters of the mystic path of self-realization and therefore known as *Siddhas,* Accomplished Ones.

They preferred the paradox to logical formulations and laid more stress on the spirit of inquiry than on intellectual solutions. Their lives were often as paradoxical as their sayings, because they despised all conventional values and used a symbolical language, in which the highest was expressed in terms of the lowest, the most sacred in profane language, inner experiences in terms of outer events. In this they revealed a trend similar to that of the followers of Ch'an and Zen Buddhism, though their meditational methods, their training and their background were vastly different from those of the Far East. And yet, all of them go back to the same origin, the conception of *śūnyatā* and the recognition of the ultimate importance of the intuitive mind.

Paradoxes, like humor, are greatly dependent on the soil in which they grow. Thus, there is a marked difference between the paradoxes which we find in the stories of the Indian Buddhist Siddhas and those of the Ch'an Masters in China and their followers in Japan. In the stories of the Siddhas the paradoxes take either the form of the miraculous, in which inner experiences are symbolized, or they show that the very thing by which man falls can be the cause by which he may rise up; that a weakness can be turned into strength, a fault into an asset, if only we are able to look at ourselves as at a stranger, without bias and prejudice, and upon the world around us as if we had never seen it before.

We are blind to reality because we have become so accustomed to our surroundings and to ourselves that we are no longer aware of them. Once we break the fetters of habit by the power of a paradoxical situation, or by a flash of intuition, everything becomes a revelation and everyday life turns into a wonder. In the stories of the Siddhas this wondrous experience which follows the great spiritual change is symbolized by miracles and the attainment of extraordinary psychic powers (*siddhi*). In Ch'an or Zen Buddhism, with its refined psychology, the scene of activity is entirely located in the human mind, and the paradoxes are of a more complex nature.

Probably it was this difference in treatment and style which prevented even serious students of Buddhism from recognizing the inner relationship between the traditions of Ch'an (Zen) and Siddhas, though thousands of miles and hundreds of years may have separated them.

The following story, which might aptly be entitled "The Man Who Met with Himself," may serve as an example. It is found in the Tibetan biographies of the Eighty-Four Siddhas (*Grub-thob brgyad-cu-rtsa-bźihi rnam-thar*), who flourished between the seventh and the eleventh century A.D.

The story runs as follows: There was once a hunter, called Savari. He was very proud of his strength and his marksmanship. The killing of animals was his sole occupation, and this made his life one single sin.

One day, while he was out hunting, he saw a stranger, apparently a hunter, approaching him from afar. "Who dares to hunt in my territory?" he thought indignantly. As he approached the stranger, he found the latter was not only as big and sturdy as himself, but—what surprised him still more—looked exactly like him!

"Who are you?" he demanded sternly.

"I am a hunter," said the stranger, unperturbed.

"Your name?"

"Savari."

"How is that?" the hunter exclaimed. "My name too is Savari! Where do you come from?"

"From a distant country," the stranger said evasively.

Savari regained his self-confidence and, trying to impress the stranger, he asked:: "Can you kill more than one deer with the shot of a single arrow?"

"I can kill three hundred with one shot," the stranger answered. This sounded to Savari like tall talk, and he wished only for an opportunity to expose his rival's ridiculous claim.

However, the stranger—who was none other than the Bodhisattva Avalokiteśvara, who had assumed this shape, because he felt pity for Savari—immediately created a herd of five hundred deer through his magic power.

Savari, who was delighted when he saw the deer emerge from the forest at not too great a distance, asked gleefully: "Will your arrow be able to go through all those deer?"

"It will go through all five hundred!" the stranger replied; but Savari suggested: "Let your arrow miss four hundred and kill one hundred only."

The stranger accomplished this feat with the greatest ease, but now Savari began to disbelieve his eyes.

"Fetch one of the deer," said the stranger, "if you have any doubt." And Savari went, as he was told.

But, alas! When he tried to lift one of the deer, he found it so heavy that he could not move it from the spot.

"What?" exclaimed the stranger, "You, a great hunter, cannot even lift a deer!" And he laughed heartily.

Now the hunter's pride was completely broken. He fell at the stranger's feet and asked him to be his teacher.

Avalokiteśvara agreed. "If you want to learn this magic shooting art," he said, "you must first purify yourself for a month by not eating meat and by meditating on love and compassion toward all living beings. I will return and teach you my secret."

Savari did as he was told, and when the teacher returned, the hunter was a changed man, though he did not yet know it. He asked the Guru for his promised initiation into the secret art of shooting.

The teacher drew an elaborate mandala (a concentric diagram, used as an aid in meditation), decorated it with flowers, and told Savari and his wife to look at it carefully.

Since both of them had seriously practiced meditation for one full month, they gazed with undivided attention upon the mandala, and lo! the ground below it seemed to become transparent, and it was as though they looked right into the bowels of the earth. There was smoke and fire, and agonizing shrieks pierced their ears.

"What do you see?" asked the Guru.

The hunter and his wife were unable to utter a word. But when the smoke had cleared away, they saw the eight great hells and the agony of innumerable human beings.

"What do you see?" the Guru asked again.

And when they looked closer, they recognized two painfully contorted faces.

"What do you see?" the Guru asked for the third time.

And suddenly, full comprehension came over them like a flash, and they cried out: "It's ourselves!"

They fell at the feet of the Guru, imploring him to show them the way of liberation. But they entirely forgot to ask for the initiation into the secret shooting art.

Savari continued to meditate on love and compassion and became one of the Eighty-Four Siddhas.

It is interesting and instructive to see the main features of this story in the garb of Ch'an or Zen, as related in Chuan-teng Lu and translated by Prof. D. T. Suzuki in his *Essays on Zen Buddhism* (Vol. II, p. 94f.):

Shih-kung was a hunter before he was ordained as a Zen monk under Ma-tsu. He strongly disliked Buddhist monks, who were against his profession. One day, while chasing a deer, he passed by the cottage where Ma-tsu resided. Ma-tsu came out and greeted him.

Shih-kung asked: "Did you see some deer pass by your door?"

"Who are you?" asked the Master.

"I am a hunter."

"How many can you shoot down with your arrow?"

"One with one arrow."

"Then you are no hunter," declared Ma-tsu.

"How many can you shoot with one arrow?" asked the hunter in his turn.

"The entire flock, with one arrow."

"They are living creatures, why should you destroy the whole flock at one shooting?"

"If you know that much, why don't you shoot yourself?"

"As to shoot myself, I do not know how to proceed."

"This fellow," exclaimed Ma-tsu, all of a sudden, "has put a stop today to all his past ignorance and evil passions!"

Thereupon, Shih-kung the hunter broke his bow and arrows and became Ma-tsu's pupil.

When he became a Zen Master himself, he had a bow with an arrow ready to shoot, with which his monks were threatened when they approached him with a question.

San-ping was once so treated. Shih-kung exclaimed: "Look out for the arrow!"

Ping opened his chest and said: "This is the arrow that kills; where is the one that resuscitates?"

Kung struck three times on the bow-string. Ping bowed. Kung said: "I have been using one bow and two arrows for the past thirty years, and today I have succeeded in shooting down only a half of a wise man."

Shih-kung broke his bow and arrows once more, and never used them again.

7
TANTRIC EXPERIENCE

THUS, EACH OF THE MASTERS developed his own method and—what is more—made each of his pupils find his own particular way. There are as many ways toward realization as there are thinking beings. This is what makes it so difficult to give a precise idea of what Zen (Ch'an) or the Siddhas stand for without overstressing individual aspects or oversimplifying the problem by mere generalizations.

They did not believe in verbal expressions of truth and only pointed out the direction in which truth might be experienced, since truth is not something existing in itself, not even as a negation of error, as a pupil of the Sixth Patriarch expressed in the following hymn:

> I do not seek the truth,
> I do not destroy the error,
> Because I know that both are nothing,
> That both are no forms (of Reality);
> The Unformed is nevertheless not "nothing,"
> But also not "not-nothing." (Shodo-Ka)

And in the same hymn we find the words: "The empty shape of transitory illusion is nothing but the shape of truth." In other words, reality is revealed in the very forms in which the world appears to us, as well as in the continual change to which these forms are subjected, because the forms as well as the change are not arbitrary phenomena but expressions of universal laws, according to which certain forms manifest themselves under certain circumstances and are dissolved or transformed into other forms. Indeed, transitoriness is only the negative term for transformation. While transitoriness expresses merely the fact of change or the dissolution of a certain form—whether that of a material "thing" or state of existence—transformation combines change with stability, which means change according to an inherent law or change in a consistent direction. This directedness of change is the principle of continuity (*santana*) and stability, which latter becomes all the more pronounced the higher a living, i.e. self-regulating and self-renewing organism, is developed.

Indeed, it is the principle of continuity which is the basic concept of the tantric view of life, a continuity that extends in both time and space, insofar as each continuous process is intersected and interwoven by innumerable simultaneously existing processes. This is what we may call the warp and woof of reality, the infinite interrelationship of all that exists in the external structure of the universe, which is repeated or reflected on a smaller scale in every living organism.

This is the great discovery of the Tantras, which made it possible to cut across all religious dogmas and formulations and thus to represent a spiritual science independent of mere beliefs or opinions, but ever verifiable by experience, because based on a strict methodology of psychological observation and meditational practice. It adds a new dimension to the profoundly true and fruitful attitude of Ch'an and Zen, in that it not only does not wait for the flashlike moment of intuitive insight but actively prepares the ground by careful guidance, according to individual propensities and faculties, thus creating an atmosphere of certainty and confidence through which the individual can establish a meaningful relationship to his own inner world as well as with the world around him.

Just as every normally gifted person has the potentiality of becoming a physician or a scientist, so every individual has the potentiality to become enlightened in the course of this life or in later existences. But just as one does not become a physician or a scientist by merely sitting and waiting, in the hope that these hidden qualities may come forth and reveal themselves, so one does not become enlightened by merely leaving it to nature. Conscious effort and aspiration are required.

This is why Buddha Śākyamuni emphasized *vīrya*, effort, energy (which is regarded as being his particular quality among the five Buddhas of our world-cycle) as one of the essential factors of enlightenment. This factor, however, depends on clear awareness (*smṛiti*; Pāli: *sati*) and insight into the Dharma, in the ethical as well as in the universal sense, i.e. the discriminating knowledge of what is Dharma and what is not (*dharma-vicaya*), out of which arises the certainty that there is something worthwhile to make an effort for, and that our energy is aimed in the right direction. Unless we behold the mountain peak in all its majesty and sublime beauty, we shall never feel the urge to climb it. *Vīrya*, therefore, is not a laborious or forced effort, but a joyful attitude, a spontaneous urge.

Thus, the very figure of the Buddha becomes the symbol of enlightenment with whom the Tantric Buddhist tries to identify himself in his meditative practice (*sādhana*). He knows that this figure is the symbol of his own potentialities. Potentiality, however, is not yet reality and, therefore, the often heard dictum "Thou art Buddha" would merely open the door to complacency and self-deception if taken as an accomplished fact instead of an assurance of our inherent possibilities.

Our "unconscious nature" (which modern psychology has rediscovered) corresponds to the latent universality of the *ālaya-vijñāna*, and as such cannot be equated with our innate Buddha-nature, because the former equally contains demonic as well as divine qualities, cruelty as well as compassion, egotism as well as selflessness, delusion as well as knowledge, blind passion and darkest drives as well as profound longing for light and liberation. Freud associates the Unconscious mainly with all negative qualities and all rejected and suppressed or unassimilated contents of the human mind, which are hidden in the "underground cellars" of our consciousness. Jung, on the other hand, is more inclined to see the Unconscious as the source of divine inspiration. Both these views are somewhat arbitrary, just as is the idea that the Buddha-nature lies "ready-made," hidden, or is already present in every sentient being and would break through in its completeness and perfection if we suppressed all thought-activities, judgments, and volitional decisions. This would amount to a complete rejection of our individuality, i.e. of a focalized consciousness, without which perception, ratiocination, discrimination, and comprehension—in fact, all mental activity—would be impossible.

If we mistake the momentary focus for a permanent and independently existing unity or an autonomous "I," then this consciousness gets fixed in a one-sided position and becomes a hindrance. However, as a relative point of reference which establishes a relationship between past and present experiences, the "I" or the notion of a perpetually self-creating inner center is an essential feature of the structure of a consciousness that is aware of itself and capable of realizing its own relativity, as well as its relationship to the world in which it lives. "The same regulating forces, that have created nature in all its forms, are responsible for the structure of our psyche and also for our capacity to think." (W. Heisenberg)

It is not enough to penetrate to the intuitive consciousness of universal unity unless we have realized also the opposite pole, the distinguishing wisdom of inner vision and spiritual discernment which awakens our sense of values and self-responsibility. It is not sufficient to identify ourselves with the oneness of a common origin or a potential Buddhahood, unless we take the decisive step toward the transformation and reintegration of the divergent tendencies or elements of our psyche.

Just as an artist creates a work of art by using the manifold materials at his disposal and by integrating them into an organic whole, in which universal laws and aspects of reality are revealed in an imaginative individual form, so the meditator should create a significant and valid inner cosmos and become one with it. This is the way of the unfoldment and reintegration of Tantric meditation, as represented in the mystic circle of the Mandala and its archetypal symbols.

As to the self-responsibility mentioned above, it clearly presupposes the development of a centralized individuality, which is as important as the fact of its dynamic (nonabsolute) character. Therefore the precondition of all meditational experience consists in becoming more and more conscious of the inner center.

> The successful I is not a rigid point but the capacity for movement around a firm standing axis, and a capacity for transformation without loss of individual form, and a penetrability which yet permits no breakdown of its boundaries.[1]

The stable axis around which our "I" revolves could be identified with the direction of karmic evolution, by which the causally connected or mutually dependent successive existences create the psychic continuity which enables us to proceed toward enlightenment in a gradual process of maturation that may stretch over many lives.

There is no doubt that this process can be hastened to a great extent by turning our attention inward and gaining a true insight into our own nature, which actually corresponds to *samyak dṛiṣṭhi*, the first and most important step on the Eightfold Path, as a precondition for the realization of all further steps. We are not concerned here with right or wrong views or opinions in the intellectual sense, but with a direct, unprejudiced, intuitive insight into the true nature of things, especially ourselves.

References and Notes

[1] Karlfried Graf von Dürkheim: *HARA, the Vital Centre of Man;* George Allen & Unwin, London, 1962; p. 88.

8

REASON AND INTUITION

IF, HOWEVER, INTUITION does not at the same time find a clear expression in our thought, it cannot have any real influence upon our life, because no force can act unless it is formed and directed. On the other hand, thoughts and truths which have been developed only on the intellectual plane must be confirmed and realized by direct experience if they are to have the power to transform our life and our deepest being.

Those who dwell merely in the realm of thought remain the prisoners of their thoughts, just as those who live in more or less vague intuitions become the prisoners of their momentary feelings and emotions.

Those, however, who can coordinate and harmonize their thoughts and their intuitions, make the best of both: they enjoy the freedom of an intuitive mind, unhampered by concepts and prejudices. They have the creative satisfaction of building the elements of intuitive experience into the exalted edifice of an all-embracing world-view and of developing a philosophy of life which is continually widening its outlook until it finds its completion in the state of perfect enlightenment.

Thus, there is no need to negate our intellect or to suppress the free flow of our thoughts and the faculty of reasoning (*vitarka-vicāra*) as long as we are conscious of the limitations inherent in all discursive thought and as long as we use our intellect within its own realm. The reasoning faculty is a valuable instrument of the human mind. Without its directing, guiding, clarifying, and stabilizing qualities, our life would turn into a chaotic nightmare.

The idea that we are already perfect, because the whole universe is present within us, and that we have only to suppress the wicked intellect in order to allow our perfection to come to the light and to reveal itself, is one of the greatest fallacies of those who see perfection only in the undifferentiated oneness of the absolute *brahman* and who try to achieve liberation or the restoration of the original state of absolute oneness by the devaluation and negation of individuality and individual consciousness. Strange as it may seem, it is just in such a theory that abstract logical thought celebrates its highest triumph.

If we really want to trust our innermost nature, and therewith the nature of the universe from which we sprang, we cannot at the same time doubt the meaningfulness of our individualization, since it is the product of that presumed primordial unity and completeness. Neither absolute oneness nor absolute differentiation can constitute a meaningful ideal, nor can perfection be identified with either an impersonal *brahman* or with the limited egocentric consciousness of a separately existing personality. Rather it is in the *middle* between these two extremes where the individual becomes the living focus of a universal consciousness.

The universal tendency toward individualization seems to aim at a focalization and intensification of consciousness that finally enables the universe to become conscious of itself. The realization of this aim occurs exactly in the middle between the smallest and the biggest "organic" system of the universe: the atom (A), and the solar system (S), between which man (M), in the order of size, stands in the middle. In other words, the size of an atom in relation to the size of man is (approximately) equal to the size of man in relation to the size of the solar system: $(A : M = M : S)$, according to the calculation of an eminent modern scientist (Lecomte du Noüy). Though this may be a very rough estimate, it is significant enough to reveal the fact that consciousness is a phenomenon that lies somewhere in the middle between two infinities: the infinitely small and the infinitely large. Infinity, therefore, is one of those ideals that, aside from their poetic feeling content, can have nothing to recommend them; and the same holds true for eternity. Both are "absolute" zero values with which we operate when we have reached the limit of the thinkable and enter the realm of pure abstraction, of nonactuality, ending in the stagnant concept of the Absolute. "All true knowledge must be a gradual revelation of the lower or more abstract in terms of the higher or more concrete aspects of reality," as J. S. Haldane expresses it. And the more concrete aspect of reality is that of the organism, the organic relationship of all forces and forms, in which no part can have a meaning by itself and "no part can be understood except with reference to the whole."[1]

Thus all reality is built upon polarity, the polarity of part and whole, of individuality and universality, of matter and energy, differentiation and oneness, time and space, form and emptiness, stability and transformation, contraction and expansion, inhalation and exhalation, systole and diastole, materialization and dematerialization, etc.; and there can be no question of "higher" and "lower" values between these polar, mutually complementary qualities. The concept of value depends on the merit of the momentary situation, the particular circumstances. Wherever there is an imbalance between the two poles, the one that is in danger of being outweighed represents the greater value. "To a God the finite should be as much a necessity as to man the infinite."[2]

To regard differentiation and individuality as mere accidents of nature or as aberrations of the original purity and unity of the divine or cosmic consciousness, is an attitude born from the arrogance of man's one-sided intellect that tries to assume the role of a judge over the very forces from which it originated. If *māyā* is the product of the universal consciousness or the divine force in its pure, undivided primordial state, the impersonal *brahman,* then it means that *māyā* is the creative aspect of the *brahman,* which we have no right to define as illusion or the power of ignorance. By doing this, we ascribe the quality of ignorance to that very *brahman,* the synonym of ultimate reality.

To the unawakened *māyā* is illusion, the cause of error and ignorance, because he tries to cling to its momentary forms, to stop their continuous flow, to possess them or to subordinate them to his narrow purposes. To the awakened one it is the creative power of the mind, the only reality we can speak of—which we had better term "actuality," because only what "acts" is real in the sense that it affects us and can be experienced. A reality that is not experienceable is only an abstract concept, a product of our speculation, a hypothesis, i.e. something without influence or relationship to our actual life. As such it has as little place in Buddhism as the Absolute, which haunts Western philosophy as a substitute for the concept of God, after having been deprived of all positive content and experiential value or relationship. There may be many levels or degrees of reality, but there cannot be any meaning in a "reality in itself" (though it may be a very logical hypothesis and an inevitable conclusion of the ever abstracting and reducing conceptual mind), a reality that is totally unrelated to anything, in other words, an absolute reality.

Is there any necessity for the conception of something absolute? Since the Absolute is not derived from experience, but is merely the opposite of the relative, it has no reality whatsoever, nor has it any conceivable meaning or effect upon our lives or actions. Life means infinite relationship; the Absolute means the very contrary, and therefore the complete denial of life. The same holds good for the idea of an unconditioned state of mind. Every form of life, every form of consciousness is conditioned and depends on the totality of all that exists or ever came into existence. The more we become conscious of this infinite interrelationship, the freer we become, because we liberate ourselves from the illusion of separateness and learn instead to experience ourselves as a true center or conscious focus of an infinite universe.

This teaches us the humility of our mutual dependence as well as the universality of our true nature and the freedom from that most deadly of all illusions, the illusion of a permanent, separate ego. Whatever resists transformation condemns itself to death. There is no death for those who accept the law of transformation. There is no bondage or limitation for those who accept the fact of their being conditioned, provided they recognize the totality of their conditioning and make use of the boundless heritage that is theirs.

The very fact that we are nonabsolute beings in a nonabsolute world gives us the freedom to experience this world in all its infinite aspects and life in all its infinite transformations. What we call illusion—*māyā*, or whatever other word we use to express the nonabsoluteness (*nairātmya*), the relativity of all that we perceive and experience—is the very outcome of the creativity of consciousness, which is as valid an expression of universal reality as the creative faculty of an inspired artist who transforms a vision into tangible, visible or audible reality. But this reality is "real" not in the sense of something that exists independently in itself, but in the sense that it reveals the true nature of an experience.

If we look at a landscape and imagine that what we see exists as an independent reality outside ourselves, we are the victims of an illusion. If, however, we see the same landscape represented in the work of a great artist, then—in spite of the fact that the painting creates the visual illusion of a landscape—we experience an aspect of reality, because we are conscious of the illusion and accept it as an expression of a real experience.

The moment we recognize an illusion as illusion, it ceases to be illusion and becomes an expression or aspect of reality and experience. The dreamer who knows that he is dreaming is already "awakened," i.e., he is no more a prisoner of his dream, no more subject to its events, no more afraid of what may happen to him.

So, let us stop deceiving ourselves with abstractions of abstractions or absolutes—words or concepts that have no content, no imaginable or tangible, experienceable, "concrete" content. People who speak about absolute truth, absolute reality, absolute unity, absolute oneness, an absolute God, or the Absolute in or by itself, indulge in empty words, words that do not relate to any experience, because experience is based on relationship—while the Absolute means unrelatedness, nonrelationship.

References and Notes

[1] Edmund W. Sinnott: *The Biology of the Spirit*, New York, 1955.
[2] Novalis: *Fragments*.

9

CONCEPT AND ACTUALITY

THE MIDDLE WAY OF THE BUDDHA—reiterated and reformulated in Nāgārjuna's Mādhyamika Philosophy and put into practice in the Tantric Sādhanas of the Vajrayāna—is based precisely on the denial of anything absolute, by proclaiming the law of dependent and simultaneous origination, in which the elements of both time (causality) and synchronicity (acausality) are combined. Even the term *śūnyatā* does not mean "emptiness" in an absolute sense, because when speaking about emptiness, we cannot conceive of or attach any meaning to this word without having at the back of our mind the question "empty of what?" The word "empty," like all words of the human language, is a relational term, just like "high" or "low," "right" or "left." This is clearly shown by the classification of *śūnyatā* into eighteen kinds of emptiness: emptiness of inner things (*adhyātma-śūnyatā*), emptiness of outer things (*bahirdha-śūnyatā*), emptiness of inner and outer things (*adhyātma-bahirdha-ś.*), emptiness of emptiness (*śūnyatā-śūnyatā*), great emptiness (*mahā-śūnyatā*), emptiness of ultimate truth (*paramārtha-ś.*), emptiness of created things (*samskrita-ś.*), emptiness of uncreated things (*asamskrita-ś.*), ultimate emptiness (*atyanta-ś.*), emptiness of limitlessness (*anavaragra-ś.*), emptiness of dispersion (*anavakara-ś.*), emptiness of primary nature (*prakrita-ś.*), emptiness of selfhood (*svalaksana-ś.*), emptiness of things (*sarvadharma-ś.*), emptiness of unttainability (*anupalambha-ś.*), emptiness of non-being (*abhava-ś.*), emptiness of self-nature (*svabhava-ś.*), emptiness of the non-being of self-nature (*abhava-svabhava-ś.*).[1]

This list could have been indefinitely extended and has itself been the subject of innumerable learned commentaries, which complicate matters even more and keep the intellect more and more busy with concepts of concepts and abstractions of abstractions, until the mind has proved its own utter emptiness and nonexistence. The Tantras cut through the whole maze of conceptual thought by leading us back to actuality, as the only reality accessible to us by experience, upon which the Buddha laid the greatest stress in view of the speculative nature of religious and philosophical theories of his time.

It is the danger of our conceptualizing intellect to get farther and farther away from life by losing itself in pure abstractions, because the more abstract a concept, the easier it is to manipulate it.

> Logic is all the more applicable in its strictest sense, the more purely hypothetical or fictitious the premises and the less they are interfered with by reality. Pure logic is only purchasable at the cost of its content of reality; it is attainable only when dealing with concepts which have lost their content of reality and which, therefore, can be filled with any desired content.[2]

Thus, emptiness in Buddhism means emptiness of anything that is existing in itself, be it as a thing or a being or an absolute concept. Even if we speak of the totality of the world or the universe, we mean thereby the totality of relations, unity in interrelated diversity. The concept of undifferentiated oneness is a concept without any content of reality. Only when the intellect is isolated from life, the fundamental fact of polarity and diversity is overshadowed by the ideal of absolute oneness. Polarity does not deny unity in any way; on the contrary, it presupposes an underlying unity, because unity in the spiritual and actual sense is not mere uniformity but the perfect cooperation of different qualities and forces and the inseparability of polar opposites. Here begins the paradox and the wonder of that mysterious faculty that we call life and consciousness.

This is the very heart of Tantric experience: the recognition of this polarity and its integration in the union of "male" and "female" qualities, of creative and receptive, active and passive, physical and spiritual, finite and infinite qualities, etc. It is the recognition that there can be no form without emptiness, no emptiness without form, that there can be no knowledge without ignorance, because knowledge can only arise out of a limitation of awareness, a focalization or concentration which consists in the exclusion of all nonrelevant elements of "reality," i.e. against a background of "ignorance," of willfully ignored elements. This "ignorance" has nothing to do with the religious term *avidyā*, which is characterized by the delusion of separate and unchangeable egohood or an absolute reality of any phenomena.

Wisdom, therefore, is not omniscience, in the sense of knowing or being aware of everything at the same time, but the recognition of our true nature as a manifestation of the totality of the universe under the unique form of our time-and-space conditioned individuality. When the texts speak of the "omniscience" of the Enlightened Ones, this can be grasped only in the sense that they fully understand the essential nature of life, an understanding that is applicable to every single phenomenon toward which they direct their attention. Their wisdom combines the polar opposites of profound feeling, or compassion (the unifying principle), with profound knowledge (the discriminating principle), the qualities of a warm heart and a clear discerning mind, represented by the Dhyāni-Bodhisattva Avalokiteśvara (the jewel in the heart-lotus) and the Dhyāni-Bodhisattva Mañjuśri with the flaming sword.

Knowledge does not consist in the accumulation of facts, but in the ever-present faculty of discernment and clear insight into the nature of things. This is possible only if we look at them ever and again with fresh eyes—as if we had never seen them before—i.e. from the standpoint of creative nescience or the creative emptiness of receptivity that allows us to experience a new dimension in a factually "known" phenomenon or an apparently familiar situation.

Here we touch at the deepest mystery of existence, the very ground from which all true meditation grows, and which Tibetans call "the wondrous (or magic) play of ignorance and knowledge" (*rig dang ma-rig cho-ḥphrul*). Would life be worth living without this nescience? Would life be bearable with perfect knowledge of every future event? Could life have any meaning, if it were coupled with omniscience? The meaning of life—like the meaning of a journey—lies not in the arrival at a certain place but in the progress toward it; in the movement itself and in the gradual unfoldment of events, conditions, and experiences. Omniscience, in the literal meaning of the word, would be utter dullness and boredom, worse than ignorance: to know everything is equal to knowing nothing. Knowledge can have meaning only in relationship to something or someone; to the knower. The knower, however, must be an individual, centralized consciousness, distinguishing itself from its surroundings, in spite of its essential unity, which may be felt and experienced so strongly that, as it is said, the knower and the known become one.

To become one, however, does not mean to dissolve into each other, to annihilate the polarity on which knowledge, like love, is based. It is the overcoming of duality in favor of polarity, in which unity and differentiation are equally present. Lovers are not annihilated in the act of "becoming one;" they lose only their ego-sense, not their individuality. Individuality is different from the illusion of egohood; the latter results in a mental and emotional imbalance and is the cause of suffering and unhappiness. Similarly, the Buddha's individuality was not annihilated in the process of enlightenment or by the experience of his universality. He did not "merge into the infinite" or "dissolve into the All," but lead an active life for another forty years.

Life means individualization, and this individualization increases with the differentiation and refinement of organs. At the same time it creates an ever-expanding consciousness which finally reaches beyond the individual and culminates in the awareness of the totality of the universe. All this proves that individualization and universality are not mutually exclusive qualities, but rather are complementary to each other. They are like two simultaneous movements in opposite directions.

Individuality pursued to its end, i.e. realized to the fullness of its possibilities, is universality. It is only when stopping halfway that individuality solidifies and shrinks to the notion of an ego that contradicts universality.

The concept of individuality as something that cannot be divided (being an indivisible unit, like any living organism), does not necessarily mean something that is completely closed in itself or shut off from everything else that exists in the world. On the contrary, it represents something that is indivisible because it has the totality of the universe at its base and is vitally related to all other phenomena similarly constituted.

For the same reason, the Tantric Buddhist does not believe in an independent and separately existing external world. The inner and the outer worlds are the warp and woof of the same fabric in which the threads of all forces and of all events, of all forms of consciousness and of their objects, are woven into an inseparable net of endless, mutually conditioned relations. Hence the word *"tantra"* (thread, web, interwovenness). Thus, "reality is not a fixed condition, but an intensifiable value whose degree depends on the intensity of our experience," as Martin Buber puts it.[3] Just as we cannot separate the sight from the seer, so reality cannot be separated from the experiencer.

The uncreative individual (as also the animal) lives in a given reality, i.e., in a reality conditioned by its senses and the coordinating faculty of the mind, depending on the level or dimension of consciousness. Each dimension produces a different reality, a different world. A two-dimensional being lives in a world of surfaces, but has no conception of space or three-dimensional objects. A three-dimensional consciousness lives in a world of corresponding space-experience, in which objects of a similar nature are perceived and regarded as material realities. On the next higher dimension these objects may dissolve into fast moving processes extending in a new direction, not contained in three-dimensional space, yet not denying the properties of the foregoing dimensions. Thus reality has as many different aspects as there are dimensions, and there are as many dimensions as possibilities of conscious awareness, which are infinite.

References and Notes

[1] For a detailed description and analysis of the Eighteen Forms of Emptiness, according to Hsuan-chang's version of the Mahāprajñāpāramitā, see D.T. Suzuki: *Essays in Zen Buddhism*, Vol. 111, pp. 236-241.
[2] Paul Dahlke: *Heilkunde und Weltanschauung*.
[3] Martin Buber: *Essays*, Zurich, Manesse Verlag.

10

THE TRANSFORMING POWER OF CREATIVE IMAGINATION

CHANGE YOUR AWARENESS, and you live in a different world, experience a different reality! The ability to change one's awareness appears only at a certain stage of reflective and creative consciousness which does not yet exist in animals and is only partially developed in man. I say "partially," because not all men have developed and made use of their creative faculties. Those who have done so are remembered as the great inspirers of humanity; through the power of their creative imagination they have given new values to life; they have changed the human outlook and world from that of a savage to that of a being capable of becoming conscious of his universal heritage.

> Of all the distinctions between man and animal, the characteristic gift which makes us human is the power to work with symbolic images: the gift of imagination. The power that man has over nature and himself lies in his command of imaginary experience. Almost everything we do that is worth doing is done first in the mind's eye. The richness of human life is that we have many lives. We live the events that do not happen (and some that cannot) as vividly as those that do. If thereby we die a thousand deaths, that is the price we pay for living a thousand lives. To imagine is the characteristic act, not of the poet's mind, or the painter's, or the scientist's, but the mind of man. Imagination is a specifically human gift.[1]

This power of creative imagination is not merely content with observing the world as it is, accepting a given reality, but is capable of creating a new reality by transforming the inner as well as the outer world. This is the very heart of the Tantric teaching and experience, which adds a new dimension to the practice of meditation and spiritual discipline.

The follower of the Small Vehicle (Hīnayāna) tries to see the world as it is—i.e. as a given reality—and turns away from it. The follower of Zen sees the world as a paradox and tries to discover the given reality behind it in his inner world, his "original face," by turning away from or denying the conceptualizing activity of the intellect. The practitioner of Tantric meditation (sādhana) agrees with the Zennist in the overcoming of conceptual thought. However, knowing that there can be no waking consciousness without content, and that to stop thought activity is as impossible as to stop a river, the Tantric Sādhaka replaces abstract (or merely "mental") concepts and the operations of a two-dimensional logic by creative and multidimensional symbols of living experience. Thus the inner and the outer worlds are transformed and united in the realization that the basic qualities of human individuality binding us to our worldly existence (*samsāra*) are at the same time the means of liberation and of enlightenment.

In short, a spiritual discipline or meditational practice which shuns the power of imagination deprives itself of the most effective and vital means of transforming human nature as it is into what it could be, if its dormant potentialities were fully awakened. But unless these potentialities are vividly represented and pictured in the human mind, there is no incentive to transform them into actualities.

However, we have to point out that there is a vast difference between creative imagination and mere aimless daydreaming, indulging in meaningless fantasies, in which the mind is drifting on the surface of our half-awake consciousness. Creative imagination builds with the "bricks of reality," as does the artist with the materials of the physical world and the potentialities of his psyche. This is done in an inwardly directed and meaningful way which crystallizes in a new and unique expression of reality—either in the form of a work of art or in that of a transformed consciousness—a transformed individual who has awakened to a new aspect of reality. The ultimate materials at our disposal are the elements of our present personality. They are the raw material which we have to convert into a supreme work of art: the completely realized human being, the symbol of which lives within us as the archetype of the Eternal Man, the exalted figure of the Enlightened One.

The very fact—and we emphasize this again—that the Buddha (or any of the great Enlightened Ones of humanity), who possessed the same basic qualities (*skandhas*) of individual existence as any other human being, was able to transform them into factors of enlightenment, proves that the very qualities which to the unenlightened are the source of illusion and deception in the endless treadmill of births and death—of *samsāra*—contain at the same time the elements of reality and the means of liberation and enlightenment.

If we can see *nirvāna* and *samsāra* as the two sides of the same reality, we should likewise be able to see the same polarity in the *skandhas* which in themselves are neither good nor bad, true nor false, real nor illusory, liberating nor binding, wholesome nor unwholesome, nirvanic nor samsaric. All depends what we make of them, how we use them. To those who have been awakened to their basic or essential potentialities, the *skandhas* are no more tendencies of self-limitation and egocentric attachment; on the contrary, they are the very factors that make the realization of freedom and enlightenment possible. That is why the Buddha regarded human birth as the best of all forms of existence.

References and Notes

[1] Jacob Bronowski (condensed from a speech to the American Academy of Arts and Letters).

PART II

THE BASIC ELEMENTS OF VAJRAYANA MEDITATION

1

THE TRANSFORMATION OF THE CONSTITUENTS OF THE HUMAN PERSONALITY

ACCORDING TO THE ANCIENT Buddhist tradition the human personality has been described as a combination of five groups or *skandhas* of interrelated functions, enumerated in the order of their increasing subtlety, and defined as:

1. *Rūpa-skandha*: a) the group of corporeality or, more correctly, the group of the sensuous, which comprises the past elements of consciousness that have formed the body and are represented by the body; b) the present elements, as the sensation or idea of matter; and c) the future or potential sensuous elements (*dharmāḥ*) in all their forms of appearance.[1] This definition includes sense-organs, sense-objects, their mutual relationship and psychological consequences.

2. *Vedanā-skandha*: the group of feelings, which comprises all reactions derived from sense-impressions, as well as from emotions arising from inner causes, i.e. feelings of pleasure and pain (bodily), joy and sorrow (mental), indifference and equanimity.

3. *Samjñā-skandha*: the group of perceptions of discriminating awareness and representation, which comprises the reflective or discursive (*savicāra*) as well as the intuitive (*avicāra*) faculty of discrimination.

4. *Samskāra-skandha*: the group of mental formations, the formative forces or tendencies of the will, representing the active principle of consciousness, the character of the individual, namely the karmic consequences caused by conscious volition.

5. *Vijñāna-skandha*: the group of consciousness, which comprises, combines, and coordinates all previous functions or represents the potentiality of consciousness in its pure, unqualified form.

In the personality of a Buddha each of the *skandhas* is transformed into an aspect of the enlightened consciousness. Thus the principle of form or corporeality is no more confined to the physical body, but comprises the totality of the universe from which it sprang and which is reflected in the structure, the organs, and the functions of the human body, and especially in the mirror-like quality of a completely stilled consciousness. Herein the enlightened mind realizes the *"Wisdom of the Great Mirror" (mahādarśa-jñāna)*, in which the forms of all things are potentially present and are recognized according to their nature as exponents of the Great Void.

The principle of feeling, instead of being ego-related and concerned only with the individual's own well-being or purely personal attractions and aversions, is widened into an all-encompassing feeling of solidarity with all sentient beings in the recognition of that greater unity of life, from which grows the *Wisdom of Equality (samatā-jñāna)*. On account of this, love is freed from possessiveness and compassion from condescension. It is the wisdom that opens us to the Greater Life.

The principle of perception is no more concerned with intellectual or conceptual discriminations or mere sense-perceptions, but is converted into the spontaneity of inner vision and spiritual discernment in the practice of meditation and thus into the *Distinguishing Wisdom (pratyaveksana-jñāna)*. Here differentiation is seen against a background of unity and in relationship to all concrete situations of life and individuality. If the Wisdom of Equality stressed the essential unity of life, the Distinguishing Wisdom teaches us to respect the differences and the uniqueness of every individual and every situation in which we find ourselves.

It is on the basis of these three preceding Wisdoms that the principle of volition turns into the Wisdom That Accomplishes All Work, (kṛtyānuṣthāna-jñāna) because it results in action without a doer, that is action which is not ego-related or ego conditioned, and is therefore "karma-free." It is action that springs from a force that has its origin in a consciousness whose roots are deeper than those of our individualized intentions: spontaneous action that expresses the totality of our being.

It is this kind of action at which Lao-tse hints when he says:

>Acting without design, occupying oneself without making a business of it, finding the great in what is

small and the many in the few, repaying injury with kindness, effecting difficult things while they are easy, and managing great things in their beginnings: this is the method of Tao.

This totality of our being becomes conscious of itself in the universality of an enlightened consciousness, in which the limited and merely coordinating faculty of the average human mind (through which we are aware of past and present objects, of time and future possibilities, and of ourselves as individuals in a stream of events and changing conditions) is transformed into the awareness of a higher dimension of reality, the law (*dharma*) that governs all phenomena of life throughout the universe: the *"Wisdom of the Dharma-Realm"* (*dharma-dhātu-jñāna*).

Thus, each of the *skandhas,* which to the average person may be a source of error and of enslaving attachment, is changed into an instrument of liberation. If we overlook this important fact, we miss the most essential message of a Buddha's actual existence in this our world; for he demonstrated by his very life that a human being is able to attain the exalted state of Buddhahood. His achievement gave rise to a powerful and far-reaching symbol and inspired some of the greatest civilizations of human history; it has endured over a span of two and a half millenniums without losing its universal appeal and importance for our time. In fact, the contemplation and realization of this profoundly archetypal symbol of the complete and enlightened man, in whom the universe is mirrored and re-created in an experienceable form, is in itself the way and the key that unlocks all problems and mysteries of our human existence: "The aim is the way!"

It is here where the Tantras and all the masters of meditation, from the early Yogacārins to the followers of Ch'an and Zen, have left the path of verbalization and intellectualization in order to reexperience the totality of man and his essential oneness with the universe in which he lives. This oneness is not sameness or unqualified identity, but an organic relationship, in which differentiation and uniqueness of function are as important as that ultimate or basic unity.

Individuality and universality are not mutually exclusive values, but two sides of the same reality, compensating, fulfilling, and complementing each other, and becoming one in the experience of enlightenment. This experience does not dissolve the mind into an amorphous All, but rather brings the realization that the individual itself contains the totality focalized in its very core. Thus, the world that hitherto was experienced as an external reality merges or is integrated into the enlightened mind in the moment in which the universality of consciousness is realized. This is the ultimate moment of the liberation from the impediments and fetters of ignorance and illusion.

We are still captured by crude similes of quantitative magnitudes in place of qualitative values, when we compare the ultimate experience of liberation with "the drop that slips into the shining sea." It would be more appropriate—though paradoxical from the viewpoint of three-dimensional logic— to say that the "sea slips into the shining drop."[2] The drop is qualitatively not different from the sea. All the oceans that cover the earth, as seen from the distance of the sun, are not more than a drop in the immensity of space; and a drop, as seen from the standpoint of a microorganism contained in it, is as vast as an ocean.

References and Notes

[1] The division in past, present and future is mentioned in Vasubandhu's *Abhidharma-kośa-śāstra*, i, 14 b. Cfr. "the Five Skandhas and the Doctrine of Consciousness" in my *Foundations of Tibetan Mysticism* (Rider, London).
[2] In the *"Divine Symphony"* by Inayat Khan, we find an interesting parallel to this thought. He says: "When I open my eyes to the outer world, I feel myself as a drop in the sea; but when I close my eyes and look within, I see the whole universe as a bubble raised in the ocean of my heart." (With grateful acknowledgement to Peter Viesnik, who drew my attention to this beautiful and significant utterance.)

2

THE FOUR SYMPHONIC MOVEMENTS OF MEDITATION

THE DEMONSTRATION of the universality of man and of his capacity to attain self-realization in the supreme experience of enlightenment—without the intervention of gods, priests, dogmas, and sacrificial rituals—on the direct way of meditation: this is what the Buddha gave to the world and which has become the very core of Buddhism, irrespective of differences created by sects, philosophical schools, or scholastic traditions, or by racial or linguistic influences.

Meditation, however, concerns not only the mind, but the whole human being, including his bodily functions and activities. Therefore the first step toward meditation consists in taking stock of the situation in which we find ourselves. Meditation means many things: it means turning inward; it means quiet observation, reflection, and awareness of ourselves; it means to be conscious of consciousness, to become a detached observer of the stream of changing thoughts, feelings, drives and visions, until we recognize their nature and their origin. These latter are the main features of the Satipaṭṭhāna practice of Theravada Buddhism.

But these are only the first steps of meditation. In the more advanced stages we change from the role of a more or less intellectual observer to that of an experiencer of a deeper reality, namely, to that of the timeless and universal source of all the phenomena we observed in the contemplation of our stream of consciousness and even in the simplest bodily functions, as for instance in the process of breathing. Breathing itself can be a subject of meditation because it reveals the very nature of life in its alternate inward and outward movement, its continuous process of receiving and releasing, of taking and of giving back, of the deep relationship between the inner and the outer world, the individual and the universe.

However, between and beyond the two alternative movements—so to say at the turning-point between them—there is a moment of stillness in which the inner and the outer world coincide and become one; there is nothing that can be called either "inside" or "outside." This moment, in which time stands still—because it is empty of all designations of time, space, and movement but is nevertheless a moment of infinite potentialities—represents the state of pure "being" or "isness," which we can only express by the word śūnyatā, as indicating the primordial ground from which everything originates. It is the timeless moment before creation or, seen from the standpoint of the individual, the moment of pure receptivity which precedes all creative activity.

It is the first movement in the great symphonic mandala or magic circle, in which our inner world appears as sound and light, color and form, thought and vision, rhythm and harmonious coordination, visible symbol and meditative experience. This first *movement*—which expression may be taken in the musical as well as in the spiritual and *emotional* sense—corresponds to the first profound meditative attitude or experience, namely "The Wisdom of the Great Mirror."

In the light of this mirror-like wisdom things are freed from their "thingness," their isolation, without being deprived of their form; they are divested of their materiality (like the reflections in a mirror, which cannot be said to be either inside or outside of the mirror) without being dissolved. The creative principle of the mind, which is at the bottom of all form and materiality, is recognized as the active side of the Universal Consciousness (ālaya vijñāna), on the surface of which forms arise and pass away like the waves on the surface of the ocean; the latter, when stilled, reflects the pure emptiness of space and the pure light of heaven (the two aspects of *śūnyatā*).

Hui-Neng, the Sixth Patriarch of the Ch'an School once said: "When I speak about the void, do not fall into the idea that I mean vacuity. . . . The illimitable void of the universe is capable of holding myriads of things of various shapes and forms, such as the sun and the moon and the stars, as well as worlds. . . heavenly planes and hells, great oceans and all the mountains. . . . Space takes in all these, and so does the voidness of our nature. We say that the Essence of Mind is great, because it embraces all things, since all things are within our nature."

If *śūnyatā* hints at the nonsubstantiality of the world and the interrelationship of all beings and things, then there can be no better word to describe its meaning than *transparency*. This word avoids the pitfalls of a pure negation and replaces the concepts of substance, resistance, impenetrability, limitation, and materiality with something that can be experienced and is closely related to the concepts of space and light.

The transparency of the mind-created body, the *vajra-kāya* or "Diamond Body," visualized in tantric meditation, symbolizes *śūnyatā* in visible form, thus bearing out the above mentioned interpretation. Here "form" is no longer in opposition to space, but form and space penetrate each other in a luminous and dynamic play of light and color.

The conception of *jiji-mu-ge* (Japanese: lit. "each thing no hindrance") has its origin in this interaction of form and emptiness, or form and space, which are experienced in the realization of the ultimate transparency of the world: the world as a phenomenon of consciousness. Without consciousness there is neither form nor its concomitant notion of emptiness. Consciousness determines the world in which we live or the particular aspect under which the universe appears to us. In itself it is neither this nor that; it is *śūnyatā*.

Thus the Mirror-like Wisdom reflects with the impartiality of a mirror the nature of all things and of ourselves, while remaining unaffected and untouched by the images it reflects. It is the attitude of the impartial observer, the pure, spontaneous awareness, which in Zen Buddhism is called *satori* or *kensho*: "looking into one's own nature."

By recognizing our own nature as *śūnyatā*, we realize that it is not different from the essential nature of all living beings. This is the "Equalizing Wisdom" or "The Wisdom of Equality," in which we turn from the cool and detached attitude of an observer to the warm human feeling of all-embracing love and compassion for all that lives. In the *Dhammapada* (Pāli) this essential equality, with others, was made the keystone of Buddhist ethics, when it was said that "having made oneself equal to others" or "recognizing oneself in others," one should abstain from hurting others. This shows that compassion in Buddhism is not based on moral or mental superiority with its inevitable attitude of condescension, but on a feeling of oneness, such as a mother feels with her child.

If, however, this feeling remains confined to the emotional plane, it may lead to a merely sentimental and one-sided attitude, in which the individual is deprived of a sense of responsibility. He may then become incapable of action and discrimination in a world that is not merely a featureless unity but an organic whole in which differentiation is as much an expression of reality as oneness, and form is as important as emptiness; both depend on each other and condition each other like light and shade.

Thus we come to the "third movement" of meditative experience in which we are concerned neither with concrete beings nor with material things. Here both differentiation and unity, form and emptiness, the purity of light and the infinite modulations of color are revealed in their infinite interrelatedness without losing their distinctive qualities and individuality of expression. This is the "Distinguishing Wisdom" in which our mundane mind, our discriminating, judging intellect, turns into the intuitive consciousness of inner vision, in which "the special and general characteristics of all things become clearly visible without hindrances" (*asaṅga*; i.e., spontaneously) and in which the unfolding of various spiritual faculties takes place.

Through this wisdom the functions of the group of discriminating processes—which we sum up under the general term of perception (*samjñā-skandha*)—are turned inward and becomes transformed and intensified into creative inner vision (*dhyāna*). Such a vision transcends mere sense-awareness and may in this sense be called "transcendental." It is a vision in which the individual characteristics of all phenomena and their general and universal relations become apparent. This wisdom is represented by the transcendental Dhyāni-Buddha Amitābha, the Buddha of Infinite Light, who is shown in the gesture of meditation (*dhyāna-mudrā*).

The "fourth movement" of meditative experience belongs to the realm of action and willpower and represents the "All-Accomplishing Wisdom," the "Wisdom That Accomplishes All Works." Here volition and its formative tendencies (*samskāra skandha*) are transformed into the selfless, "karma-free" action of a life dedicated to the realization of enlightenment, motivated by compassion and based on the understanding of both the individual and the universal aspect of life and phenomena, as experienced in the previous three movements. In the *Vijñaptimātra-Siddhi-Shāstra* it has been said that "this kind of consciousness manifests itself for the benefit of all living beings . . . in the three kinds of transformed actions . . ." namely, those of body, speech, and mind, "according to the vow." The vow is that of the Bodhisattva, whose "body" is the universe (*dharma-kāya*), whose "speech" is the *mantric* word, the word of truth and power, and whose "mind" is the universal consciousness.

3
THE MEANING OF GESTURES

EACH OF THE FOUR MOVEMENTS of meditative experience is represented by a gesture (*mudrā*) of one of the respective four Dhyāni-Buddhas, who symbolize these states of meditative experience and are grouped around the figure of the central Dhyāni-Buddha, in whom the four movements are integrated. These five Buddhas thus form a mandala, a sacred circle, in which each of them occupies a particular place, according to the successive movement and spiritual attitude expressed by the position of their hands.

The movement or the position of our hands is highly significant for our mental or emotional attitude. The Sanskrit word *mudrā*, therefore, signifies much more than a casual gesture of the hands; it denotes a spontaneous expression of our deeper consciousness, even though we may not be aware of it normally. It is the "seal" or the visible imprint of our mind that characterizes the flow and the direction of our consciousness.

The main *mudrās* seen in Buddha images are not only based on an accepted conventional code—which would be valid only within a certain tradition and within the frame of a particular cultural or racial environment—but are of a nature that can be universally understood and accepted. They are based on knowledge and experience of general human psychology.

The palms of the hands have always been regarded as important centers of psychic energy, secondary only to the main centers, located in the brain, the throat, the heart, the navel, and the reproductive organs, in which this energy is generally accumulated and transformed in accordance with the different levels of conscious, subconscious, and unconscious activities. All can be raised to the plane of spiritual awareness in the process of awakening and integrating the activities of these *cakras* through meditation and specialized yoga techniques.

If the main centers of the body, which are connected through the nerve channel of the spinal column—the axis of our psychosomatic organism—are harmonized and integrated, the secondary centers, like those of the palms of the hands, are capable of radiating the focalized energy, or of projecting and transmitting conscious forces into the immediate surroundings especially into any objects or living beings with which they come in touch.

The experience of this power of transmission is the basis of all ritual gestures of blessing. It finds its strongest expression in the laying on of hands, a practice known through millenniums and often demonstrated by its observable results, namely, the power of healing mental as well as physical afflictions. That this power can be generated only by persons who have attained a high degree of spiritual or psychic integration goes without saying. Only a person who has himself become "whole" can make others whole. This is the reason why the power of healing or the capacity of conferring blessings is generally ascribed only to saints and enlightened beings.

However, this does not minimize the importance of these secondary centers of psychic energy, even for the less developed individuals. In the gesture of prayer, in which the hands are raised and lie flat against each other so that the palms are almost touching, while the fingers are stretched upward, resting against each other, the energies emanating from the palm-centers are intensified and reabsorbed into the circuit of individual forces in the direction of the highest supraindividual center, in which the universal consciousness has its potential seat.[1] Prayer is the first step toward its awakening.

Prayer is an act of opening ourselves to these universal forces within or beyond ourselves. It has its root in the heart-center, where our deepest emotions—such as love, faith, compassion—are born. Therefore the hands are raised to the level of this center and point upward, as if to support or express the upward trend of our aspirations, in which the individuals submits to the universality of the spirit. This does not mean that the individual submits to something outside of himself, but rather to something that is already present within his innermost being, though only dormant and not yet realized.

However, as there are and have always been Enlightened Ones who have realized this universality, we may express our veneration of them by raising the joined hands to the forehead or above the crown of the head in salutation and in recognition of their supreme attainment, which we hope to realize within ourselves by arousing and activating these higher centers toward a similar awakening. This form of salutation is a common feature in the ritual worship practiced all over the East, often combined with prostrations, in which the forehead touches the ground. This is at the same time an exercise in humility—which Westerners often find difficult to perform. It hurts their pride, their vanity, their ego or their false sense of dignity. In reality the touching of the ground with the highest center of consciousness is an act of humility. It is also a symbol of the fact that the highest consciousness must descend into the depth of material existence, that the "lowest" and the "highest" are interchangeable (being one in essence, but different in appearance or function), and that the very "earth" is the basis, the womb, and the breeding-ground for the unfoldment and the realization of the spirit.

The first gesture of the Buddha under the Tree of Enlightenment was the touching of the earth (*bhūmisparśa-mudrā*), calling the earth to witness. The earth here stands for the totality of his past, which is as old as the world, in which he has practiced innumerable acts of renunciation which entitle him to his present position and enable him to gain enlightenment. The earth is also the symbol for the totality of all that has *become,* that has taken concrete, tangible form as the materialized past, not only of one, but of all beings living in this world, who have to take this world in its present aspect as the firm basis and starting point for their further development or their final liberation.

Without facing this past and recognizing it as the world in which we live, we cannot become free from its bondage, which becomes stronger the more we try to reject it. We become free, not through rejection or aversion, but through knowledge, through understanding and accepting things as they are, in their true nature. This is the first aspect of meditation, represented by the Dhyāni-Buddha Akṣobhya: the pure awareness of things as they are and the awareness of being conscious of them and of ourselves.

It is here that the ocean of consciousness becomes conscious of itself, by reflecting all things as in a mirror: without attachment and without aversion, without discriminating or

MUDRĀ Gestures	LEVELS	SKANDHA Constituents	TRANSFORMED Into:	REPRESENTED By:	
Bhūmisparśa-m Earth-touching (right palm inward)	basic level	*Rūpa* Form & Corporeality	Wisdom of the Great Mirror	*Akṣobhya*, the Unshakable Touching the Earth	Intro- spective
Dāna-mudrā Giving (right palm outward)		*Vedanā* Feeling	Wisdom of Equality (Essential Unity of Life)	*Ratnasambhava* The Jewel-born giving	Commu- nicating
Dhyāna-mudrā Meditation (both palms upward)	middle level	*Samjñā* Perception	Wisdom of Distinguishing Inner Vision	*Amitābha* Infinite Light Meditating	Intro- spective
Anhaya-mudrā Fearlessness (right palm outward)	upper level	*Samskāra* Volition	The All-Accom- plishing 'Karma'-free Action	*Amoghasiddhi* The All-Accom- plisher, Blessing	Commu- nicating
Dharma-mudrā Universal Law (left palm inward; right palm outward)		*Vijñāna* Coordinating Consciousness	Wisdom of the Universal Law (Dharmadhatu)	*Vairocana* The Radiating One. Setting in Motion the Wheel of the Law.	Integrating

Left hand in lap, palm upward

Palm turned outward

Both hands

judging, merely taking in the totality of all that is within and without ourselves, the totality of our past and our present as it offers itself to our spiritual eye. This is the Wisdom of the Great Mirror.

The stilling of the mind, therefore, is the first step of meditation, and this stilling is possible only if we recognize the firm ground of our present position and the world in which we live. We have created this world through our own past, in so far as the latter determines that which our senses are capable of perceiving and experiencing. Thus the touching of the earth is the recognition of our past in the mirror of our present consciousness, and the firmer we take our stand on this "earth," the more perfectly can we reflect the light of "heaven," the universality of the mind.

The palm of the hand that is touching the earth is turned inward and therefore relates to our inner center. The outward turned palm establishes communication with others. It indicates both an opening of ourselves toward others and an outflowing of psychic forces. A gesture of blessing, for instance, would be inconceivable, if the back of the hand were turned toward the object or the person to be blessed. In the laying on of hands the palm rests on the head of the person receiving the blessing, because it is from the palms that psychic force is supposed to emanate.

The turning of the palm outward in the reversal of the earth-touching gesture constitutes, therefore, a complete reversal of the conscious attitude, namely the change from the cool, detached and uninvolved "objective" observer to the warm and profoundly caring attitude of one who not only recognizes and realizes the unity of all life, but feels involved in all its forms, sharing other beings' joys and sorrows, and thus giving himself in love and compassion to all beings.

This was the attitude of the Buddha after his enlightenment when, instead of enjoying the bliss of emancipation for himself alone and entering into the final state of *parinirvāna*, he returned into the world, taking all its suffering upon himself again, in order to share his great vision and his liberating knowledge with his fellow-beings. Thus he gave to the world not only his teaching, but himself, his complete life. This is symbolized in the gesture of giving (*dāna-mudrā*) which expresses the Wisdom of Equality, or the essential oneness of all life, embodied in the form of the Dhyāni-Buddha Ratnasambhava, whose right hand is stretched across his knee with the palm turned *outward* and his fingertips barely touching the earth.

The most general attitude of meditation, in which all levels of the mind are engaged, is represented by the Dhyāni-Buddha Amitābha, the Buddha of Infinite Light, who embodies the Wisdom of Distinguishing Inner Vision. Both his hands with palms turned upward, rest upon the soles of his upturned feet, the active right hand upon the passive left hand. The upward turned palms, so characteristic of this gesture of meditation (*dhyāna-mudrā*), signify a receptivity toward the eternal qualities and forces of the universe. The palms are like open bowls, ready to receive the gifts of heaven. In this gesture the body is in perfect symmetry, completely centered, balanced, and relaxed.

Only out of this centered and relaxed attitude can spontaneous and selfless action be born. This is represented by the Dhyāni-Buddha Amoghasiddhi, who embodies the Wisdom That Accomplishes All Works. His right hand, with the palm turned *outward* and the fingers stretched upward, is raised to the height of his shoulders in the gesture of fearlessness (*abhaya-mudrā*), reassurance, and blessing. Amoghasiddhi is the embodiment of that highest freedom in which an Enlightened One moves through this world without creating new karmic bonds through his actions, because they are motivated by selfless love and compassion.

The passive left hand of all the four above-mentioned Dhyāni-Buddhas is always shown as resting in the lap with its palm turned upward in an open, receptive attitude, because our essential, though unconscious, relationship to the universe (or its corresponding forces within us) is common to all stages of meditation. Besides the direction of the palms we have to consider the three planes or levels of these gestures. The first two *mudrās* are on the basic level and point toward the earth. The *Dhyāna-mudrā* is on the middle level, which represents "man," in whom "heaven" and "earth" are united. The fourth gesture is on the universal level, where wisdom turns into spiritual action.

On this level we also find the fifth gesture, which belongs to the central Buddha of the mandala: Vairochana, the Radiating One, who represents the sum total of the Four Wisdoms, namely the Universal Law. His gesture is the "Setting in Motion the Wheel of the Law" (*dharma-cakra-mudrā*). In this gesture both hands are active on the level of the heart center, the left hand turned inward, the right turned outward. Thus the inner and the outer worlds are united in the ultimate realization, as well as in the primordial state of universality.

References and Notes

[1] In contrast to this natural gesture of praying, which has been depicted in numberless ancient paintings and sculptures of various religions, is another gesture, in which the fingers are interlocked in such a way that it appears as if the praying person were shackled or straining in a feeling of helplessness and despair, or struggling to obtain something by sheer force of will. It is significant that this gesture—which apparently was unknown or not favored in early and medieval Christianity and even during the Renaissance, as we can see from numerous well-known paintings—has now, as it seems, been generally adopted in Western countries. Does it not reflect the tense, if not cramped, attitude of the Western individual?

4

ORIENTATION, COLOR, AND TIME-SEQUENCE IN THE MANDALA

FROM THE FOREGOING it becomes clear that the position of the Dhyāni-Buddhas in the mandala is not only concerned with a spatial arrangement and their mutual relations, but also indicates a sequence in time, a development or unfolding of spiritual qualities in the process of meditation, which comprises the totality of the human consciousness and all its faculties, as indicated in the five *skandhas*.

The mandala is like a map of the inner world, which we want to explore and realize in the great venture of meditation. But just as a map conveys nothing to one who is not familiar with its conventional symbols or the geographical names and designations, in the same way a mandala can have no meaning for people who have no idea of the underlying tradition and symbology. Just as we have to know the language and the alphabet before we can read a book, we have to know the language of symbols and colors before we can read and appreciate the message of a mandala! But people nowadays talk about mandalas, collect and produce mandalas and look upon them as merely aesthetic compositions or decorations, or as magic devices to induce meditative trance states. They fail to realize that mandalas have a precise meaning and that every detail in them is significant and does not depend on arbitrary moods or whims of an artist, but is the outcome of centuries of meditative experience and a conventional language of symbols as precise as the sign-language of mathematical formulas, where not only each sign, but also its position within the formula determines its value.

Even an ordinary geographical map presupposes that we know, for instance, that blue stands for oceans and lakes, blue lines for rivers, black or red lines for roads and railways, green for low-lying plains, different shades of brown for mountains of different altitudes, etc. But even these indications would be of little use to the observer if the map were not oriented according to the four quarters of the compass. Unless we know that the top of the map is north and the bottom south, so that the east is to the right and the west to the the left, the map would not help us to find our direction.

The same holds true for the mandala. But if people take it for granted that the mandala is oriented like a geographical map, they miss the meaning and confuse the time-sequence of its details. North, south, east, and west in a mandala are not indications of three-dimensional space, but of movement within the inner space of meditational experience. And this movement, like the course of the sun, begins in the east. Consequently, the entrance into the mandala is from its eastern quarter, where the sun rises, in other words, from where the meditative experience starts. Since the mandala was originally drawn or composed on the ground in front of the meditator, the entrance is the point nearest to him and, therefore, designated as east, and as the movement from there proceeds clockwise, following the course of the sun, the left side of the mandala is designated as south, the right side as north and the farthest point opposite to the meditator as west. If such a mandala is reproduced in a *thangka* and hung on a wall like a map, what is up would be the west (and not the north) and what is down the east (and not the south). This has been misunderstood and misrepresented so often (by reproducing mandalas the wrong way round), that it is necessary to point this out as clearly as possible.

The prototype of all mandalas is the great *Stūpa* in Sanchi, a massive tumulus, in which some of the relics of the historical Buddha Sākyamuni, were enshrined. The *Stūpa* is surrounded by a monumental stone railing with gates *(toranā)* opening toward the four quarters of the universe. The emphasis on the four open gates, symbolizing the universal character of Buddhism, which welcomes all seekers of truth with the Buddha's words, "Come and see," has been preserved in the mandalas of the Vajrayāna, where the ground-plan of a square temple with four open gates surrounds the inner circle.

Between the stone railing and the base of the *Stūpa* was a path for ritual circumambulation *(pradaksina-patha)* in the direction of the sun's course. The orientation of the gates also corresponds to the sun's course: sunrise, zenith, sunset, nadir. As the sun illuminates the physical world, so does the Enlightened One illuminate the spiritual world. The eastern gateway represents the Buddha's birth, the southern his enlightenment, the western the proclamation of his doctrine, and the northern his final liberation *(parinirvāna)*.

Circumambulating the *Stūpa*-sanctuary thus meant to re-experience the Buddha's path of liberation; and this is exactly what the tantric mandala means. But instead of following the chronological order of events in the life of the historical Buddha, the infinitely more complex and developed mandala of the Vajrayāna follows the psychological structure of the human mind and the elements of the human personality, as contained in the Buddha's original teaching and definition of the *skandhas*.

Thus, the Wisdom of the Great Mirror, as embodied in Akṣobhya, occupies the eastern quarter of the mandala; Ratnasambhava, the embodiment of the Wisdom of Equality, occupies the southern quarter; Amitābha, the embodiment of the Distinguishing Wisdom of Inner Vision occupies the west; Amoghasiddhi, the embodiment of the All-Accomplishing Wisdom, the north; and Vairocana, the sum total of all these Wisdoms, occupies the center.

To each of these quarters and their presiding Dhyani-Buddhas is assigned a particular color: to the east the dark-blue of the sky before sunrise, to the south the yellow of the sun at noon, to the west the red of the setting sun, and to the north the mysterious blue-green of the moon-lit night. The center, the integration of all colors, is white.

In this way the colors of the Dhyāni-Buddhas and their respective quarters of the mandala express a particular mood and spiritual attitude which—combined with their gestures—give each of them an outspoken character and an easily visualized image. The very colors in which these images appear free them from any conception of materiality and raises them to the level of an intense psychic reality—a reality that is as actual as the mind that experiences them.

However, the capacity of experiencing them depends on the creative faculties of our intuitive consciousness and the depth of our feeling. Both can be developed by the practice of guided visualization and mantric evocation, as taught in the *sādhanas* (practices) and liturgies of tantric meditation. These again are based on a deep understanding of our depth-consciousness and a general knowledge of human psychology. This was regarded as more important than occupation with metaphysical problems and speculations, as we can see from the early Abhidharma literature, out of which the later tantric *sādhanas* with their meticulous psychological details and mandalas grew.

> Every shape and form that arises in the soul, every link which in a mysterious way, joins us to the Universal Life and unites us, maybe without our being aware of it, to Man's most ancient experience, the voices which reach us from the depth of the abyss, all are welcomed with almost affectionate solicitude. Buddhism does not desire that such life of the soul should be scattered. It is of no importance if these images, visions, fears and hopes are not entirely suited to our own vision. They are a legacy which Man carries with him from his birth. They have a positive, real existence like the things we see and feel. They are an irrepressible element of our persons. If, with the rule of reason, we should desire to thrust them back down into the depth of our souls, they would burst forth, all the same, sudden and destructive. It is better, then, to assume possession of them at the first and then by degrees to transfigure them, just as one passes from the outer enclosure of the mandala, successively, through the others until one reaches the central point, the primordial equipoise regained after the experience of life.[1]

Even the negative aspects of our *skandhas*, our passions, aversions, attachments and delusions have to be truly recognized and painfully experienced before they can become stepping stones for our progress on the way to liberation, before they can become transformed into the light of higher wisdom.

> The aim of all the Tantras is to teach the ways whereby we may set free the divine light which is mysteriously present and shining in each of us, although it is enveloped in an insidious web of psyche's weaving.[2]

In this aim all Buddhist systems of meditation are united, though their ways may differ. But as long as they recognize the Four Wisdoms as the basis of all meditative practices, they shall never lose that spiritual balance on which the final success of them all depends. That this was recognized not only in the Mahāyāna literature and in Indian and Tibetan Tantras, but equally in Chinese Ch'an and Japanese Zen, becomes evident in Rinzai's (Lin-chi was his Chinese name) "Fourfold Contemplation."[3]

Explaining his meditational method Rinzai made the following statement:

> At the first instance I destroy the Man and not the object.
> At the second instance I destroy the object but not the Man.
> At the third instance I destroy both: the man and the object.
> At the fourth instance I destroy none of them: neither the Man nor the object.

This statement, which on the surface sounds like a paradoxical Zen *koan,* is in reality a sober assessment of the subject-object relationship in the experience of the Four Wisdoms:

In the Wisdom of the Great Mirror the pure *objective* awareness prevails, while the notion of the subject (Man) is absent.

In the Wisdom of the Essential Equality of all beings, the *subject* (Man) becomes the only conscious reality, without an object.

In the Wisdom of Distinguishing Vision both subject and object lose their independent reality and are seen in their mutually dependent relationship on the universal stage, and in their eternal interplay of emptiness and form, in which materiality, thingness, and the illusion of separate entities gives way to the transparency of creative vision. It was this experience, according to the Buddha's own words, that characterized his enlightenment.

In the All-Accomplishing Wisdom of selfless action, subject and object are restored to their functional status of polarity on the plane of the three-dimensional world of existential—i.e. relative—reality. Thus, "neither the Man nor the object" is destroyed, and we have returned into our familiar world, where "mountains are again mountains and waters are again waters" (to use the well-known Zen phrase), but where we see them with new eyes, no more veiled by the illusion of egoity and separateness and freed from craving and possessiveness as well as from enmity and aversion. *Saṁsāra* has turned into *Nirvāna*; the mundane world has turned into a gigantic mandala, in which every form has become an expression of total reality and every living being a unique manifestation of a greater life and a universal consciousness.

Thus, the meditative experience of the Four Wisdoms has revealed itself as a tremendous symphony of four movements, in which the pendulum of experience results in the transformation of *all* faculties of man, until he has become complete.

This completeness cannot be achieved through negations—for which reason the Buddha rejected asceticism—nor through one-sided affirmation of the one or the other of our basic faculties. Feeling has to be balanced by knowledge, intuition by clear thought, contemplation by action. Those who believe that by mere passive sitting they can attain enlightenment, are as far from the mark as those who believe that they can achieve liberation by mere learnedness or pious recitation of sacred texts. This was pointed out by the ancient Ch'an Master Tai-hui when he wrote to his disciple Chen-ju Tao-jen:

> There are two forms of error now prevailing among followers of Zen, laymen as well as monks. The one thinks that there are wonderful things hidden in words and phrases. The second goes to the other extreme, forgetting that words are the pointing finger, showing one where to locate the moon. Blindly following the instructions given in the *sūtras*, where words are said to hinder the right understanding of the truth of Zen and Buddhism, they reject all verbal

teachings and simply sit with eyes closed, letting down the eyebrows as if they were completely dead. Only when these two erroneous views are done away with, is there a chance for real advancement of Zen.[4]

This sound advice is as true nowadays as it was then; it applies not only to Zen, but to all methods of meditation.

References and Notes

[1] Giuseppe Tucci, *The Theory and Practice of the Mandala*, (Rider & Co., London), p. 83.
[2] Ibid.
[3] *Katto-shu,* part 11, folio 27b-28a, quoted by Ohasama-Faust in *Zen, der lebendige Buddhismus in Japan,* Perthes A.G., Gotha, 1925.
[4] Dwight Goddard, ed., *A Buddhist Bible,* New York: Dutton.

5

MANTRAS AS SEALS OF INITIATION AND SYMBOLS OF MEDITATIVE EXPERIENCE

WE HAVE CONSIDERED ORIENTATION, color, and time-sequence in the inner space of the mandala, as well as the *mudrā*, the spiritual and emotional attitudes of meditation, represented in the form of Dhyani-Buddhas. The symbols so far employed belong mainly to the realm of visible, tangible, or spatial qualities of meditative experience; but equally important is the audible, the sound.

In fact, sight, sound, and touch are the main elements from which our outward directed consciousness builds up our three-dimensional world of sense awareness. If, however, our consciousness is directed inward, these same elements create a world of many more dimensions than the three of our external world.

Even the element of touch, which we ordinarily associate merely with the corporeal world and its surface experience, takes on a new and much deeper aspect, namely that of intuitive feeling, affecting not only our senses but the core of our being. We say that we are "touched," if we are deeply moved by acts of love, kindness, compassion, or gratitude or any other great quality of the human heart.

In a similar way sight is transformed into creative vision, in which forms and colors take on new meaning and relationship and a transparency in which forms interpenetrate and colors oscillate, so that all become exponents of a living and universal continuum, and not only concepts of an objectifying intellect.

Likewise sound is transformed into dynamic force, not only in the sense of a vibration or physical motion, but in that of a deeply felt emotion. Our whole being vibrates in a new rhythm and creates a space experience that lifts us out of our limited individual space into a universal realm in which "the harmony of the spheres" is revealed and from which all great music, poetry, and mantric power are born.

> The forms of divine life in the universe and in nature break forth from the seer as vision, from the singer as sound, and are there in the spell of vision and sound, pure and undisguised.[1]

Vision and sound are integrated in the mantra. Therefore the mantra has the power to call up the inner image. Out of the pure and primordial mantric sound (*bīja*, the seed) arises the word, and the word turns into speech and thought. As long as word and speech flow with the rhythm of the divine song of the poet and seer, in harmony with the eternal flow of life, so long the word has mantric power. But when the word hardens into a mere concept or evaporates into a lifeless abstraction, the vision is lost and the world is estranged into a collection of things and objects. This estrangement is aptly characterized in a passage by Alan Watts:

> Perhaps the ghastly mistake was just that step in man's evolution which made it possible for him to reflect, to comment upon life as a whole. For in being able to stand aside from life and think about it, he also put himself outside it and found it alien. Perhaps thinking about the world and objecting to its whole principle are simply two aspects of but one activity. The very words suggest, do they not, that *we must object to everything that becomes an object?* But aren't there also times when we speak of something that we know as a subject—the subject of this book, the subject I am now studying. I wonder,

then, would it be possible to *subject to life instead of objecting* to it?[2]

In the mantra, indeed, we "subject" ourselves to the powerful aspects of our inner life by opening ourselves and identifying ourselves with them. Mantras, like songs and poetry, are the expression of direct experience, and as such they are capable of evoking similar experiences in those who know how to listen and to open themselves to their subtle vibrations. Though nonverbal in origin, song and poetry use not only sound and rhythm, but word symbols evocative of images which the listener re-creates in his own mind and thus identifies with himself. Thus the mantra is not only the product of direct experience, but the means by which this experience can be re-created. This is implied in the literal meaning of the word mantra: "the tool of the mind."

But like any other tool, its power lies not in itself but in the way it is used. In other words, without knowledge of how to handle it, the mantra is as useless as a chemical or mathematical formula to one who knows nothing of chemistry or mathematics. By merely repeating H_2O we cannot produce water; and people who mindlessly repeat mantras which have no meaning to them, merely waste their time and cheat themselves. When I speak of "meaning," I do not mean an intellectual or verbal content, but a connection with the experiential background with its emotional, religious, and cultural aspects, associations and subtle allusions, especially those related to the realm of the sacred, transcending our finite sense-perceptions or mundane linear logic.

Mantras are seals of initiation, in which a long process of spiritual training culminates. They are the condensation of the essential experience and knowledge acquired in the course of this training and in the act of initiation which consists in the transference of consciousness from Guru to Chela (Skt. *cela,* pupil). This is also called the "transference of power" (Tib. *dBang-bsKur*), because it empowers the pupil to follow the direction toward full realization. He has had a foretaste of this through having shared the consciousness and the achievement of his Guru in the moment of initiation. It is this that gives the pupil the certainty of an attainable aim, the knowledge of its nature, and the incentive to pursue it. He is no more a blind seeker but one who knows where he goes. And he is filled with joyful confidence, which makes his *sādhana* into a matter of deep satisfaction instead of a religious duty or the mere adherance to spiritual discipline. The mantra, moreover, will ever and again call up the presence of the Guru, who thus becomes a continuous inspiration and guide toward the ever deepening realization of the contents and meaning of each of the mantras conveyed by him. Because each mantra is the key to a particular aspect of the human mind.

Thus the mantra, apart from its inherent character as an archetypal symbol in its own right, crystallizing out of centuries of meditative practice and experience, acquires an emotional and individually significant character which connects Guru and Chela; it calls up the very moment of initiation, in which a new dimension of consciousness was opened to the adept.

It is a tragedy of our time that hardly had the West overcome the prejudice against the use of mantras—which had been ridiculed and condemned as meaningless gibberish, even by well-known Indologists and Tibetologists—a number of self-appointed teachers of the East with half-baked scientific ideas began to make a parody of the ancient mantric tradition by employing them as mechanical devices of pseudo-psychiatric practices devoid of any intelligible meaning or religious value.[3] Others, without knowledge of Western mentality, naively tried to import Eastern religious practices without creating the necessary approaches through which Westerners could gain a reasonable understanding of Eastern thought and feeling, without violating their common sense or abandoning the genuine values of their own culture. The widely advertised and commercialized Guru invasion of Western countries has led to such a lowering of all religious and spiritual standards that even the good work that has been done by some of the more serious exponents of Eastern thought is in danger of being misjudged and misinterpreted.

References and Notes

[1] H. Zimmer: *Ewiges Indien*, p. 81.
[2] Alan Watts: *Cloud-Hidden, Whereabouts Unknown*, p. 7, Pantheon Books, New York, 1973.
[3] "It is interesting to observe various metaphysical churches and occult groups tacking the word 'science' to their organization. There is 'religious science,' 'occult science,' etc. all misnamed, but which try to tap the great

prestige presented by the label 'science.' If the common person were to choose the discipline of greatest power in affecting reality, science would have to be it. There is a pervasive knowledge of the power of the literal, quantifying consciousness which is fundamental to science. However, there are other modes of consciousness which are nonlinear, nonsequential and intuitive in operation." (*Dream Reality* by James J. Donahoe, Bench Press, Oakland, CA., 1974)

It is these intuitive, nonlinear and nonsequential modes of consciousness with which we are concerned in meditative and mantric practices. They are neither measurable nor susceptible to biofeedback. But it is typical of the shallow-mindedness of the general public that it promptly falls into the trap of pseudo-scientific spirituality, which believes in measuring and quantifying mental states and experiences, as if the "amount" of energy involved had anything to do with the value or the spiritual significance of the resultant state of mind.

6

MANTRA AS PRIMORDIAL SOUND AND AS ARCHETYPAL WORD SYMBOL

MANTRAS ARE NEITHER MAGIC SPELLS whose inherent power can defy the laws of nature, nor are they formulas for psychiatric therapy or self-hypnosis. They do not possess any power of their own, but are means for arousing and concentrating already existing forces of the human psyche. They are archetypal sound and word symbols that have their origin in the very structure of our consciousness. They are, therefore, not arbitrary creations of individual initiative, but arise from collective or general human experience, modified only by cultural or religious traditions.

> A symbol is, on the one hand, the primitive expression of the Unconscious, on the other hand, it is an idea that corresponds to the highest premonition of the conscious mind. Such things (like archetypal symbols) are not to be thought out, but must grow up again from the dark depth of oblivion, in order to express the outer premonition of the conscious mind and the highest intuition of the spirit, so as to integrate the uniqueness of a consciousness, that is fully aware of the present, with the primordial past of life.[1]

The mantra thus connects our peripheral consciousness with our depth consciousness, which represents the totality of our past. Our past, however, reaches back to a time before the creation of structured language and fixed word forms or concepts. Thus the earliest mantric expressions or seed-syllables (*bīja*) are prelingual, primordial sounds which express feelings but not concepts, emotions rather than ideas.

Just as music conveys meaning, though this cannot be expressed in words, basic mantric sounds convey vibrations which affect our attitudes, our moods, our states of consciousness. They also affect different psychic centers in our bodies which are not connected with thought-activity but with space-feeling, inner movement, emotion or other psychic qualities, because consciousness is located not only in the brain but in various other centers (*cakras*) of psychic energy. When we are moved by a song or a certain passage in music, we cannot even say why this is so. There are no logical reasons. We simply feel that something begins to swing or to vibrate within us like a chord of the same wavelength.

The basic vowel sound of a mantric seed-syllable (*bīja*)—if coming from the depth (both physically and spiritually) of the performer of a sacred ritual, involving his whole body and mind—produces an effect that is difficult to imagine, if we consider that sound merely as represented by a printed syllable in a book or pronounced in a spoken word. Though it is true that ultimately every sound has potential mantric qualities, there is a clear distinction between a mere linguistic vowel sound and that of a mantric seed-syllable. The mantric nature of the latter is indicated by a small circle or dot (*anusvara*) on top of the written character, signifying that the outflowing sound is closed off and turned inward, where it merges from the audible into the inaudible inner vibration. The latter is the real *shabda,* or inner sound which sets in motion the respective psychic forces or *cakras* and frees them from the restrictive entanglements, by loosening the "knots" (*granthi*) into which they have bound themselves, due to our negligence or misuse of them.

As in music we can discern a different vibrational character in all mantric vowels: the O is a rounded, all-inclusive sound, and it is certainly not by chance that in Greek and Roman scripts it has been symbolized by a circle. By superimposing the *anusvara* upon this sound, it is converted into the mantric seed-syllable OṀ. As such it has always been regarded—from the earliest times of Indian history until the present day—as the universal sound. In the words of Rabindranath Tagore, "OṀ is the symbolic word for the infinite, the perfect, the eternal. The sound as such is already perfect and represents the wholeness of things. All our religious contemplations begin with OṀ and end with OṀ. It is meant to fill the mind with the presentiment of eternal perfection and to free it from the world of narrow selfishness."[2]

Buddhism shares with the teachings of the Upanishads the recognition of man's potential universality, but it is equally conscious of the importance of individuality, without which this universality could not be experienced and realized. The Buddhist way, as we may say, begins where that of the Upanishads ends. Although the mantric symbol OṀ is shared by both, its evaluation is not the same, since it depends on the position which the symbol occupies in the particular mantric tradition and in relationship to other symbols within this tradition. OṀ, therefore, in Buddhist tradition stands at the beginning of every mantric formula, but never at its end. (OṀ also is never pronounced or written as A-U-M, a purely scholastic interpretation for the purpose of accommodating the afterthoughts of metaphysical speculation, which has nothing to do with the simple mantric sound.)

OṀ is like the opening of our arms to embrace all that lives. It is like a flower that opens its petals to the light of the sun. The crown-chakra (*sahasrāra-cakra*), in which the OṀ traditionally is placed, is indeed depicted as a thousand-petalled lotus. However, the energies thus received do not remain in the petals of the flower; they have to descend into the darkness of the roots in order to be transformed into a life-giving and life-sustaining force. In the same way, the universality experienced in the OṀ, the primordial sound of timeless reality, must descend and be realized in the depth of the human heart in order to be transformed into vibrant life.

OṀ is the ascent towards universality, HŪṀ the descent of the state of universality into the depth of the human heart. OṀ and HŪṀ are like counterpoints in a musical score. OṀ is the infinite; but HŪṀ is the infinite in the finite, the eternal in the temporal, the timeless in the moment, the unconditioned in the conditioned, the formless as basis of all form: it is the Wisdom of the Great Mirror, which reflects the void as well as the objects and reveals the emptiness in the things as much as the things in the emptiness.

The OṀ stands like the sun in the center of the mandala, the place of Vairocana, the "Sun Buddha," the Radiating One; the HŪṀ stands in the east, the place of Aksobhya. Though the east is the entrance-point into the mandala, the HŪṀ cannot precede the OṀ in any mantric formula, because the presence of the center is the *conditio sine qua non* of the mandala, which in Tibetan is rightly translated as "center [and] circumference" (*dKhyil-hKhor*). In other words, we must have passed through the experience of OṀ in order to reach and to understand the still deeper experience of HŪṀ. Many have experienced moments of universality, but very few have been able to realize and to incorporate them in their life.

The only person among the great leaders and thinkers of modern Hinduism who could see this clearly—without in any way being conscious of the parallelism between his own philosophy and that of the Buddhist Vajrayāna—was Srī Aurobindo. He emphasized the importance of the descent of the "Supramental" into human life and consciousness after the highest spiritual attainment of universality—thus going beyond the original aim of upanishadic thought.

The basic vowel sound of the long Ū in HŪṀ is the sound of depth, vibrating forth in the *anusvara,* which merges into the inaudible. The vowel "u" (=oo) expresses a downward movement and represents the lower limit in the tonal scale of the human voice, the threshold of silence, which in Tibetan is called "the door of the inaudible" (*U-ni thos-pa-med-pahi sgo*). The aspirate "h" which precedes it, is the sound of breath (*prāna*), the subtle life-force. The sonorous inwardly directed, inwardly vibrating final sound of the nasalized "m", representing the *anusvara,* stands as it were between consonants and vowels, being in fact the combination of both, thus hinting at a state beyond duality. This is why the *anusvara* is the characteristic mark of practically all seed-syllables (*bīja-mantras*), which distinguishes them from ordinary vowel sounds.

An exception is the long ĀH, the third most important mantric sound and, at the same time, the basic sound of all language. In its short form it is potentially inherent in all consonants, according to Sanskrit rules, so that in Devanagari (and also in Tibetan), it need not be written, except when it bears the full sound of a long "ā", when it is indicated by a vertical line, added to the preceding consonant. The sound "Ā", in its tonal as well as in its mantric value, stands in the middle between the all-inclusiveness of "Ō" and the depth of "Ū". It is horizontal in movement and expresses the faculty of speech and thought (corresponding to *"logos"* in Western tradition). It is the first sound of the new-born child. It is the first expression of communication with and recognition of others and the surrounding world. It is the expression of wonder and direct awareness. As the *bīja-mantra* of Amoghasiddhi it represents the Wisdom That Accomplishes All Works: the spontaneous action, prompted by the realization of both the unity of life and the uniqueness of each of its forms. These two principles are embodied in the two preceding stages in the temporal order of the mandala, namely in Ratnasambhava's Wisdom of the Essential Oneness of Life and in Amitābha's Distinguishing Wisdom of Inner Vision.

OṀ

ĀḤ

HŪṀ

represent three planes of reality:

the universal,

the ideal, and

the individual

and three dimensions of consciousness, incorporated in three psychic centers:

the Crown Center (*sahasrara-cakra*)

the Throat Center (*viśuddha-cakra*)

the Heart Center (*anāhata-cakra*).

Therefore we find that in Tibetan Thangkas (painted scrolls or temple banners), depicting Buddhas, Bodhisattvas, prominent religious personalities or fierce protectors of the Dharma, the respective *bīja-mantras* are written on the reverse side of the painting, on the places corresponding to the crown of the head, the throat, and the heart of the Thangkas central figure.

Thus, OṀ - ĀḤ - HŪṀ represent the three great mysteries of the Vajrayāna, namely the "Mysteries of Body, Speech, and Mind" (*kāya, vāk, citta*). What is meant here by "body" is not the physical body, but the whole universe which represents our cosmic body, of which our physical body is only a miniature replica. The Enlightened One, whose mind embraces the universe, thus lives in the *Dharmakāya*, the universal body.

The Mystery of Speech is more than that of mere words or concepts; it is the principle of all mental representation and communication, be it in form of audible, visible, or thinkable symbols, in which the highest knowledge is conveyed and imparted. It is the mystery of the creative sound, of mantric speech, of sacred vision and intelligible thought, from which flows the Dharma-revelation of an Enlightened One. "As in the first awakening of [primordial] sound, there was a magic compulsion which by its directness and immediacy overpowered the seer-poet through image and word, so it is for all following ages which know how to use mantric words, a compelling magic tool for calling up immediate reality: the appearance of gods, the play of forces."[3]

Indeed, the Mystery of Speech is the mystery of mantric power and creative imagination, from which dreams, ideas, thoughts, art and culture, religion and science, are born. It is from this mysterious quality of the human mind that the conception and visualization of the luminous bodies of Dhyani-Buddhas and Bodhisattvas have sprung: known as the "Bodies of Spiritual Enjoyment," or of "Bliss and Inspiration" (*sambhoga-kāya*).

The Mystery of the Mind, however, is more than can be conceived and grasped in thoughts and ideas: it is the realization of the spirit in this our world of individual existence in the depth of the human heart. It is the transformation of the mortal body into the precious vessel of the *Nirmāṇa-Kāya*, the Body of Transformation, the visible manifestation of the *Dharma-Kāya*.

From the level of the universal law (*dharmadhātu*) to the plane of ideal perception and ideation (*sambhoga-kāya*) of mantric sound and inner vision, consciousness finally crystallizes on the plane of human realization (*nirmāna-kāya*). Thus the three Mysteries of Body, Speech, and Mind, whose experience has been condensed into the *bīja-mantras* OṀ - ĀḤ -

HŪM, are intimately related to the doctrine of the Three Bodies or the principles in which an Enlightened One, a Buddha, manifests himself on the three planes of reality: the universal, the ideal, and the individual.

In the next chapter we shall discuss the fourth most important *bīja-mantra* associated with Amitabha, the seed-syllable HRĪḤ.

References and Notes

[1] C. G. Jung: *The Secret of the Golden Flower* (translated from the original German edition, p. 32).
[2] Rabindranath Tagore: *Sādhanā*.
[3] Heinrich Zimmer: *Ewiges Indien*.

7

MEANING OF THE MANTRIC SEED-SYLLABLE "HRĪḤ"

THE MANTRIC SEED-SYLLABLE HRĪḤ has the nature of the flame: it has its warmth, its intensity, its upward movement, its radiance and its color. It is the sacred sound-symbol of Amitābha, whose color is red and whose seat in the mandala of Dhyāni-Buddhas is in the West, the place of the setting sun and the hour of meditation (*upāsana*), when the day's work is done and peace descends upon the world. Physical activity has come to rest and gives place to inner activity: the mind is freed from the fetters of mundane cares and soars up to the spiritual realm of Amitābha, symbolized in Sukhavati, the abode of bliss.

Contemplating the setting sun, the meditator (*sādhaka*) visualizes the radiant deep-red figure of Amitābha, glowing with love and compassion for every sentient creature; and as this radiance surrounds and fills the *sādhaka*, the petals of his heart are opened, and in deep devotion he repeats the mantra "OṂ AMITĀBHA HRĪḤ."

In the OṂ he makes himself as wide as the universe (the sound "O" is all-embracing; its movement is like opening one's arms), so as to make room for the Infinite (*amita*) Light (*ābha*) that is Amitābha, and in the HRĪḤ he kindles the upward-leaping flame of inspiration and devotion, by which he partakes of the very nature of Amitābha.

Nothing could give a more adequate expression of his feelings of devotion than Milarepa's heart-stirring prayer:

> Lord, from the sun-orb of Thy grace
> The radiant rays of light have shone
> And opened wide the petals of the lotus of my heart,
> So that it breathes forth the fragrance born of knowledge,
> For which I am for ever bounden unto Thee;
> So I will worship Thee by constant meditation.
> Vouchsafe to bless me in mine efforts,
> That good may come to every sentient being.
> Not one movement of my body will I give to any worldly purpose:
> But body, speech and heart I dedicate to winning Buddhahood.[1]

Amitābha's "Distinguishing Wisdom" (*pratyaveksana-jñāna*) is the wisdom of inner vision (*dhyāna*); in other words, it is not intellectual analysis or discrimination, but a perfect and unprejudiced awareness of the manifold forms of life and phenomena against the background of fundamental oneness. The significance of this awareness and the acknowledgment that differentiation is as important as unity (because both condition each other) becomes apparent in Amitābha's manifestation on the plane of individuality and action, when he appears in the form of Avalokiteśvara, in whom the rays of his infinite light are transformed into innumerable helping arms and outstretched hands. In the palm of each of these hands appears the "eye of wisdom," to show that *upāya* (skillful means, i.e., the power of love and compassion) must always be accompanied by *prajñā* (transcendental wisdom). Only in this way can Avalokiteśvara be the guide and helper of all those who are desirous of liberation.

Thus, on the plane of individuality and action, the *bīja-mantra* HRĪḤ, like a living and growing seed, expands and blossoms out into the formula OṂ MAṆI PADME HŪṂ. MAṆI, the jewel, is Avalokiteśvara, who is being realized in the "lotus (*padma*) of the heart" also known as the *anāhata cakra*.

In other words, HRĪḤ is the sum total of OṂ MAṆI PADME HŪM; it is the seed from which this mantra springs and into which it is integrated again. Therefore the HRĪḤ is generally added to the OṂ MAṆI PADME HŪM. It goes without saying that the above-mentioned interpretation of this mantra does not exhaust its meaning, because every mantra is multidimensional and can be applied to various planes of experience. Therein consists its living value and its creative faculty.

On the first plane we have to consider the pure sound value of a mantra and its psychological associations; on the second plane its verbal meaning (as far as this can be established) and its mental and traditional associations; on the third plane its creative or evocative value (which depends on the particular experience of initiation in the supreme moment of the transference of power); and finally its growing and expanding spiritual value in the practice and experience of progressive *sādhana*.

In such a *sādhana* the mantra takes on different dimensions and evokes different mental images and visualizations, depending on whether the mantra is applied to the universal realm of the *Dharmakāya*, or to that of the *Sambhogakāya*, the realm of creative vision and spiritual enjoyment, or to that of the *Nirmanakāya*, the realm of action and transformation of both body and mind.

In the case of *bīja* or seed-syllables, we have furthermore to consider in which connection or combination they are used, because—as in a chemical formula—it is the combination that determines their specific meaning. For this reason we can discuss here the seed-syllable HRĪḤ only on the first and second of the above-mentioned planes.

"H" is the sound of the vital principle, the sound of breath, the symbol of all life. "R" is the sound of fire, the seed-syllable of which is RAM. The "I" stands highest in the tonal scale of vowels; it has the greatest intensity, the highest rate of vibration and, therefore, represents the highest spiritual activity and differentiation. The aspirated after-sound (*visarga*), which we have transcribed as "H", has no tonal value and is used in Tibet only as a written symbol (the two small circles after the main body of the letter), without being pronounced.

It distinguishes the seed-syllable from the ordinary use of the word and emphasizes its mantric character.

The literal meaning of *"hrī"* is "to blush" (which consists in taking on the color of Amitābha), "to feel shame." In the Pāli Abhidhamma *"hiri"* takes the third place in the list of wholesome or "beautiful" (*sobhana*) factors of consciousness, next to faith (*saddha*) and mindfulness (*sati*). If we analyze the psychological origin of the feeling or innate faculty of shame, we shall find that it is based on the noblest quality of the human character, namely an inborn sense of values and responsibility. It is one of the strangest and most subtle of phenomena, in which the deepest forces of the human soul act independently of our desires, our will, and our intellect, and set in motion physical reactions (diversions in the bloodstream) which likewise are not under our control.

What is this intangible, mysterious force? It is the inner voice, the moral law (*dharma*) within us, the voice of conscience, of inner knowledge (*bodhi*)—not the intellectual, but the intuitive, spontaneous knowledge—due to which we do the right thing without expectation of reward or advantage. It is the guiding principle and the special virtue of the Bodhisattva, who acts without being bound by the results of his action (*karma*), because he has renounced its fruits, being bent on the enlightenment of all, unconcerned with his own welfare. He is like the sun which shines equally for sinners and saints; he is one who has realized the force of HRĪḤ, of Amitābha's wisdom of inner vision.

This may suffice to give an introduction to the inner meaning of the seed-syllable HRĪḤ. But just as written music cannot convey the emotional and spiritual impact of heard or performed music, so the sound-symbol of a mantra and its intellectual analysis cannot convey the experience of an initiate and of the profound effects it creates in the course of prolonged practice (*sādhana*).

Though the first impetus is given by the Guru through his "transference of power" (*abhiṣeka*, Tib. "Wangkur") (and how much he can transfer depends on his own status, as well as on the preparedness and receptivity of the recipient), it depends on the *sādhaka*, whether he is able to keep the mantra alive and to put it into practice. A man may possess a formula for atomic power; yet, unless he knows how to put this formula into practice, he remains as impotent as before. A mantra has

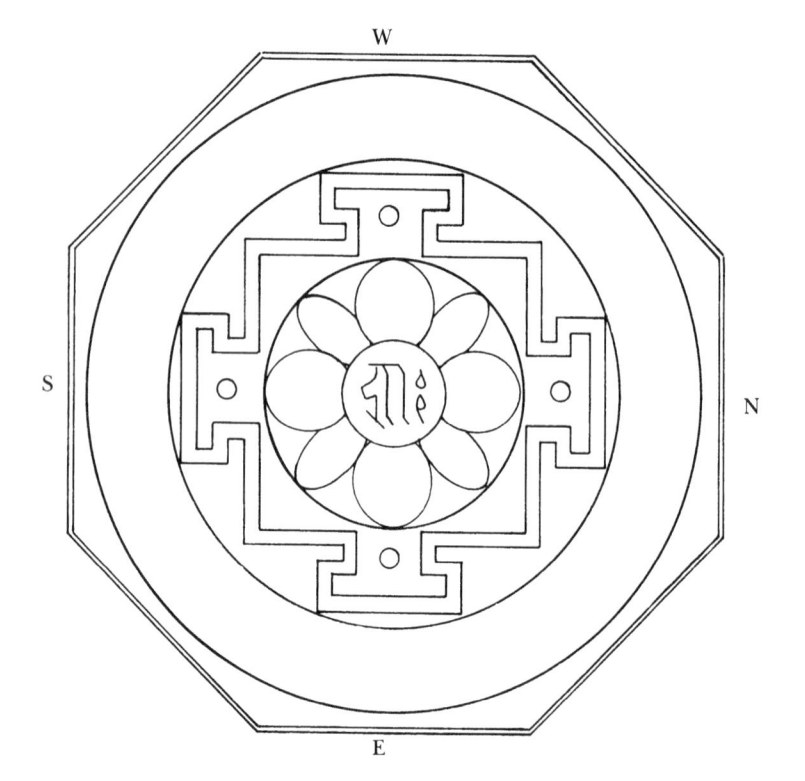

MANDALA OF AMITĀBHA

in which the seed-syllable HRĪḤ is put into the center, while OṂ is put into the place of the west (on top), which originally was occupied by Amitābha's HRĪḤ.

This means that the central figure or its seed-syllable, like the key in musical notation, determines the character of the mandala and modifies the meaning of all its other parts.

The above reproduced mandala, which has been greatly simplified in order to bring out more clearly the most important features, shows the square ground-plan of the universal temple, open towards the four directions of space. It is surrounded by three protective circles: an inner circle of lotus petals, a middle circle of diamond scepters (vajras) and an outer circle of flames, —symbolizing purity of heart, the steadfastness and determination of a concentrated mind, and transcendental knowledge. (More about this on pp. 95 & 193) no power in itself, but only serves to concentrate and to direct and release those forces and faculties which are always present in the individual but beyond his reach.

A mantra, like a *koan*, defies rationalization, but at the same time it has the advantage of *starting* with a direct experience (and not only perchance leading to one) and of containing a specific direction, which leads the *sādhaka* into ever deeper realms of awareness, irrespective of whether he succeeds in reaching the ultimate realization. And what is more—it never can mislead, because it does not seek the solution of a problem but rather the dissolution of impediments, the loosening of the knots (*granthi*) into which we have entangled ourselves consciously and unconsciously by our desires, prejudices, and the accumulated effects of our attachments.

Every thought creates a new thought, and every answer a new question. But it is only when our thoughts have come to rest and our consciousness regains the state of pure luminosity and sensitivity, that the gates of the great mysteries of the spirit are opened and the fullness of power, or realization, descends upon us.

If I use the word "power," I do not mean it in the sense of something that acts outwardly or can be used for personal ends or for our own aggrandizement, but as something that brings about a complete transformation of the individual in whom it is present. And it is this transformation into an exponent of super-individual reality that can act upon others.

Thus a Guru is able to perform the rites of initiation and the transference of power only if he has generated this power with himself through years of hard training—and even then he will generally spend many days and nights in deep meditation before performing any of these rites.

Only those who have had the good fortune to witness the physical and spiritual transformation which takes place in the Guru can imagine what it means and how it is possible to confer upon others something of the bliss and inspiration of a realm beyond words: the realm of the Buddhas, the realm of Enlightenment.

References and Notes

[1] Translated by Lama Kazi Dawasamdup, in *Tibet's Great Yogi Milarepa*, ed. by W. Y. Evans-Wentz, p. 143.

MULTIDIMENSIONALITY OF SEED-SYLLABLES (BĪJA)

IT IS SIGNIFICANT that the main mantric seed-syllables (*bīja*) of the Vajrayāna, and in particular those used in the basic structure of the mandala of the Dhyāni-Buddhas, are based on simple vowel sounds, like o, ā, ū, ī, corresponding to four movements; the circular (all-inclusive), the horizontal, the downward, and the upward movement.

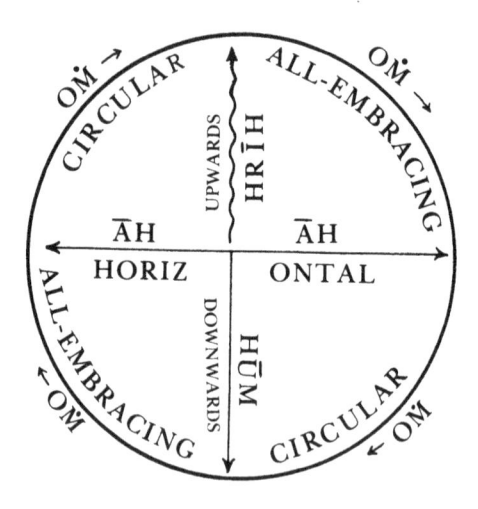

THE FOUR MOVEMENTS OF MANTRIC SOUND

The upward and downward movements of HRĪḤ and HŪṂ also correspond to the movements of the respective elements with which they are associated in the mandala: fire moves upward, water downward. Earth and air, associated with the *bījas* TRĀṂ and ĀH stretch out horizontally.

Just as water and fire are opposites in movement, so Akṣobhya and Amitābha stand opposite each other in the mandala. But their polarity, i.e. their compensatory nature, is indicated by the fact that they belong to the same axis in the diagram upon which the mandala is constructed. Their common factor is that both represent introspective attitudes; their difference consists in the fact that Akṣobhya's attitude is mainly a reflective and receptive awareness, while Amitābha's attitude is that of discerning or distinguishing vision, i.e. active and creative.

Their corresponding mudrās show the same tendency. Akṣobhya's reflective attitude is expressed by the inward turned palm of his right hand, Amitābha's distinguishing vision by the upward turned palm of his right hand. Thus the (vertical) east-west axis of the mandala may be called the axis of intro-

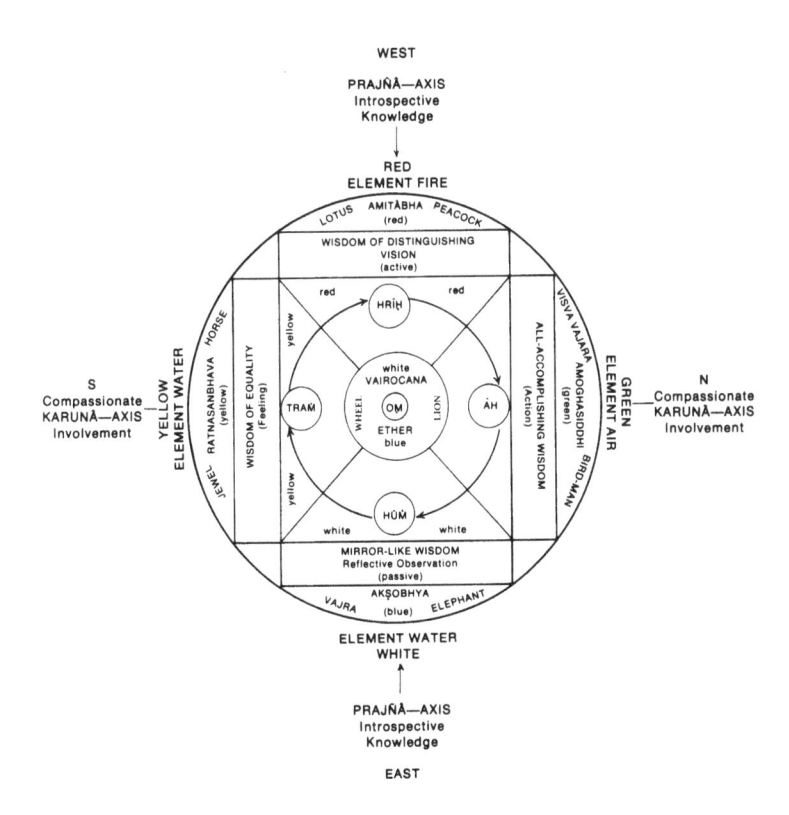

BASIC STRUCTURE OF THE MANDALA OF
THE FIVE DHYĀNI-BUDDHAS:
THEIR BĪJA-MANTRAS, WISDOMS, ELEMENTS,
COLORS AND SYMBOLS

spective knowledge (*prajñā*). In contrast to this the (horizontal) north-south axis may be called the outwardly directed axis of compassionate involvement.

Just as earth and air are opposites in density and movability, so Ratnasambhava and Amoghasiddhi are the polar opposites in the horizontal axis of the mandala: Ratnasambhava represents feeling and emotion, while Amoghasiddhi represents volition and action. Both are extravertive or communicative, i.e. directed toward other beings, either in the feeling of love and compassion or in the selfless action motivated by these feelings. This outward-directedness and communication is expressed in the mudrās of both Ratnasambhava and Amoghasiddhi, whose right-hand palms are turned outward.

From all this it becomes evident that the mandala reveals a double polarity: first, that of *prajñā* and *karunā*—the axis of introspective knowledge and the axis of compassionate involvement—and second, the inner polarity of each single axis, such as reflective awareness and creative vision of the east-west axis, or feeling and action (or emotion and volition) of the south-north axis.

But a mandala is not merely a static structure of the mind; it represents the inner space in which we move. And our movement here again reveals a third kind of polarity insofar as we are alternating between inward and outward directed states or mental attitudes. In the clockwise movement beginning from the eastern starting point, the meditator proceeds from the inward directed attitude of introspection (Akṣobhya) to the outward directed attitude of communication (Ratnasambhava). In the third movement he turns again inward in the attitude of meditative absorption (Amitābha), and in the fourth movement again outward in action (Amoghasiddhi).

This is indicated by the respective alternating mudrās, as mentioned before. However, the change in attitude does not mean a break in the continuity of the *sādhana* or a negation of the previous experience. On the contrary, each experience forms the basis for the subsequent step and is thus integrated in the new attitude and experience.

Without the Wisdom of the Great Mirror, which reveals to us our true nature and our position in the world, we could not conceive the essential oneness of life and our solidarity with other sentient beings. And likewise, the Wisdom of Distinguishing Vision is possible only on the basis of the essential unity of life, which enables us to see the interrelatedness of forms and individual beings. The underlying unity makes it possible to appreciate the value and the beauty of differentiation and the significance of individuality. Without it unity would be meaningless and mutual understanding impossible. And again, it is on this basis of recognizing and understanding both individuality and the essential oneness of life, that unselfish and spontaneous action can succeed in bringing happiness and liberation into the world.

The *bījas* proceed in a similar way. The OṀ is contained in the HŪṀ, as it precedes every mantra, as for instance that of Akṣobhya: "OṀ Akṣobhya HŪṀ." And likewise, if we now proceed from Akṣobhya to Ratnasambhava, the experience of HŪṀ (and OṀ) is included in the TRAṀ, while both the experience of the HŪṀ and of the TRAṀ are included in the HRĪḤ, and correspondingly all these *bījas* are present in the experience of ĀḤ.

When now we return to the HŪṀ of Akṣobhya, we experience his Mirror-like Wisdom on a much higher level, a level that comes much nearer to that of the center. And, in fact, if we arrive on the highest level of Akṣobhya's Wisdom, it no longer reflects merely the individual situation of the *sādhaka*, but the universality of Vairocana's *Dharma-dhātu Wisdom*, which is now reflected in the Great Mirror.

When this is the case, Akṣobhya under the name Vajrasattva-Akṣobhya (the Diamond Being) becomes identical with the center of the mandala. It is for this reason that Akṣobhya and Vairocana become interchangeable. This relationship is clearly expressed by the colors associated with them. The body-color of Akṣobhya is blue, the radiation of the Mirror-like Wisdom emanating from his heart is white (like the reflection and the color of the element water). The body-color of Vairocana is white, and the radiation of the Dharmadhātu Wisdom, emanating from his heart (i.e. from his essential being) is blue, (like the color of the element ether).

According to the emphasis upon the one or the other aspect of these Dhyāni-Buddhas, the triangular field on the eastern side of the mandala is either white or blue, in which case the circular space around Vairocana takes the opposite color, i.e. blue when Akṣobhya's field is white (as in the case of our diagram of the basic mandala), and white when Akṣobhya's field is blue.

A deeper explanation can be found in the statement of the Viññānavādins that *mano-vijñāna,* the empirical consciousness (from which we start at the beginning of our meditation) and the universal consciousness are overlapping in what has been defined as *manas,* whose object is not the sense-world, but that ever-flowing stream of becoming (*santāna*) which is limited neither by birth and death nor by individual forms of appearance, but contains the sum total of all our past, enshrined in the depth of our innermost being. It is the manifestation of the basic universal consciousness or *ālaya-viññāna.*

While the *mano-vijñāna* sorts out and judges the results of the five kinds of sense perceptions, the *ālaya-vijñāna* has been compared to the ocean, on the surface of which waves and currents are formed when disturbed by outer influences, but which reflects the clear light of heaven when undisturbed by emotions, desires or aversions, thus becoming the Great Mirror of Akṣobhya's Wisdom.

Mediating between the universal consciousness and the individual intellect is the spiritual consciousness (*manas*), which takes part in both sides. It represents the stabilizing element of the human mind, the central point of balance, upholding the coherence of its contents by being the stable point of reference. But for the same reason it can also be the cause for the conception of a permanent ego in the unenlightened individual, who mistakes this relative point of reference for the real and permanent center of his own personality. Or, as the Laṅkāvatāra Sūtra expresses it: "Intuitive mind (*manas*) is one with Universal Mind (*ālaya-vijñāna*) by reason of its participation in Transcendental Intelligence (*ārya jñāna*) and is one with the mind-system (the five senses and the intellect) by its comprehension of differentiated knowledge."

Thus it depends whether this intuitive mind is directed toward the world of differentiated sense impressions or toward the universal [depth-] consciousness. In the first case it reflects our momentary position in the present world; this is the situation with which we begin our meditation. In the latter case it reflects our true universal nature and our identity with the *Dharmadhātu,* at which we arrive after we have moved through the mandala many times in ever narrower circles which finally merge into the center.

Since thus Akṣobhya is the reflection of Vairocana on the plane of human consciousness, the mantra HŪṀ represents the humanized experience of the *Dharmakāya*: the realization of the *Dharmakāya* in the human body, which thus becomes *Nirmāṇakāya*. Herein lies the special importance of HŪṂ, because it brings down the supramental upon the human plane, which is the aim of Buddhahood. OṂ is, so to say, the raw material, the universe in its pure suchness and objectivity, or the *conditio sine qua non* of all that is or appears in form. But the HŪṂ contains the *experience* of this suchness plus that of all its modifications. It comprises both unity and diversity.

OṂ may be compared to the purity of the child, in whom all possibilities of development are present in a latent form, while HŪṂ is the return to the purity and simplicity of the child after a life of human experience and with the knowledge and compassion that grow out of deep suffering and exalted joy. It is the attitude of an Enlightened One who has "gone the Way," who has arrived at the "other shore" (*param*). Thus the HŪṂ in its highest potential contains the OṂ and all the other mantras of the Dhyāni-Buddhas.

In those schools of the Vajrayāna which follow the mystic or inner path of Vajrasattva (the Adamantine Being)—the active reflex or emanation of Akṣobhya—in whom the rays of the combined Wisdoms are integrated, Vajrasattva-Akṣobhya becomes the exponent of all transformed *skandhas,* integrated into the "purified aggregate of consciousness," while Vairocana becomes the exponent of the "purified aggregate of bodily form," i.e. the principle of spatial extension, or of space as the precondition of all bodily existence. In this case the HŪṂ assumes a higher dimension than the one that stood at the beginning of the meditative path. It is the integration of all the experiences and spiritual attitudes and Wisdoms encountered in the process of the four movements around the center of the mandala. This may be summarized in the following formula:[1]

$$\left.\begin{array}{l}\text{OṂ}\\ \text{HŪṂ}\\ \text{TRAṂ}\\ \text{HRĪḤ}\\ \bar{\text{A}}\text{Ḥ}\end{array}\right\}\left\{\begin{array}{l}\text{OṂ-HŪṂ}\\ \text{OṂ-HŪṂ-TRAṂ}\\ \text{OṂ-HŪṂ-TRAṂ-HRĪḤ}\\ \text{OṂ-HŪṂ-TRAṂ-HRĪḤ-ĀḤ} = \text{HŪṂ}^5\end{array}\right.$$

The same idea is expressed in a more graphic form, in which the seed-syllable HŪṂ is visualized in the colors of the five Wisdoms and their respective Dhyani-Buddhas.

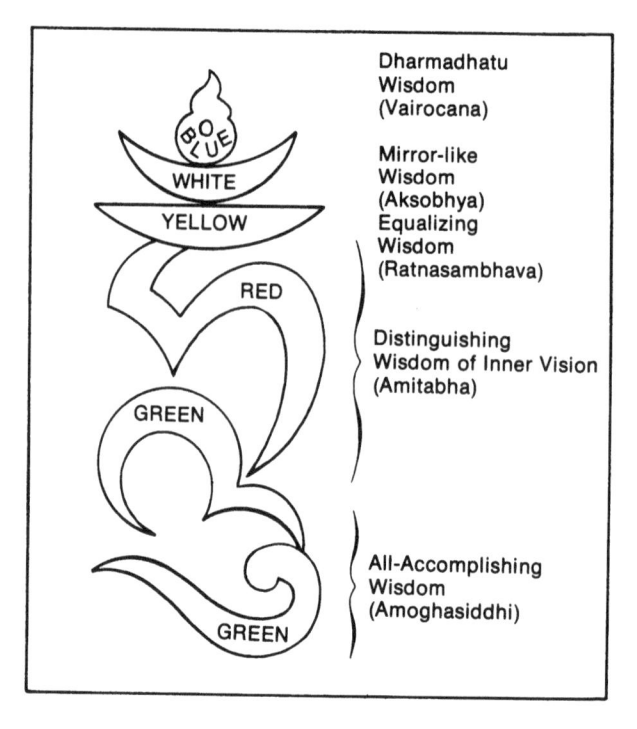

```
                    Dharmadhatu
                    Wisdom
                    (Vairocana)

                    Mirror-like
                    Wisdom
                    (Aksobhya)
                    Equalizing
                    Wisdom
                    (Ratnasambhava)

                    Distinguishing
                    Wisdom of Inner Vision
                    (Amitabha)


                    All-Accomplishing
                    Wisdom
                    (Amoghasiddhi)
```

References and Notes

[1] This formula shows, as the name *seed*-syllable (*bīja*) indicates, that it is not a static but a growing thing, which extends into ever higher dimensions through its steadily accumulating experiential content and spiritual as well as intellectual relations.

9

MULTIDIMENSIONALITY OF MANTRIC FORMULAS AND THEIR RELATIONSHIP TO THE HIGHER PSYCHIC CENTERS

IN CONTRAST to the prelingual seed-syllables, or primary mantric sounds (*bīja*), their combination with religious symbols or names may fittingly be called secondary mantras, though they are in no way inferior or secondary in importance. In fact seed-syllables are rarely used by themselves, and most of the important mantras are either preceded by or placed between *bījas*. The *bījas* are both the motive-power as well as the indication of the levels of reality toward which the mantra is directed. They may also indicate the place in the basic mandala, which is divided into five "families," headed by one of the Dhyāni-Buddhas and symbolized by the specific emblem of each of them. The Buddha family is symbolized by the Wheel of the Dharma, which belongs to the center of the maṇḍala and is characterized by the *bīja* OṀ. The eastern section of the mandala is occupied by the Vajra Family, whose *bīja* is HŪṀ. The southern section is occupied by the Jewel Family (*ratna*), the western sector by the Lotus Family (*padma*), and the northern sector is occupied by the Karma Family, whose symbol is the *viśva-vajra* or the sword and whose *bīja* is ĀḤ. Practically all mantras begin with OṀ, because it is the universal basis for all Buddhas and Bodhisattvas. But any mantra containing the seed-syllable HRĪḤ would be related to the western sector of Amitābha, while the HŪṀ would be related to the Vajra Family of Akṣobhya, Vajrasattva, Vajradhara etc. However, it must be pointed out that the Vajra Family, as already indicated by the importance of the seed-syllable HŪṀ, has a very special position in the meditational system of the Vajrayāna, because it occupies at the same time the heart center (*anāhata cakra*), i.e. the place of realization on the human plane, which to the tantric Buddhist is of paramount importance, because it is the plane of decision.

As it is impossible to delineate all the laws and modifications that govern the mantric tradition of the Vajrayāna within this limited frame, we may confine ourselves to the following general observations and a few appropriate examples.

Most mantras are a combination of seed-syllables and symbol-words of evocative power. What constitutes evocative power depends on the cultural and religious background of the individual, i.e. on the connections which the symbol establishes with visible, tangible, imaginable, or experienceable objects or with deep-rooted emotions. In other words, the symbol must stimulate the imagination and therewith the creative qualities of the human mind, or it must call up emotions that are strong enough to carry the *sādhaka* into a state of exaltation, devotion or inner unification. Devotional symbols are generally connected with the names of deities (as some of the Hindu mantras and some of the mantras connected with local deities or protective powers in popular Buddhism) or enlightened beings, such as Buddhas and Bodhisattvas or their counterparts in meditative experience, according to the spiritual level and the religious background. Where this background is missing, the symbol has no emotional appeal, and therefore no power, nor any intellectual value. This is the reason why mantric formulas of this kind cannot be taken over by people who have not grown up in the particular religious tradition from which these mantras have sprung, or people who have not grown *into* such a tradition through understanding, practice, training and spiritual experience or assimilation.

In tantric *sādhana* the sound of the mantra calls up the visible symbol or image, its color, its emotional attitude, its movement or gesture, its place or direction in the maṇḍala and its relationship to all the other features or qualities of the spiritual symphony that represents the totality of the human mind and the universe it reflects. And in the same way as we cannot understand or even less create a symphony (in the musical sense) without having studied or practiced each basic instrument and the laws of their coordination and cooperation, in the same way we cannot understand or make use of a maṇḍala unless we have studied and practiced each single item that makes up the maṇḍala.

Mantra, yantra, mudrā and maṇḍala form a perfect unity of sound, visible symbol, gesture, and mutual interrelationship. In the Karaṇḍa Vyūha it is said that Avalokiteśvara refused to teach the six syllables of his sacred mantra without initiation into its deeper meaning and the maṇḍala connected with it; because as each word gets its specific meaning through the context in which it is used, so each mantric sound or word derives its particular meaning from the way it is combined with others and placed in the maṇḍala.

> If Avalokiteśvara does not want to communicate the six syllables without a description of the maṇḍala, this has its reason in the fact that the formula as a creation in the realm of sound is incomplete and useless if its sisters in the realm of inner and outer vision and in the sphere of gestures are not combined with it If this formula is to transform a being and to lead it

to the state of enlightenment . . . it must be able to occupy all spheres of reality and activity of the initiate: speech, imagination, bodily attitude, and movement.[1]

If the mantra does not occupy the complete human being, his mind, his senses, his body and his imagination, it cannot lead to an integration of all his faculties and make him into a whole man (a "holy one" in this sense), which is the precondition of enlightenment. Without the multidimensionality of the mantra, it would not be able to combine the diverse realms of outer and inner reality, of body and mind, emotion and action, the visible and the audible, the tangible and the intangible, the concrete and the ideal, actuality and imagination.

Through the combination of seed-syllables and symbol-words we enter from the realm of prelingual sound-symbols into the sphere of imaginative thought and poetic speech, speech that reaches beyond the meaning of words to the essence of things and feelings. The words of ancient poets and seers were words of power which formed the human mind, created religions and cultures, art and literature, and all that spurred human beings to push on beyond the needs of the day, beyond the dictates of necessity, into the realm of freedom, of self-expression, of fulfillment of human dreams and aspirations.

The powerful six syllables of Avalokiteśvara's mantra OṀ MAṆI PADME HŪṀ HRĪḤ have filled a millenium of Tibetan history with a superhuman aspiration, reflected by millions of inscriptions, carved on stones and rocks and displayed in gigantic letters on mountainsides, until the whole country was saturated with the consciousness of the great compassionate Bodhisattva, the emanation of the infinite light of Amitābha's *Dharmakāya*.

This mantra is a good example of the combinations of seed-syllables and symbol-words. The words Maṇi and Padma can easily be translated as Jewel and Lotus, which led to the facile and deceptive interpretation, "O Thou Jewel in the Lotus, Amen!"—which only shows that mantras cannot be simply translated or approached by philological means. They cannot be understood without their experiential background and the manifold associations of their word-symbols.

Maṇi is a synonym of *ratna,* and signifies not only a jewel in the concrete sense, but anything that is precious; and in the religious parlance of Buddhism *ratna* is associated with the Buddha, his doctrine (*dharma*) and his community of those who have realized the Dharma (*sangha*). *Maṇi* is also associated with the idea of the magic wish-fulfilling stone (*cintamaṇi*). Thus *maṇi* stands for the Enlightened One, or the enlightened mind in general, while *padma* is not only the lotus blossom, but indicates the spiritual faculty of unfoldment. In this capacity it is a synonym for *cakra*, the center of psychic forces which are consciously activated, so that they unfold themselves like the petals of a lotus and radiate like the rays of the sun. The *cakra* itself is a sun symbol: the spokes of the wheel emanating from the nave like the rays of the sun.

In this connection *maṇi-padme* (locative) symbolizes that the Light of Amitābha (whose red color indicates the western sector of the mandala) is realized in the lotus of the Heart Center (*anāhata cakra*). This is iconographically represented by the figure of Avalokiteśvara who holds a red jewel before his chest, at the level of the Heart Cakra.

This gesture has often been misinterpreted as the gesture of praying (*āñjali-mudrā*), instead of the lotus-mudrā (*padma-mudrā*), when the hands form a chalice in which the jewel rests. Even if the jewel is absent (as in many representations) the lotus-mudrā distinguishes itself from the praying or worshipful gesture (*namaskāra-mudrā*), insofar as the fingertips are slightly apart, while the roots of the hands are touching each other.

If we now see the whole mantra in the light of the Three Bodies (*trikāya*) and their corresponding Three Mysteries, the formula takes on a wider meaning: In the OṀ we experience the *Dharmakāya* and the mystery of the universal body, in *Maṇi* the *Sambhogakāya,* the jewel of the inspirational "Body of Bliss," in which the Enlightened Ones appear before the inner eye in the splendor of their virtues and accomplishments. From this wondrous vision flows the inspiration of all immortal art, highest wisdom and profound truth, expressed in mantric speech and poetry. In *Padma* we experience the spiritual unfoldment of the *Nirmāṇakāya,* and in HŪṀ we experience the *Vajrakāya* as the integration of the Three Bodies and the Three Mysteries of Body, Speech, and Mind. In the HRĪḤ, finally we dedicate the totality of our transformed personality—which thus has become the *Vajrakāya*—to the services of Amitābha.

In the advanced practice of meditation, the various forms in which Amitābha appears are transmitted to the corresponding psychic centers of the *sādhaka*. Thus the *dharmakāya*-aspect of Amitābha is visualized on top of the Crown Center (*sahasrāra cakra*), seated upon the "thousand-petalled lotus." In his *sambhogakāya*-aspect, in which he appears as *Amitāyus*, the Buddha of Boundless Life, crowned with the crown of the Five Wisdoms and adorned with the ornaments of his spiritual qualities and accomplishments, he is visualized in the Throat Center (*viśuddha cakra*). And in his *nirmāṇakāya*-aspect as Avalokiteśvara, he is visualized in the Heart Center (*anāhata cakra*).

As a further example of the multidimensionality of mantras we may take a quick look at one of the chief mantras of the Tibetan Nyingma School, whose founder, Padmasambhava, is the earliest exponent of the Vajrayana in Tibet. This is his mantra:

OṀ ĀḤ HŪṀ / VAJRA GURU PADMA SIDDHI HŪṀ!

OM	ĀH	HŪM	VAJRA
DHARMAKĀYA	SAMBHOGAKĀYA	NIRMĀNAKĀYA	UPĀYA
Universality	Potentiality	Realization	Means of Realization
Sahasrāra Cakra (Crown)	Viśuddha Cakra (Throat)	Anāhata Cakra (Heart)	Selfless Action

GURU	PADMA	SIDDHI	HŪM
PRAJÑĀ	KARUNĀ	JAYA	VAJRAKĀYA
Wisdom	Compassion	Accomplishment (Victory)	Integration
Padmasambhava in whom wisdom and compassion are united		The Enlightened One	

There is also another version that connects the second part of this mantra directly with the maṇḍala of the Dhyāni-Buddhas. After having experienced the *Dharmakāya* of universality in the OṀ, the *Sambhogakāya* of inspirational delight in the ĀḤ!, the *Nirmāṇakāya* of spiritual transformation and realization on the human plane in the HŪṀ, one will experience the Mirror-like Wisdom in the transparent adamantine sceptor of the *Vajra,* the Wisdom of Equality in the *Guru,* the Distinguishing Wisdom of Inner Vision in the *Padma* (the unfolding lotus blossom), the All-Accomplishing Wisdom in the *Siddhi* (attainment), and the integration of all these Wisdoms in the final HŪṀ of the *Vajrakāya.*

References and Notes

[1] *Avalokiteśvara-gupa-karaṇḍa-vyuha,* edited by Satya Bratu Samasrami, Calcutta, 1873.

10

THE TWO PHASES OF MEDITATION AND THE PSYCHIC CENTERS OF THE BODY MAṆḌALA

THUS THE MANTRA grows out of the primordial sound, and out of the mantra the visible or visualized form of the divine figure (which is said to be an "explosion of *śūnyatā,*" the creative Void), in which the *sādhaka* projects the highest faculties of his mind, his essential and experiential being, into visible form. And slowly one divine figure after another emerges, according to the directive tendencies and the inherent plan of the *sādhana,* and takes its place in the inner space of the maṇḍala. This however, can be achieved only after each of the mantras has been kept present in the mind for a considerable time, and this can be done only by repeating each particular mantra (which calls up a particular form or vision) for hundreds, nay, even thousands of times, until the *sādhaka* has completely identified himself with its visualized form and color, and penetrated to the inner core of its meaning.

The structure of the maṇḍala itself, which precedes the visualization of the divine figures, must have been thoroughly fixed in the mind before the actual meditation begins. The maṇḍala is built in the form of a universal temple on top of the sacred mountain, representing the axis of the universe (and corresponding to the spinal column of the meditator). This temple is open to the four directions of space, and in each of the four entrances stands one of the guardians of the threshold. The temple is surrounded by three protective circles: first a circle of lotus petals, symbolizing the purity of heart, as basis for the ten transcendental virtues; second, a circle of diamond scepters (*vajras*), symbolizing the strength and determination of the concentrated mind; and third, a circle of flames, representing the purifying force of higher knowledge, in the fire of which all dross and impurities are burned away, and in which everything that had coagulated is liquified and integrated into one great upsurging experience.

The same process of integration will finally be achieved when the inner sanctum of the maṇḍala is filled with the emanations of the enlightened mind, which in ever narrower concentric circles surround the center until they become one with it. Thus, there are two phases of meditation: the creative or productive (*utpanna-krama*) and the dissolving and integrating (*laya-krama*). Once the maṇḍala-technique has been fully practiced, the process need not start from the periphery, i.e., from the building up or visualizing of all the separate aspects and qualities of the enlightened mind, but from the center itself, from which emanates the complete spiritual universe in all its diverse aspects, and into which it is withdrawn in the final act of integration.

It is through this that the *sādhaka* realizes and partakes of the universal breath of creation and reintegration, which manifests itself in the very function of physical breathing, of inhalation and exhalation, which is one of the basic experiences of meditative body-consciousness. Only in the alternate movements of differentiation and unification can there be an actual experience of reality and life. And this experience has to be re-created again and again, until it becomes the natural rhythm of conscious life.

If we do not dissolve or integrate the creations of our mind, we will get attached to them and become their prisoners, as a man who becomes possessed by his possessions. If, on the other hand, we remain in a state of irrevocable finality, we will be frozen in a state of complete stagnation. Every experience has to be integrated in our deepest consciousness or in the totality of our being, until we have reached the state in which our consciousness has become an exponent and meeting place of all living forces of the universe, and our body the multistoried temple and maṇḍala of these forces. Though our body, according to the Buddhist view of life, is created, crystallized and formed by the directive forces of the mind, yet we are apt to identify ourselves only with those faculties of consciousness which are located in the brain. Thus we forget or neglect the other centers of psychic force, corresponding to different levels of dimensions of consciousness, associated with vital, sexual, regenerating functions, as well as with emotional and intuitional faculties. A typical reaction to the one-sided emphasis on the intellectual qualities of our brain-consciousness in the past—to give only one example—is the sudden upsurge of an equally extreme sex-consciousness in our present time. It is the revenge of nature for the misuse or neglect of important and necessary qualities on which the harmony of our conscious existence as human beings depends.

According to ancient Chinese wisdom, man stands between heaven and earth, being the meeting place and the mediator between cosmic and terrestial forces. Tibetan tradition reflects this idea by dividing the psychic centers of the human body into three zones, corresponding to the principles of "heaven, earth and man": an upper zone, to which the Crown Center and the Throat Center belong; a middle one, represented by the Heart Center; and a lower one, to which the Solar Plexus and the Root Center (including the organs of reproduction) belong.

The upper zone is the realm of spiritual or psychocosmic forces (corresponding to the Chinese concept "heaven"); the middle zone is the realm of human realization; the lower zone is the realm of earth-related vital forces. In ascending order they correspond to the vital principle of the element Earth (stability), the vital principle of the element Water (fluidity) the vital principle of the element Air (movement,

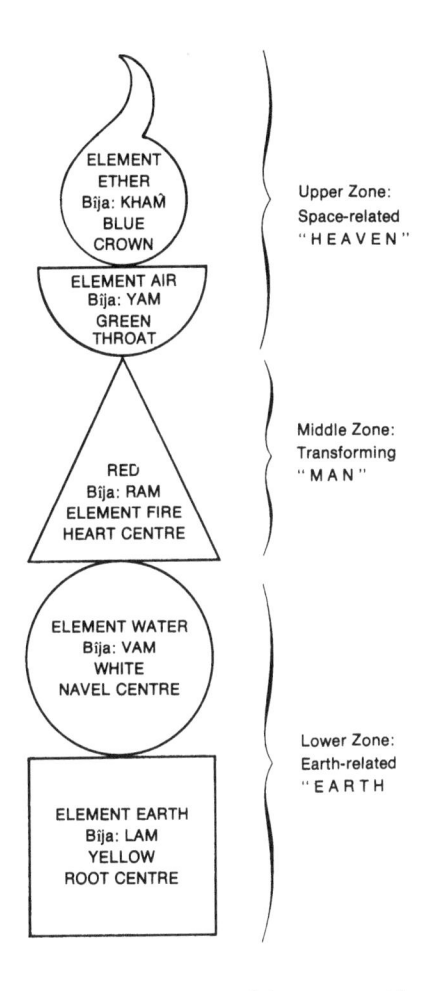

```
         ╱‾‾‾‾‾╲
        │ELEMENT│
        │ ETHER │
        │Bija: KHAṀ│         Upper Zone:
        │ BLUE  │           Space-related
        │ CROWN │           "HEAVEN"
        ╲_____╱
       ╱ELEMENT AIR╲
      │ Bija: YAM   │
      │  GREEN      │
      │  THROAT     │
       ╲_____╱
           /\
          /  \
         /    \
        / RED  \               Middle Zone:
       /Bija: RAM\              Transforming
      /ELEMENT FIRE\              "MAN"
     /HEART CENTRE  \
    /_____\

        _____
       /           \
      │ ELEMENT WATER│
      │  Bija: VAM   │
      │   WHITE      │
      │ NAVEL CENTRE │
       _____/
                                 Lower Zone:
      ┌──────────────┐           Earth-related
      │ ELEMENT EARTH│             "EARTH"
      │  Bija: LAM   │
      │   YELLOW     │
      │ ROOT CENTRE  │
      └──────────────┘
```

It may be noted that the elementary *bījas* are not identical with those of the Dhyāni-Buddhas or those of the Three Mysteries. When the latter are consciously projected into the respective *cakras*, the nature of the *cakras* is being modified and their forces are transformed into qualities of higher awareness and potentiality.

The geometrical symbols (square, circle, triangle, semi-circle, and acuminated circle) are transformed into three-dimensional forms in the construction of *stūpas* or *chortens*, religious monuments representing simultaneously the *cakras* of the human body and the elements of the universe. The above-mentioned symbols accordingly change into cubic, spheric, conic, or pyramidal forms, the semicircle into a cup-shape and the acuminated circle into a "flaming drop" (*bindu*) or a small ball from which a flame issues. (More about this in my *Psycho-Cosmic Symbolism of the Buddhist Stūpa*, Dharma Publishing House, Berkeley, California, 1971) vibration), and the vital principle of the element Ether (radiance). From this it becomes clear that the middle zone is the most important and decisive, because it mediates between "heaven and earth," and combines both in transforming them into the human experience of enlightened freedom, expressed by the seed-syllable HŪṀ in the human heart. The Muṇḍaka Upanishad too speaks of the meeting of Heaven and Earth in Man: "He in whom Heaven and Earth and the Middle Region are united, together with the mind and all life-currents—know him to be the one Self; give up all other talk; this is the bridge of immortality."

When this is realized, the human body is transformed into the sacred temple of the spirit and into the maṇḍala of the Dhyāni-Buddhas. However, it has to be observed that the Buddhist Cakra-Yoga is not concerned with fixed or static values, but with the dynamic aspects of living forces and their ever-present ability of transformation. Thus, the natural qualities of the psychic centers are modified by the conscious projection of the qualities or visualized forms of Dhyāni-Buddhas into them, a technique which presupposes an intensive training in this particular yoga and, therefore, goes beyond the purpose of our present attempt to give a general idea of the main elements of creative meditation, accessible not only to specialists, but to all interested readers. The following part of this book will, therefore, be devoted to the wider and more accessible aspects of meditation.[1]

References and Notes

[1] More detailed information about the Buddhist Cakra-Yoga can be found in my FOUNDATIONS OF TIBETAN MYSTICISM, Rider & Co., London, or Samuel Weiser, New York.

PART III

MEDITATION AS DIRECT EXPERIENCE AND SPIRITUAL ATTITUDE

1

POLARITY AND INTEGRATION

THE EAST DISCOVERED the eternal recurrence of the same conditions and similar events. The West discovered the value of the uniqueness of each event or existential condition. The East kept its gaze fixed upon the cosmic background, the West on the individual foreground. The complete picture, however, combines foreground and background, integrating them into a higher unity. The complete human being, the man who has become whole (and therefore "holy"), is he who unites the universal with the individual, the uniqueness of the moment with the eternity of the cyclic recurrence of constellations and existential situations.

In the knowledge of immortality the East neglected the mundane life. In the knowledge of the uniqueness and value of the present moment, the West neglected the immortal. Only in the deepest aspects of the Vajrayāna (the Mystic School of Tibetan Buddhism), as well as in the *I-Ching* (the oldest book of Chinese wisdom), the attempt has been made to connect the vision of the foreground with that of the background, to connect the momentary with the eternal and the uniqueness of every situation with the ever recurring constellations of universal forces.

Only he who, while fully recognizing and understanding his Western heritage, penetrates and absorbs the heritage of the East, can gain the highest values of both worlds and do justice to them. East and West are the two halves of our human consciousness, comparable to the two poles of a magnet, which condition and correspond to each other and cannot be separated. Only if man realizes this fact will he become a complete human being. "In man life becomes conscious of itself, and with this it develops into a task and into freedom, so that it can receive anew, make a new start, that it can regain its beginning, its heritage and its origin, and can be reborn." (Leo Baeck)

Man's life is suspended between the poles of Heaven and Earth. Let us retain within us the width of Heaven, but let us not forget the Earth that bears us. Earth and Heaven are the symbols of the finite and the infinite, in which we share equally. It is not our task to choose between these two poles of our existence or to give up the one for the sake of the other, but to recognize their mutual interdependence and to integrate them into our very being. Our problem, therefore, is not "either-or" but "as-well-as," because man is the center between Heaven and Earth, the place where Heaven and Earth meet.

For this reason the Buddha praised human birth as the best, because only in human life do we find the opportunity to realize the Middle Way which unites Heaven and Earth and which alone can give meaning to our existence by freeing us from our attachment to the one or the other extreme. Existence means limitation, but limitation in this sense is not synonymous with narrowness and ignorance; rather it consists in the creation of meaningful form, concentration upon essentials, renunciation of all that is superfluous or nonessential, the giving up or restraining of desires and cravings—a restraint which results in greater freedom. The wisest man is he who is able to convey much with few words, the greatest artist he who can express the deepest experience in the simplest form. Therefore it has been said, "Simplicity reveals the master."

In other words, it is the finite that gives meaning to the infinite, because the infinite can express itself only through finite form. And vice versa: where the finite clings to existence for its own sake, without reflecting the infinite, it becomes meaningless and carries the seeds of death within itself.

Uniqueness in time and expression is the preciousness of form. It is precious because it is transient as a flower which blossoms and wilts, but which nevertheless expresses the eternal character of all flowers and of all life. It is the preciousness of the moment, in which timeless eternity is present. It is the preciousness of individual form, in which the infinite is revealed.

Therefore the Buddha silently held up a flower, when the pious pilgrim Subhadra wanted to know the quintessence of the Buddha's teaching. The flower, which opens itself to the light of heaven, while yet being rooted in the earth, belongs to the deepest symbols of the East. The darkness of the earth and the light of heaven: the powers of the depth, in which the experiences of an infinite past—of aeons of individual life-forms—are stored, and the cosmic forces of supra-individual, universal laws, are united in the blossom of spiritual unfoldment into conscious form.

The Buddha—like all Enlightened Ones— is represented as sitting on a lotus throne. The lotus is the prototype of all mandalas, all centralized systems of a spiritual universe of intricate relationships. It is the prototype of all Cakras or psychic centers, in which the chaos of unconscious forces is transformed into a meaningful cosmos, and in which individual existence finds its fulfillment in the final realization of Enlightenment, the state of completeness (the state of being entirely "whole," which we call "holy").

The purpose of Buddhist meditation, therefore, is not merely to sink back into the "uncreated" state, into a state of complete tranquilization with a vacant mind; it is not a regression into the "unconscious" or an exploration of the past. It is a process of transformation, of transcendence, in which we become fully conscious of the present, of the infinite powers and possibilities of the mind, in order to become masters of our destiny by cultivating those qualities which lead to the realization of our timeless nature: to enlightenment. Thus, instead of contemplating a past that we cannot change, and upon which we cannot have the slightest influence, meditation serves to sow the seeds of final liberation and to build *now* bodies of future perfection in the image of our highest ideals.

In order to do this, it is not sufficient merely to "spiritualize" our life; what we need is to "materialize" our spirit. To despise matter for the sake of the spirit is in no way better than mistaking matter to be the only reality. Novalis once said that the outer world is nothing but the inner world in a state of mystery. If thus we look at the world with the eyes of a poet—that is with the eyes of the spirit— we shall discover that the simplest material object, nay, anything that is *formed*, be it by man or by nature, is a symbol, a glyph of a higher reality and a deeper relationship of universal and individual forces than we ever expected. And since these forces are the same as those which make up our consciousness, our inner life, our very soul, the words of Novalis are not poetic exaggeration, but a profound truth. We have become accustomed to associate the word "matter" with something low and valueless in contrast to what we call "spiritual" and have thus deprived ourselves of the very means to penetrate to the core of reality and to give meaning to our life, to our individual existence in this material world. We have torn apart the profound unity between the inner and the outer world, by declaring the one to be "spiritual" and the other to be merely "material" and, in the last resort, "illusory."

It is the special function of meditation to re-unite the inner and the outer worlds, instead of renouncing the one for the sake of the other. Meditation is not an escape from the world, but a means of looking deeper into it, unhampered by prejudices or by the familiarity of habit which blinds us to the wonders and the profound mysteries that surround us. In both philosophy and religion the concepts of oneness, of universality, infinity, boundlessness, formlessness, emptiness, changelessness, timelessness, eternity, and similar one-sided abstractions of a purely conceptual type, became the summum bonum, the hallmark of an intellectual spirituality which tried to isolate them from their counterpoles: diversity, individuality, form, materiality, movement in time and space, change, growth, transformation, etc., which were depreciated and scorned as qualities of a lower order and as a negation of ultimate reality. This is a typical example of mere word-thinking and logical ratiocination, which is as far from an understanding of reality—or, let us say, the nature of reality, which may have many dimensions—as the attempt to isolate the positive from the negative poles of an electric or magnetic field.

We may break a piece of magnetized steel as often as we like, we shall never be able to separate the positive from the negative pole; each fragment will always have both. This shows that polarity is an aspect of unity, not an arbitrary duality but an inseparable whole.

Our abstract thinkers, however, want to have unity without diversity, infinity without anything finite, eternity without change, universality without individuality, emptiness without form, substance without quality, energy without matter, and mind without body. They fail to realize that unity is meaningless without diversity, or infinity without the finite; that universality cannot be experienced except in the individual, and that the individual on the other hand derives its meaning and value from the realization of its universal background and interrelationship. In other words, universality and individuality are not mutually exclusive or irreconcilable opposites, but the inseparable poles or aspects of the same reality. We cannot attain to universality by negating or destroying individuality. Individuality, however, is not identical with egocentricity. We are all individuals, but we are not necessarily all egoists. By overcoming our ego we do not lose our individuality but, on the contrary, we enrich and widen our individuality, which thus becomes the expression of a greater and more universal life. So long as the illusion of a permanent, unchangeable, and separate egohood exists, we put ourselves into opposition to the very nature of life, because life means movement, change, growth, transformation, unfoldment, and integration into ever more meaningful forms of relationship. By seeing the world from the perspective of our limited little ego and our ephemeral aims and desires, we not only distort it; we make it a prison that separates us from our fellow-beings and from the very sources of life. But the moment we become truly selfless, by emptying ourselves of all ego-tendencies, of our power hunger and all possessiveness and craving, we break down the walls of our self-created prison and become conscious of the immensity and boundlessness of our true being. That true being comprises the infinite forms and potentialities of life and conscious awareness, in which each form represents a momentary constellation of forces and aspects in the continuous stream of life. The fact that no form or aspect of life is a self-contained, unchangeable unit, but exists only in relation to others and ultimately to the totality of all that exists, is hinted at by the Buddhist term *śūnyatā*, which literally means "emptiness," namely, empty of self-nature, or permanent and enduring substance.

This emptiness, however, cannot be realized without being conscious of its opposite pole, i.e., without realizing form. Nor can the function[1] of form be realized without emptiness. Just as objects can exist only in space, and space can be conceived only in relation, so objects, form, and emptiness condition and penetrate each other. They co-exist inseparably, for which reason *śūnyatā* has aptly been circumscribed by the expression "plenum-void," the all containing, all-producing emptiness. In its deepest metaphysical sense, it is the primordial ground, the ever-present starting point of all creation. It is the principle of unlimited potentiality which can be experienced only in moments of complete, unconditioned freedom, in moments of spontaneous insight, in which we are lifted out of the net of cause and effect and find ourselves faced with a sense of pure being. On the intellectual plane *śūnyatā* is the relativity of all things and conditions, insofar as no thing exists independently but only in relationship to others—and ultimately in relationship to the whole universe. This relationship is more than a mere causal, time-space relationship; it is one of a common ground and a simultaneous presence of all factors of existence, although certain factors may take a momentary precedence over others. Thus *śūnyatā* is not "nothingness" but rather "no-*thing*-ness." It is the beginning and the end of all things. If we want to make *śūnyatā* an experience instead of a mere concept of relativity (useful as this may be from the standpoint of philosophical understanding), we must consciously go through the process of creation and dissolution, of becoming and dissolving and reintegrating in meditation. We must *experience* that form is emptiness and emptiness is form by consciously creating form, until it is visible to the inner eye and filled with life and significance, in order to reabsorb it bit by bit and stage by stage into *śūnyatā*, the all-embracing inner space. This is the dual process of meditation; it does not consist merely in the reversal of the creative process or in the negation of form, but contains both form-creation and form-dissolution, because *śūnyatā* can never become a living experience unless we have realized both poles of its incommensurable nature.

References and Notes

[1] I speak of the "function" of form because form is not static.

2

THE INWARD WAY

IN ORDER TO UNDERSTAND *śūnyatā* in its deepest sense "one must experience sitting at the center of existence and viewing things from this hub," as D. T. Suzuki once expressed it. In order to get to the hub of existence, into the center of our being, *we must reverse the direction of our mental outlook and turn inward.* This turning about in the depth of our consciousness is called parāvritti, and is the main purpose of all meditation.

So long we have looked from within outward, scattering our attention upon the self-created objects of our sense awareness and our mental activities. Now we reverse the direction and go back the way we came, untying the knots by which we have tied ourselves to our present human existence.

The Buddha, according to the Śūrangama Sūtra, explained this process by tying a knot into a silk handkerchief, holding it up and asking Ānanda, his favorite disciple: "What is this?" Ānanda replied: "A silk handkerchief, in which you have tied a knot."

The Buddha, thereupon, tied a second knot into it, and a third one, and continued doing so until he had tied in this way six knots. And each time he asked Ānanda what he saw, and each time Ānanda replied in the same way.

Thereupon the Buddha said: "When I tied the first knot, you called it a knot; when I tied the second and third, etc., you still maintained the same answer."

Ānanda, not comprehending what the Buddha was driving at, became puzzled and exclaimed: "Whether you tie a single knot or a hundred knots, they always remain knots, though the handkerchief is made of variously coloured silk threads and woven into a single piece."

The Buddha admitted this, but he pointed out that though the piece of silk was one, and all the knots were knots, yet there was one difference, namely the order in which they had been tied.

To demonstrate this subtle and yet important difference, the Buddha asked how these knots could be untied. And at the same time he started pulling at the knots here and there, in such a way that the knots, instead of being loosened, became tighter. Ānanda said, "I would first try to find out how the knots were tied."

The Buddha exclaimed: "Right you are, Ānanda! If you wish to untie a knot, you must first find out how the knot was tied. For he who knows the origin of things, knows also their dissolution. But let me ask you another question: can all the knots be untied at the same time?"

"No, Blessed Lord! Since the knots were tied one after another, in a certain order, we cannot untie them unless we follow the reverse order."

The Buddha then explained that the six knots correspond to the six sense organs, through which our contact with the world is established.

In a similar way, meditation must begin from the level of our present state of existence, of which our body is the most obvious manifestation. Instead of getting entangled in beliefs and opinions, theories and dogmas, spiritual ideas and high-flown hypotheses, we have to untie the knots of our body and mind. We must relax our tensions and stresses and so establish a state of perfect harmony and balance. In order to establish this balance, our body must be centered and effortlessly resting in itself. Only if our body is centered and all its functions are at rest, can our mind become centered so that we can attain a state of concentration, the first prerequisite of meditation. Concentration should not mean an intellectual effort toward the solution of a problem, but rather a resting of our mind within its own center of gravity, which is revealed and activated by the interest aroused in the subject of contemplation.

"Interest" means to be within it (*inter-esse*), not to look at it merely from without, but to identify ourselves with it. This is possible only if the subject of our meditation inspires us. But what can we identify ourselves with? Certainly not with an abstract idea, a mere concept, a moral principle, or a philosophical thesis, but only with an ideal embodied in man and capable of being realized by man. It is here that the image of the perfected man, the perfectly Enlightened One, the Buddha (or, as we may say, the model of the Complete Man) comes in. This is the reason why, at the beginning of the path of meditation, an element of devotion, faith in the higher qualities (or the divine nature) of man and the dedication to a supreme ideal, are the main forces that carry us along toward final realization. Those who believe that meditation can be practiced without this faith are indulging in mere intellectual acrobatics; they will never penetrate into the realm of the spirit.

Devotion removes the main hindrance of meditation, the ego, and opens us toward a greater life, while inspiration draws us toward the realization of our aim. Without establishing a comprehensive and convincing aim of meditational practice, meditation cannot succeed. It is for this reason that we have first to state our aim and convince ourselves of its value as well as of the possibility of attaining or realizing it. Therefore we have to create a mental background and a spiritual climate before we can begin with the actual practice of meditation. Without this background and the power of an inner conviction (or faith), meditation becomes a tedious exercise to which we have to force ourselves, instead of being drawn to it. This is psychologically of the greatest importance, as it corresponds to the natural, and therefore spontaneous, behavior of conscious organic life.

> The behavior of an organism results from its being drawn to something, desiring something, whereas orthodox psychology, grounded in physiology and the physical sciences, is obliged to think of behavior as the result of a push or drive (For instance, hunger, sex, fear, ambition, etc.) They are thought of as resulting from a chain of physical causes fundamentally like those that drive a machine ... it does not explain the precise directiveness of behavior. Drive will provide an organism's motive power, as it does for a car, but without something to steer it the car will have no goal, and its direction will be amiss.[1]

> The difference between the contrasting concepts of "drive" and "goal," of being pushed or being drawn, seems to me much more than a quibble. It involves two unlike views of the basis of all organic activity. We are so mechanically minded, that the concept of drive seems more natural to us. Actually, the idea of being drawn provided a more accurate picture of our motives as we experience them.[2]

Meditation should not be a task to which we force ourselves "with gritted teeth and clenched fists;" it should rather be something that draws us, because it fills us with joy and inspiration. So long as we have to force ourselves, we are not yet ready for meditation. Instead of meditating we are violating our true nature. Instead of relaxing and letting go, we are holding on to our ego, to our will power. In this way meditation becomes a game of ambition, of personal achievement and aggrandizement. Meditation is like love: a spontaneous experience—not something that can be forced or acquired by strenuous effort. If I may be allowed to paraphrase Martin Buber's beautiful words about "true philosophy" by replacing "philosophy" with "meditation," I would formulate the quintessence of meditation in the following way: "True meditation is the meditation of a lover. He who practices such meditation, to him the hidden meaning of things is revealed, the law of things that has not yet been revealed to anybody before and which is not like something outside himself, but as if his own innermost spirit, the meaning of all his life-time and destiny, of all his painful and exalted thought, were suddenly revealed to him."

Though the consummation of love consists in the becoming one with the object of our love, this presupposes that love cannot exist without an initial object that inspires us to such an extent that we can finally identify ourselves with it. Similarly, in order to have our heart in meditation, we must be inspired by its aim and even by its initial object, because meditation is not just musing or a state of reverie, but directed consciousness or conscious awareness which cannot exist without an object. There cannot be consciousness without content.

To be conscious means to be aware of something. People who claim to meditate with an "empty mind" deceive themselves. They may be daydreaming or they may fall asleep, but that is not meditation. Consciousness is a dynamic force, in constant movement, a continuous stream. One can stop it as little as one can stop a river. If we could stop it, there would be no river, because the nature of a river consists in flowing. However, though we cannot stop a river, we can control it by diverting its flow in the desired direction. In the same way, though we cannot stop the mind, we can give it direction. That means: meditation is directed consciousness.

This holds true even for those who do not choose an immediate subject for their meditation, because they definitely change the direction of their consciousness by turning inward. This results in a momentary or temporal sense of peace, because by turning our consciousness toward itself, we slow down its flow, as a river may be dammed up and form a quiet lake until it overflows and moves on again. This is what we may call "letting the mind rest in itself," the first step of meditation, in which the consciousness for the time being is stilled and thus remains in a state of "reflection." In this state the contents of our consciousness are mirrored on its surface, so that we can observe them as a spectator.

But this alone is not sufficient, nor can we hold this state for long, because, like flowing water that is dammed up and begins to flow over in various directions, so also our mind—unless it is channeled in a predetermined direction—begins to move here and there. By merely observing the meandering of our thoughts and emotions and mental images, we may get a certain insight into the functions of consciousness, but nothing more. It is here, as well as in the observation of dream-states, that modern psychology stops, after analyzing and interpreting the contents of consciousness thus observed. But interpretations based on an intellectual analysis of mental images and archetypal symbols is as unsatisfactory as describing music in words, or colors to a blind man.

The language of words (on which our intellectual activity is based) and the language of symbols (which combine visible, audible, and emotional features in which our deeper consciousness expresses itself), are two different mediums of expression and conscious awareness. The one is based on more or less fixed one-dimensional concept with a two-dimensional logic ("either-or"), the other on more or less fluid multidimensional images with a correspondingly multidimensional logic. The realm of vision and the realm of thought may partly overlap, but they are never identical. The higher dimension contains the lower one, but not vice versa. Meditation, therefore, must go beyond word-thinking, beyond thinking in concepts; it must encompass the whole human being, i.e. not only his intellect, but also his feeling, his vision, his emotional and intuitive capacity. Those who try to throw away their intellect—they are generally those who never had one—are just as mistaken as those who try to avoid all emotions (they are generally those who are afraid to face them). Only where heart and mind are united, can genuine intuition spring up. The language of intuition, however, is that of the symbol, which presents itself as a form of inner vision; because vision replaces the causal, time-conditioned relationship of the different aspects of a multidimensional object or process (which in thought can only be grasped one after another, i.e. as a succession in time) with a simultaneous awareness of all salient aspects of the envisaged symbol, in accordance with the plane on which it is experienced.

Such a symbol is the figure of the Buddha, as the representative of the complete human being, a symbol that is not only visible, but can be experienced in mind and body in the act of meditational and devotional practice, and with which the meditator can identify himself in his innermost being, even though he may still have a long way to go toward his final realization.

When contemplating a Buddha statue, even a man who knows nothing of the Buddha's teaching will come to the conclusion that this, indeed, is the perfect representation of the spiritualized man who, without losing the solid ground of reality beneath his feet, accepting and ennobling his corporeality without clinging to it and without being dependent on it, is at peace with himself and with the world. What serenity and happiness are mirrored in his face; what equanimity and tranquility in every limb of his body; what profound silence and harmony! A harmony that is contagious and penetrates the beholder! There is no more desire, no more want, no restlessness, no insecurity, no chasing after external things, no dependence on anything. There is the highest bliss—in one word, completeness.

He who can create and bring to life this image before his mental eye or, still more, he who can experience it within himself, as the great masters of meditation did and still do, in wordless devotion and complete self-surrender: such a one has taken the first step toward inner transformation and liberation, because he has found the attitude from which the knowledge of the Eternal in Man was and ever is born.

This image of the perfected or complete man, which has crystallized out of the millenniums of meditative experience, does not represent an arbitrarily isolated moment in the career of the Buddha, but the sum total, the quintessence of his spiritual activity—something that is valid for all times and all human beings, something that is an expression of the true nature of man. We may not be able to define or to envisage this ultimate nature of man in its fullness and universality. But we can imagine and visualize to some extent a human being in whom are embodied all the qualities which lead to the realization of this exalted state. And since our striving needs an understandable, tangible, concrete aim which is able to fill us with courage and certainty, there can be nothing more suitable than the figure of the Perfect Man as embodied in the spiritual image of the Buddha. By transforming our own body into the living symbol of this image, in assuming the bodily posture and attitude of meditation while withdrawing the mind from all outer objects and letting it rest in its own center, we are preparing the way for the experience of final realization.

References and Notes

[1] *The Biology of the Spirit*, Edmund B. Sinnott; (The Viking Press, New York; 1955), p. 64.
[2] *Ibid.*, p. 66.

3

BODY-CONSCIOUSNESS

MEDITATION IN THE BUDDHIST SENSE could best be defined as "the overcoming of outer perception in favor of inner awareness."[1] If we perceive our body in its outward material form or appearance, we are dealing with an object among other objects of the external world: We can take it to pieces, dissect it, analyze it, dissolve it into its chemical or molecular constituents, or observe its mechanism and measure the electrical impulses that operate it. From this point of view—which is strictly scientific—we can completely dissociate ourselves from our body and declare our spiritual independence by denying all responsibility for our bodily existence.

But if we are *inwardly aware* of our body, we are no more dealing with a merely material object, a thing among other things; we are confronted with a living organism which, according to the Buddha's teaching, is the product of our mind, of the basic tendencies of our consciousness, acquired through aeons of our development and maintained or modified through our present words, deeds, and thoughts.

In other words, our body is a form of materialized consciousness. But since this consciousness has an infinite past, it necessarily is a condensation of all universal laws and forces, focalized in the process of individualization and carried on through innumerable incarnations along the line of its inherent impetus toward an ever increasing awareness and unfoldment of qualities, forces, or experiences accumulated in our depth-consciousness.

> This gathering up of consciousness during time can be followed also through space. It stretches up through time from the placid mass of cells on the drying mud, through reptiles browsing on the branches of trees and the little mammals peeping on them through the leaves, up to Proust in his exquisite, agonizing web. So too, at this moment of time I can feel consciousness stretching from the crystalline virus that blights tomato plants, through fish, reptiles and mammals to the minds of men. Indeed, it is obviously only an expedient convention to stop with the forms of life that are earliest in time, or the simplest in space. Consciousness must surely be traced back to the rocks which have been here since life began and so make a meeting place for the roots of life in time and space, the earliest and the simplest. Why, indeed, stop with this planet? Even if nothing like the human psyche and intellect have developed elsewhere, it is necessary in an indivisible universe to believe that the principle of consciousness must extend everywhere. Even now I imagine that I can feel all the particles of the universe nourishing my consciousness just as my consciousness informs all the particles of the universe.[2]

The fact that this consciousness is a living force and not a stagnant state makes it clear that no permanent bodily form can represent or do justice to its nature. The very change—or, better, the faculty of continual transformation—is a profound expression of the dynamic character of the mind. By looking at this change from a prejudiced, possessive point of view, we interpret it merely as a negative quality, instead of realizing the positive side of this process, which is not arbitrary or meaningless destruction, but a process of continual transformation according to the inherent law of the living spirit within us.

> I died from mineral, and plant became;
> Died from the plant, and took a sentient frame;
> Died from the beast, and donned a human dress;
> When by my dying did I e'er grow less?[3]

Those who despise the body because of its transiency therewith only prove their mental immaturity. For them the body will become a prison, while to those who recognize the body as a creation and the visible expression of the very forces that constitute our innermost being, it becomes the temple of the mind. A temple, however, by its very structure reflects the qualities and functions of its indwelling spirit. A temple that houses a universal spirit must itself represent the universe. And this is exactly what the Tantras maintain. The functions of our body correspond to the functions and laws of the universe which gradually unfold and strive to become conscious within us. The more we realize this process, the greater will be the harmony and cooperation between body and mind, the inner and the outer world, until we finally realize their essential oneness. In that moment we know that the universe itself is our true body and that we are not confined to our present physical frame in which our universal body expresses itself on the temporal, three-dimensional plane.

The most obvious and the most vital function of our psychosomatic organism is the function of breathing. How vital and basic it is we can gauge from the fact that we can live without food for a number of weeks, without drink for a few days, but without air hardly for a few moments. We can relinquish even consciousness—as in deep sleep or under narcosis or in states of catalepsy—but we cannot relinquish breathing as long as we are alive. Breathing, therefore, is the most subtle function of our organism, a function that can be both conscious and unconscious, volitional and nonvolitional. This is in contrast to most of our other organic functions such as the beating of the heart, the circulation of the blood, the currents of nervous energy, the functions of digestion, assimilation, and secretion, etc. Breathing is the only vital function which, in spite of its independence from our normal consciousness and its self-regulating and self-perpetuating subconscious character, can be raised into a conscious function, accessible to the mind. Due to this double nature, breathing can be made the mediator between mind and body, or the means of our conscious participation in the most vital and universal functions of our psychosomatic organism. Breathing, thus, is the connecting link between conscious and unconscious, gross-material and fine-material, volitional and automatic functions, and therefore the most perfect expression of the nature of all life.

Those exercises that lead to the deeper states of meditation, therefore, begin with the observation and experiencing of breath, which in this way is converted from an automatic or nonvolitional function into a conscious one, and finally into a medium of spiritual forces. As such, it has been called *prāṇa* in ancient Sanskrit. This is a term that combines the physical as well as the psychic and spiritual qualities of breath, similar to our word "inspiration," which can be used in the sense of "inhalation" as well as in that of direct spiritual awareness and experience, or as the Greek word *pneuma* can signify "spirit" as well as "air."

The ancients apparently had a profound insight into the nature of breathing and treated it not merely as a physical function but as a conveyor of cosmic energy. If, therefore, we try to impose our will upon this function, without a deeper knowledge of its laws and its far-reaching effects, we are liable to cause irreparable damage to our health. On the other hand, if we try to cooperate with it consciously, without interfering with our will (our selfish intentions, our hankering after power and domination), but merely filling it with our consciousness and undivided attention (*smṛti*), then the function of breathing will not only be raised from a physical process to the level of a spiritual experience, but the whole body will be penetrated with vital energy and become conscious in its entirety, so as to be transformed into an instrument of the mind. Thus, instead of analyzing and dissecting, or merely diverting our consciousness to external movements or secondary functions of our body, we become again complete in the integration of body and mind, in which every single function derives its meaning only in relationship to the whole. The mere awareness of minor functions, isolated from their essential relations, is meaningless.

If thus we see the function of breathing against a still wider background than our momentary individual organism, we realize that it is a link not only between the conscious and the unconscious functions of our body, but between two worlds: the inner and the outer, the individual and the universe. It is for this reason that the Upanishadic idea of the *ātman,* the universal principle in man, is equated with the dynamic *prāṇa,* the breath of life, the vital force that streams through man, so that he partakes of the Greater Life, in which the individual and the universe are one. And for the very same reason the Buddha had to reverse the ancient terminology, when the connotation of *ātman* had hardened into a stagnant, abstract concept of a changeless, immortal soul, which to the average man was indistinguishable from a glorified ego. Therefore the Buddha replaced the *ātman* by the *anātma-vāda,* the teaching of "egolessness," which reestablished the dynamic nature of life, without thereby denying what is immortal in man. In fact, he reestablished the universality of man—not as an abstract principle—but as something that can be realized by overcoming the limitations of our ego-illusion.

One of the most effective means for bringing about this realization is the practice of *ānāpānasati,* the contemplation and conscious experience of the process of breathing, as described in some of the most important Pāli texts (like *Majjhima-Nakāya* and *Dīgha-Nikāya*). The Pali word *pāna* corresponds to the Sanskrit term *prāṇa,* while *sati* is the equivalent of *sarti* (mindfulness, remembrance, collection) in Sanskrit. Thus *ānāpānasati* literally means "mindfulness in [the process of] inbreathing and outbreathing." The text describes in simple words how the meditator, after having retired to a lonely place and having taken the traditional crosslegged position of meditation, consciously observes his breath: "Drawing in a long breath, he knows: 'I am drawing in a long breath.' Exhaling a long breath, he knows: 'I am exhaling a long breath.' Drawing in a short breath, he knows: 'I am drawing in a short breath.' Exhaling a short breath, he knows: 'I am exhaling a short breath,' " etc. It goes without saying that he does not verbalize this observation, he simply is fully aware ("he knows") of each phase of the process of breathing, without mental interference, without compulsion, without violation of the natural functions of the body. Hereby not only the breathing becomes conscious, but with it also the organs through which it flows.

If it were only a matter of intellectual observation and

analysis of the breathing process, this exercise would more or less come to an end at this stage. The purpose of this exercise, however, is exactly the contrary, namely, the gaining of a synthesis: the experience of the body as a whole, and finally the synthesis of body and mind. Our text, therefore, continues with the words: "Experiencing the whole body (*sabba-kāya*) I will inhale; experiencing the whole body I will exhale."

The next step is the stilling of all functions of the body through the conscious rhythm of the breath. From this state of perfect mental and physical equilibrium and its resulting inner harmony, grows that serenity and happiness which fills the whole body with a feeling of supreme bliss, like the refreshing coolness of a spring that penetrates the entire water of a mountain lake.

Thus breathing becomes a vehicle of spiritual experience, the mediator between body and mind. It is the first step toward the transformation of the body from the state of a more or less passively and unconsciously functioning physical organ into a vehicle or tool of a perfectly developed and enlightened mind, as represented by the radiance and perfection of the Buddha's body.

The next steps are devoted to the incorporation of spiritual functions in the process of breathing, i.e. whatever may be the object of our widening awareness, feelings, emotions, thoughts, and perceptions, etc., is being associated with the functions of breathing, projected into them, experienced in them, supported by them—becoming one with the universal body of the breath. It is a process that cannot be explained, but only experienced, and which therefore can be understood only by those who have a practical knowledge of meditation, which can be gained by all those who have the patience to proceed step by step, in which case each step will on its own accord open the way to the next higher one, in accordance with the character and the level of spiritual development of the meditator. It is for this reason that all Eastern *sādhanas* (meditative practices) are couched in general terms, which merely serve as landmarks, but leave the individual experience untouched. This may appear as a disadvantage or a defect of those *sādhana*-texts while in reality it is only a sensible precaution against the danger that arises from trying to imitate other peoples' experiences instead of gaining one's own. Meditation is a strictly individual affair, in spite of certain common factors of human psychology. Just as a physician cannot prescribe the same medicine to all patients, so the same *sādhana* cannot be given to all who want to practice meditation.

References and Notes

[1] H. Zimmer's definition of Yoga.
[2] *An Aside on Consciousness* by Jacquetta Hawkes (wife of J. B. Priestly) taken from her book on England, *A Land*, forming part of an Anthology edited by Whit Burnett under the title *The Human Spirit* (George Allen & Unwin, London, 1960).
[3] *Jalal Ud-Din*, in H. L. Myers' version.

4

THE CONTEMPLATION OF BREATH AND THE MEANING OF PRĀṆA

THERE ARE CERTAIN TYPES of practice which are based on such universal principles that they can be applied to all normal human beings, like general rules for the maintenance of physical health. The practice of *ānāpānasati* is the most important of them, and this is why the Buddha recommended it as the best starting point for any kind of creative meditation (*bhāvanā*). In fact, among the forty subjects of meditation mentioned in the early Pāli texts, *ānāpānasati* is one of the few that lead to the deepest state of absorption (*appanā samādhi*).

But even the description of this *sādhana* can give only the framework of this meditation, which has to be filled with the meditator's own experience. Though a sunset—as a factual occurrence—is the same for whoever witnesses it, no two people experience it in the same way. Consequently, any description of personal meditation experiences should not be regarded as a model to be imitated, but only as an example or indication of the possibilities contained in this kind of *sādhana*. It helps to bring about the same inspirational impetus as a poem or any other work of art created by others, which encourages us to pursue our own creative experience in a similar direction, without trying to imitate anything or to hinder the spontaneity of our mind by endeavoring to force it into a preconceived form.

It is in this respect that *ānāpānasati* distinguishes itself from *prāṇayama* (which has been popularized by many yoga teachers in the West, who follow the usual Hindu tradition): it does not try to control (*yama*) the process of breathing, in the sense of trying to impose our will upon it—which would only assert our ego-sense or the power-aspect of our ego, instead of overcoming it—but it tries to make us fully aware of this vital process by identifying ourselves consciously with its rhythm and its profound implications.

Thus we experience the very nature of life by surrendering ourselves to its rhythm, instead of interfering with it, because it is the rhythm of the universe that breathes through us. Instead of thinking ourselves as the agents and originators of this movement ("*I* am breathing in; *I* am breathing out," etc.), we should rather feel "the universe breathes in me, streams through me; it is not *I* who is breathing, but the universe through me."

And while experiencing this, we receive and accept the vital forces (*prāṇa*) of the universe with our whole being with every inhalation, and we surrender ourselves wholly with every exhalation. This makes us realize that life consists in a continuous process of taking and giving, of receiving and relinquishing, of integration and renunciation, of a continuous exchange and a profound interrelationship of all individual and universal forces. Whatever we receive, we have to give back; whatever we try to hold on to or to keep ourselves, will kill us. Therefore the saying: "Whosoever shall seek to save his life shall lose it." I expressed this in one of my meditation poems in the following lines, under the title "The Rhythm of Life."[1]

> Threefold is the rhythm of life:
> taking,
> giving,
> self-forgetting.
>
> Inhaling I take the world within me,
> Exhaling I give myself to the world,
> Emptied I live within myself —
> live
> without self
> in voidness supreme.

> Inhaling I take the world within me,
> Exhaling I give myself to the world,
> Emptied I experience abundance,
> Formless I fulfill the form.

We should suffocate if we tried to retain the air that we have inhaled, just as we would be poisoned if we tried to keep the food we had eaten. The necessity to receive and to accept what is not ours should demonstrate to us our dependence on something greater than ourselves and make us humble, because only those who are humble have a real chance to make use of what they have received. On the other hand, to give up again what we have received should make us selfless and strengthen our capacity of renunciation. Renunciation, however, should not be looked upon as an act of asceticism, but rather as a means of freeing ourselves of unnecessary possessions, cravings, and unworthy ambitions, by which we burden ourselves and make a prison of our existence. Renunciation, therefore, if it is genuine, is not an act that should be accompanied with a feeling of regret or grief, but should be a cause of joy, an act that carries in itself a feeling of deep satisfaction, like the feeling of release and satisfaction that we experience in every exhalation.

There are people who believe that under all circumstances renunciation is to be regarded as one of the highest qualities of the human mind, an opinion that has been favored by all more or less ascetic and other worldly religions. But neither acceptance nor renunciation is a value in itself. Those who proudly renounce the world, and because they are unwilling to accept or to receive it with an open heart and mind, will go the way of self-annihilation, of spiritual death, as will those who want only to receive, without giving back what they owe to the world and to their fellow beings.

Thus, the process of breathing, if fully understood and experienced in its profound significance, could teach us more than all the philosophies of the world. By raising this process into the light of consciousness, we not only become aware of the basic functions of life, but we have a chance to get access to the formative forces of the subconscious, so that the integration of all qualities of body and mind is made possible.

> The hidden formative power of Nature takes on its fullest meaning and effect for man's higher development only when he becomes conscious of its mysteri-

ous working. *Man* matures and completes himself only by becoming conscious of those great laws which, at the level of unconscious Nature, are simply lived. But this is a special form of becoming conscious. It is a question not of becoming intellectually or objectively conscious of the breath of life and its rhythmical order as manifested in breathing, but of becoming aware of it as a living movement in which oneself is also included, without fixing it or standing apart from it. This *awareness* of life working within us is something fundamentally different from observing, fixing and comprehending from the outside. In such observing and comprehending, he who comprehends stands apart from the comprehended and observed. But in becoming *aware,* the experience remains one with the experiencer and transforms him by taking hold of him.[2]

So long as we regard breathing merely as a physical function which consists only in filling our lungs with air and expelling it after having absorbed some of the oxygen contained in it, we are far from a real understanding of what *prāṇa* means. The breath of which the ancient texts speak is more than merely air or oxygen; it is the expression of a dynamic experience of vital force, generated with every inhalation. It does not end in reaching our lungs, but continues in our bloodstream, transforming itself into ever more subtle forms of energy conducted through the intricate system of our nerves, and thus it courses through our whole body, down to the furthest extremities until we can feel it reaching even our toes and the tips of our fingers, creating a new kind of body-consciousness.

Thus, *prāṇa* is not only subject to constant transformation, but is able to make use of various media without interrupting its course. Just as an electric current can flow through various substances, whether solid, fluid, or gaseous and can even flash through empty space or move in the form of radio waves if the tension or the frequency is high enough, so the current of psychic force can utilize the breath, the blood, or the nerves as conductors. At the same time it can move and act beyond these media by radiating from the focal points of concentrated nerve-energy or centers of consciousness *(cakras),* if sufficiently stimulated and intensified through conscious awareness of the whole psychosomatic parallelism represented by our physical body.

This can be achieved by the traditional posture of meditation in which the body not only achieves its maximum centeredness, but also rests in its own center of gravity (without requiring any outer support), as seen in the familiar images of Buddhas, seated in the lotus-position *padmāsana*), in which a closed circuit of vital and psychic energy is created. This current flows in two interconnected circles, formed by the upper and the lower limbs, which meet in the joined hands, resting upon the upturned soles of the feet, in front of the solar plexus or navel center (*manipura-cakra*).

The importance of this posture, i.e., the way of sitting (*āsana*) and the position of the hands (*mudrā*) which characterize the attitude of meditation (*dhyana-mudrā*), becomes evident if we contemplate the attached reproduction of a meditation picture, which was created spontaneously in a kind of after-trance state, following a vivid meditational experience of a steadily expanding body- and space-consciousness. It shows very clearly the currents of force, in which an upper and a lower circuit—the upper one formed by chest, arms and hands, the lower one by abdomen and folded legs—are joined in the hands, so as to form a consecutive or infinite current in the shape of a figure 8 (which, if written horizontally ∞, becomes the symbol of infinity). The fact that the hands, in which the upper and the lower circuits meet, are resting in front of the vitally important navel center, makes them into the focal point of conscious forces. From here these forces radiate in ever widening circles or spiral movements, until the surrounding space—which so far was only an intellectual notion—is transformed into a space filled with consciousness, into conscious space. Since this movement extends not only horizontally, but equally upward and downward, the effect is that what until now has been regarded as solid ground is felt as space—as immaterial and intangible as the air around the body. This results in a feeling of levitation, of hovering in empty space. The meditator has lost all feeling of heaviness, and even the things surrounding him seem to have lost their materiality. They are perceived in a peculiar way: not singly, or sequentially, but simultaneously, because, in place of a focal consciousness, a diffused kind of awareness has emerged. It does not cling to the surfaces of things but penetrates them. Thus the process of becoming conscious of the surrounding space is at the same time a trans-

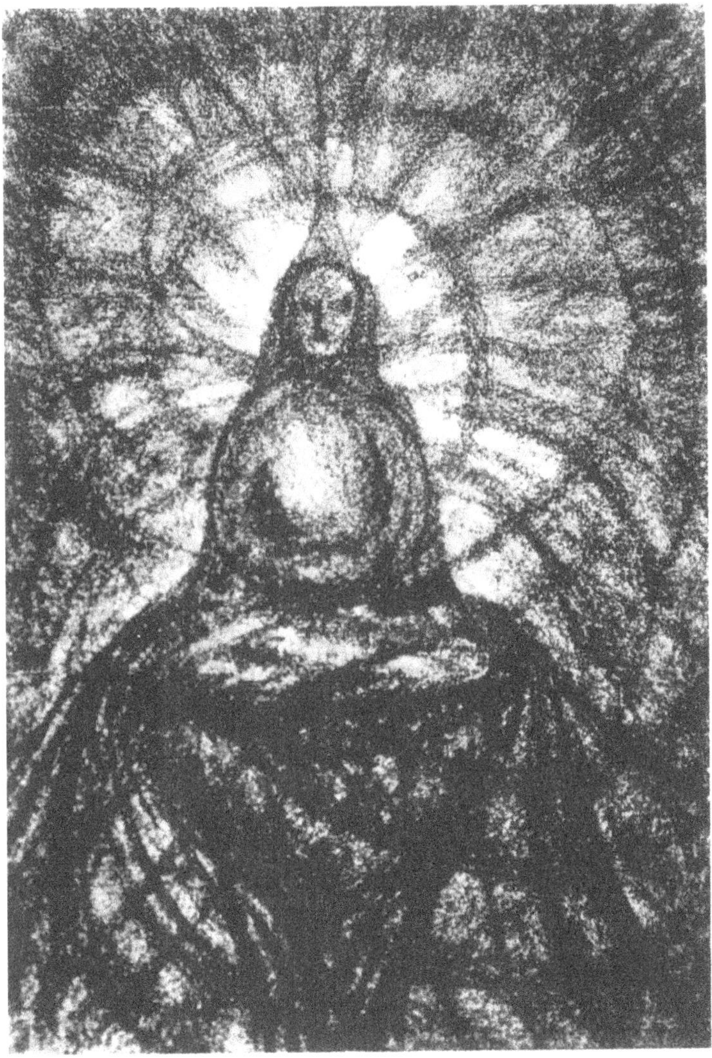

formation of consciousness into space, a creative unfoldment of conscious space, which is more than an intellectual or visual awareness of three-dimensionality. The fact that it emanates not from the head, which we generally regard as the seat of consciousness, but from the navel region, where the hands rest within each center, shows the importance of this center in connection with a different kind of space experience, which has its roots in a deeper region of conscious or subconscious awareness than that of the intellect. An inkling of this may be conveyed by the strange feeling in the solar plexus caused by being confronted suddenly with empty space at the edge of a precipice.

Since it is from the navel center that our body has been nourished and grown (i.e., extended itself into space) in its embryonic state, we can well understand why this center has been regarded as the vital and basically most important center in man. In China and Japan it is even thought of as the seat of the human soul. The Japanese call it *Hara* and regard it as the basic center of Life (i.e., a life that is not merely an individual property, but something greater than the individual).

> Just as the growth and unfolding of the crown of a tree depends directly on its root-system, so also the vital development of man's spirit depends on his being true to his roots, that is, to an uninterrupted contact with the primal unity of Life, from which human life also springs.[3]

If, therefore, meditation is to serve the development of man's spirit and the completeness of his psychosomatic nature it has to descend to the roots of life before it can rise to the heights of the spirit.

References and Notes

[1] From a collection of my poems under the title *Mandala* (Origo, Zurich, 1961).

[2] Karlfried Graf von Dürckheim: *HARA, the Vital Centre of Man*, p. 158f. (George Allen & Unwin, London, 1962).

[3] Op. cit., p. 18.

5

THE FOUNDATIONS OF MINDFULNESS

TO BE FULLY CONSCIOUS in all situations and conditions of life, is what the Buddha meant when he said that we should be mindful while sitting, standing, lying down, or walking. But "fully conscious" does not mean to be conscious of only one aspect or function of our body or our mind, but to be conscious with and of our whole being, which includes body and mind and something that goes beyond body and mind: namely that deeper reality at which the Buddha hinted in the term *Dharma* and which he realized in the state of Enlightenment.

The most effective way to become conscious of our whole being and to dwell in a state of perfect concentration and equanimity is as we have seen, the practice of *ānāpānasati*. This is the basis of all meditation, because it is through breathing that we are able to come in contact with and connect all our physical and psychic faculties with our conscious mind. Through breathing we achieve the synthesis of all our functions and realize the dynamic and universal nature of life and the impossibility of the idea of a separate and unchangeable egohood, as expressed in the Buddha's *anātma*-doctrine. Only on this basis can the subsequent steps of the Satipatthāna-meditation have any meaning and prevent its deterioration into a mere intellectual analysis and negation of all positive aspects of human life.

It is characteristic and significant for the negative and prejudiced attitude of those who propagate a modern Burmese Satipatthāna practice, that they suppress precisely that part of the original Satipatthāna upon which the Buddha laid the greatest stress. They replace it by the most superficial of all methods, namely the observation of the rising and falling of the abdomen—thus diverting the attention of the meditator from the real experience of the breathing process. If one needs such desperate methods of focusing one's attention, it is better to abandon the practice and fix one's concentration on something more inspiring, something which holds our interest naturally and spontaneously without the use of force or sheer willpower, which only strengthens our ego-sense.

To concentrate on the visible mechanism of moving, the functions of limbs and muscles, i.e., the merely material side of one's body, is focusing one's consciousness on the lowest form of illusion and purely intellectual analysis. It does not bring us one step nearer the truth, but misleads us into believing that we have isolated certain facts, while in reality we have only forced our materialistic interpretation upon them. The deception consists in overlooking the fact that we cannot isolate any sense impression, since each sense impression is already an enormously complicated process. We can only reduce it to the point of emphasizing its most superficial aspect by suppressing all other factors. It is ridiculous to call this an act of unprejudiced observation or awareness, because the intentional exclusion of the spiritual factor, namely the force that moves or causes movement, the will—and, equally important, the mind which observes its own actions and reactions—and finally the conditions which make the movement possible: the universal forces which form the background and the *conditio sine qua non* for all phenomena of matter and movement, of consciousness and will power, of life and death, inertia and flux.

The falsification of the Buddha's Satipatthāna can be seen in the artificiality of such phrases as "touching, touching, touching"—"lifting, lifting, lifting" etc., by which each movement is verbalized—as if the lifting, the touching, the putting down, etc., were something that happened by itself. The Buddha was free from such deceptive devices of narrow dogmatism. He was not afraid of using the word "I" or the first person singular of the verb expressing individual action. He, for instance, simply and naturally said: "When making a long inhalation, I know that I make a long inhalation, when making a short inhalation, I know that I make a short inhalation; and similarly, as the case may be: I go, I stand, I sit, I lie down."

The fact that all movements are related to a central force, to an individual consciousness, does not mean that this force is an absolute, unchangeable and personal ego. Quite the contrary: he who has realized the fundamental significance of the breathing process—which is a continuous taking and giving back, assimilation and transformation, acceptance and release—knows that the essence of individual life cannot be a stagnant, immovable ego or separate entity—separate from the body which it inhabits, as well as from the world in which it lives—but a dynamic force, a focus of infinite relationships. The effort to separate the various functions and to look upon them as if they were autonomous, unrelated to anything else, is a gross violation of truth and reality. If there is visible movement, its reality does not lie in the object that is moved, but in the force which moves it.

If a stone falls, no amount of analytic investigation as to the nature of the stone can explain the reason for its fall. Only when we realize the force and principle of gravitation do we begin to understand the universal significance of that simple phenomenon observed in the falling of a stone.

By suppressing one half of the fact, namely the conscious process of our subjective act of willing, which miraculously (and what greater miracle could there be, than the direct action of mind upon matter!) causes the movement of our limbs—by suppressing this fact, I say, we violate the truth and degrade reality to a mechanical and perfectly senseless phenomenon. Apparently Admiral Shattock had come to a similar conclusion when he asked Mahasi Sayadaw the question: "What is the connection between the mind that thinks and gives orders, and the physical brain that carries them out in the body; and how does it work?" Here he touched upon one of the most profound mysteries of life—the interrelationship of mind and matter (*mano-maya*), which leads to the understanding that the body is not only a tool, an instrument of the mind, different from or even foreign to the essential nature of the mind, but that it is a crystallization of our consciousness, built up through aeons of organic evolution in harmony with universal laws, which reveal themselves in every function of the body and its organs. Instead of taking this opportunity to give some hints concerning the true nature of the mind and its creative power (*mano pubbangama dhammā*), the Sayadaw gave the following amazing reply: "The Sayadaw cannot possibly give you an opinion about a matter which has not been included by the Buddha as one for instruction; it would be impossible for him to have an opinion on such a thing." The Buddha never forbade his disciples to think for themselves, nor did he establish a dogma that excluded such questions.

By trying to undo the spontaneous interaction of body and mind by submitting it to a slow-motion analysis and a superficial verbalization, we reduce ourselves to a state of artificial imbecility which—if pursued to its logical end—would lead to a complete standstill of all functions of life, to physical and spiritual suicide by way of schizophrenia. Because what we actually do is to drive a wedge between the functions of the body and the mind by splitting their unity into an observing intellect (an isolated part of our surface consciousness) and the outer effect of a physical function (an isolated part, or the mere end product of an intricate psychophysical process which has its roots in the deeper layers of our consciousness). The effect of the insertion of our analytical or intellectual consciousness into the spontaneous functions of our bodily organism, which through millenniums of practice have been freed from the burden of conscious effort, has been humorously described in Ogden Nash's well-known poem about the centipede who was immobilized the moment he tried to observe consciously the movements of his legs:

> The centipede was happy quite,
> Until a toad in fun
> Said: "Pray, which leg goes after which?"
> This worked his mind to such a pitch,
> He lay distracted in a ditch,
> Considering how to run.

The fact that all the major functions of the body have become automatic, i.e. self-regulating, unconscious, and—with the exception of breathing—beyond the interference of will power or intellect (the beating of the heart, the circulation of blood, the currents of nervous energy, the processes of digestion, assimilation of foodstuffs or expulsion of unsuitable substances, etc.), is an achievement of our biological evolution or the supra-individual powers of our depth consciousness. Without these we would not have the freedom to develop a spiritual life reaching beyond the frontiers of the body, beyond merely physical needs and egocentric desires, or the limitations of momentary situations and conditions. If we had to make a conscious effort to keep the heart beating or to maintain the function of breathing, our whole attention would be absorbed merely in keeping alive. There would be neither the time nor the opportunity to exert the mind in any other direction; and to fall asleep would mean certain death.

As pointed out in the preceding chapter, there is only one vital function which, in spite of its independence from our waking consciousness and its self-regulating and self-perpetuating subconscious character, can be transformed into a conscious function and submitted to our will. This is the function of breathing and, due to its double nature, it can be made the mediator between mind and body or the means of our conscious participation in the most vital and universal function of the body. However, if we try to impose our will upon this function, without a deeper knowledge of its laws and its far-reaching effects, we may violate its natural rhythm and cause irreparable damage to our health. If we try to cooperate with it consciously, without interference by our will, merely filling it with our consciousness and undivided attention (*smṛti*), then not only will the function of breathing be raised from a physical process to the level of a spiritual experience, but the whole body will be penetrated and consciously experienced in its entirety and transformed into an instrument of the mind. Thus, instead of analyzing and dissecting, or merely diverting our consciousness to external movements or secondary functions of the body, we become again complete (whole) in the integration of body and mind, in which every single function derives its meaning in relationship to the whole. The mere awareness of minor functions, isolated from their wider background and their essential relations, is meaningless. An isolated experience or an isolated fact, or a fragment of knowledge taken out of its context, has no value, unless it is brought into proper perspective and into relationship with other pieces of information. The faculty of coordination is more important than the faculty of storing bits of knowledge, i.e., learning. Awareness, remembrance, and coordination are the three essentials of the mind. "Pure awareness" is pure nonsense, because one cannot be aware without reference to previous states of awareness, stored up in memory. Only by reference to previous experiences and coordination with their contents and results, can awareness have any spiritual value.

The term '*smṛti*' (Pāli: *sati*) confirms this view, as it represents not only the quality of awareness, attention, and thought, but also the faculty of remembrance. In fact, the Sanskrit root "smṛ" means "to remember, to think of." Thus the idea of "pure" or "bare awareness," which the Burmese School wants to make the basis of meditation, cannot be maintained as a characteristic of Satipatthāna. Moreover, the central element of all meditative practice is missing in the Burmese method, namely, *prīti* (Pāli: pīti): rapture, enthusiasm, or, better still inspiration. This is the joyful, forward-driving element which is the central factor of meditation (defined as: *vitaka, vicāra, prīti, sukha, ekāgratā*) and which in the final stages of meditation merges into *sukha*, the bliss and happiness of emancipation. The Burmese method is a veritable *tour de force*, in which the meditator rigorously subdues all natural impulses by sheer willpower. Concentration, however, should be achieved by an attitude which naturally draws everything toward one point and creates cooperation with all other forces of the human psyche. A concentration achieved by the suppression of these elements is like crippling or mutilating an organism in order to make it comply with dictates of brutal force.

By breaking up the function of walking into its various phases, for instance, we only destroy the unity of movement and replace it by an artificial division, which merely makes movement a torture without bringing us one step nearer to the understanding of its nature. It is the antithesis of spontaneity, the undoing of all that the Masters of Zen regard as the highest achievement of the mind: intuition. It is the victory of the narrowest kind of intellect over the liberating forces of the unifying, intuitive mind.

Anybody with even the slightest knowledge of meditation knows that suppression is not the way to the mystery of the mind, nor that of the body, the feelings, or the emotions. What unites the mind, what prevents it from straying, is "*pīti*," which is a good deal more than the curiosity of the brain in conducting a scientific experiment to discover the mechanism of mind and body. It is the rapture of inspiration, which we may find in the stillness of nature, at the foot of a tree, in a lonely hermitage and in the quiet chamber of the heart. Inspiration is the spontaneous movement from the lesser to the greater, from the lower to the higher. It contains no element of force or violence.

6
THE FUNDAMENTAL PRINCIPLES OF MEDITATION

INSPIRATION IS THE VERY HEART, the central force of all meditation. But since inspiration is a spontaneous faculty (also interpreted as "rapture"), it cannot be created on command, but only induced by arousing our interest or our admiration. Thus, before we can get inspired, we must prepare the ground, create the mood, the receptivity of the mind, and for this there are two requirements: relaxation, quietness, peace, and harmony on the one hand and, on the other, something that gives direction and concentration to the mind, i.e. either a mental subject or a visible object of contemplation that is sufficiently attractive to hold the attention of the meditator.

The beauty of nature or of a poem, a moving prayer as a devotional chant, the remembrance or the image of a charismatic personality or an Enlightened One in whose footsteps one wishes to follow, all these are conducive to meditation. Other good preparations are music, incense, flowers, and light, or the ritual of offering them in a temple or at a shrine (as was usual in every Tibetan home, as well as in most Indian homes of Buddhists and Hindus alike). In short, the elements of beauty and devotion are the most powerful incentives of meditation. Both these elements are united in Tibetan Thankas, which may explain the strange fascination they exert on the modern mind and especially those interested in spiritual values and meditative practices. For devotional temperaments prayer itself becomes an entrance to meditation; in fact, prayer in a deeper sense, as a "direction of the heart" (as we shall see in the next chapter) is itself a form of meditation. Whatever we love becomes an easy subject of contemplation, because it requires no effort, but follows the natural inclination of mind and heart.

However, even intellectual pursuits, the exploration of ideas and phenomena of our ordinary life and its problems, may be a starting point of our meditation, though there is always the danger of getting stuck on the intellectual level and resting contented with rational solutions, instead of reaching the level of direct experience in which the problem dissolves. Nevertheless, the faculty of thinking is as important in the initial stages of meditation as any of the other factors involved in the process of meditation. This is clearly indicated in the first two factors of the most ancient definition of Buddhist meditation: *vitarka*, initial thought, and *vicāra*, sustained thought; in other words, thinking and reflecting, the two aspects of discursive thought. This gives direction, coherence, and concentration to our consciousness, whose stream of ever-changing thoughts, feelings, impressions, and images we cannot stop, but only channel, restrict, and direct, by giving it a strong incentive, a central point of interest or attraction. KLong-chen-pa, one of the most renowned spiritual teachers of the Tibetan Nyingma Sect, who lived in the early fourteenth century and was known as a great master of meditation, exclaimed in one of his works on *The Natural Freedom of the Mind*:

> Alas! Those people professing to meditate but suppressing all thought, are conceited about a conceptless state which they call a "presence," and for this reason being stupid like cattle, turn themselves into animals by habituating themselves to this state. And if they do not, they themselves have no chance of becoming free from Samsāra, even if they "meditate" on the sphere where no forms obtain. Therefore, the more conceited they grow, the more they are possessed by the demon of their own systems.[1]

Thinking (*vitarka*) according to the psychology of the ancient Abhidharma, destroys sloth and torpor, reflecting (*vicāra*), or sustained thought, clears up doubt; inspirational joy or rapture (*prīti*) prevents hatred; happiness (*sukha*) counteracts restlessness; and one-pointedness counteracts greed. Buddhism has never spurned clear thinking, but on the other hand it has never fallen into the trap of believing that conceptual thought and logic can solve metaphysical or spiritual problems. But before we can trust our intuitions, or rather discern between genuine intuitions and mere *wishful* thinking or vague feelings, we have to learn how to use our reason and our faculty of thinking. Buddhism has always insisted on clarity—not only on clarity of thought, but equally on clarity of vision—which is abundantly demonstrated in tantric *sādhanas* and Tibetan Thankas, where every detail is clearly defined and delineated as in a surrealistic picture. It might be said that Buddhist mysticism consists in a heightened sense of reality and actuality.

Thus, thinking and reflecting are only the beginning and lead to an intuitive state of consciousness in which the processes of thinking and reasoning come to an end and some kind of deeper vision or direct experience takes over. The first step in this direction is the experience of the infinity of space, in which consciousness loses its limitations and leads to the experience of the infinity of consciousness. This experience of boundless extension and freedom leads to the realization of *śūnyatā*, which in the early Pāli texts is described as the sphere of no-*thing*-ness (*nañcāyatana*).

Beyond this no words can describe the actual experience of the meditator who, therefore, is described as having arrived at the state of "neither-perception-nor-non-perception," the realm of the ultimate limit of perception, because the distinction between the experiencer and the experienced object has disappeared; subject and object have become one, perfect unification (*samādhi*) has been achieved.

According to the Abhidharma the different stages of the meditative process can be defined in the following way: in the beginning thinking, reflecting, inspiration, happiness, and one-pointedness are present; in the second stage the initial thought disappears; in the third stage the discursive thought process comes to an end, leaving only a feeling of inspiration, happiness, and one-pointedness. In the fourth stage only happiness and one-pointedness remain, and in the fifth stage, there is only the experience of oneness, whose bliss is beyond words.

The process of concentration can be graphically depicted by the following triangle of steadily decreasing factors of meditative consciousness:

vitarka-vicāra-prīti-sukha-ekāgratā
vicāra-prīti-sukha-ekāgratā
prīti-sukha-ekāgratā
sukha-ekāgratā
ekāgratā

As we can see from this systematic representation of the five stages of absorption, no attempt is made to give any particular content. They merely form the general frame, and into this frame we may fit any meditational subject, whether it is based on a discursive thought or on visualization. The first of these two methods has been mainly favored by the Hīnayāna Schools —with the exception of the ten Kasina exercises, i.e. meditations on "hypnotic circles"[2] while the practice of visualization was increasingly favored by the Manāyāna Schools and developed to perfection in the Vajrayāna. In accordance with this trend, the Pāli term, *jhāna,* which has generally been translated as meditative "absorption" or, most misleadingly, as "trance" or "ecstasy" (although "instasy" would have been more adequate), was rightly interpreted in its Sanskrit equivalent *dhyāna* as "vision," both in the sense of nonverbal intuitive experience and as "visualization," instead of mental abstractions.

The Buddha himself said that his teaching is deep, profound *(gambhīra),* beyond the realm of speculation and word-thinking *(avitarka, avicāra),* comprehensible only to the wise. The only way, however, to free ourselves from the tyranny of words and concepts is the imaginative method of visualization, or the replacement of our one-track logic by the multidimensional symbol. Even a strict science such as mathematics has developed a language of multidimensional symbols and visual formulations in which the position of each sign or symbol in the general context of a formula determines the meaning and value of each particular sign. The meditative experience of Buddhism developed a similarly intricate system of visual symbols based on archetypal forms or images which evolved from the depth of human consciousness and proved their efficacy through millenia of meditative practice.

The special significance of inspiration *(prīti)* is not only evident by its central position among the five factors of meditation, but also by its similar position among the seven factors of enlightenment *(bodhyanga),* which it divides into two groups, of which the first contains three active factors, while the other contains three corresponding passive factors:

1) *smṛti*   — awareness, recollection, mindfulness;
2) *dharmavicaya* — discernment of what is *dharma* and what is not;
3) *viryā* — energy, effort;
4) *prīti* — rapture or inspiration;
5) *praśrabdhi* — quietness, serenity;

6) *samādhi* — entasy, unification
7) *upekṣa* — mental balance, equanimity.

Thus, awareness is balanced by equanimity, discrimination by unification, and effort by quietness, while inspiration holds the center.

For those who think that *samādhi* is an end in itself or the highest achievement in meditation, it may come as a surprise that *upekṣa* is the final item in this group. The reason is that though *samādhi* may be the culmination in the meditative experience, we cannot remain in that state (which would mean stagnation) but have to return to the world, to the pursuits of normal human life. It is here that the achievement of *samādhi* is put to the test, and if it is a real attainment, it is equanimity. While *samādhi* is a peak experience, equanimity is its long-range effect on life.

In a similar way, concentration has often been regarded as almost synonymous with meditation. But a state of intense concentration is not necessarily meditation; in fact, in most cases it is not. An accountant who is bent on his figures or an astronaut who is concentrated on his switchboard or his instruments is certainly not meditating. The difference is that meditation leaves us a certain amount of freedom in the movement toward and around our subject. It is this freedom which may be described as a concentric movement around the subject of meditation, rather than an arrow-like frontal approach in a straight line, which corresponds more to the one-sided viewpoint of Western perspective and logic.

Thus, concentration, although an important factor in meditation, is not the whole of it, but only a precondition, insofar as it excludes disturbing influences and diversions. But even here we have to be careful not to go to the extreme of narrowing our attention or our outlook to such a degree that we isolate our subject and cut it off from all possible relations with other things or with its general background.

According to Patanjali's three principles of yoga, meditation can be defined as a combination or successive integration of *dhāranā, dhyāna,* and *samādhi.* The function of *dhāranā* is the fixing of the mind on a certain subject, or in a certain direction. This may be achieved through the recitation of sacred texts, mantric formulas (*dhārani*), prayers (*prani-*

dhāna), or other acts of devotion (*pūjā, vanadanā*), concentration on breathing, on an image or maṇḍala, etc. After the mind is thus fixed and directed, it is able to contemplate or to visualize without conscious effort any thought-object or symbol that is able to arouse genuine inspiration. Thus a state of *dhyāna*, of deep absorption and inner vision, comes into existence and leads to *samādhi* in which the contemplative experience is integrated in the completely unified consciousness of the meditator. He is now able to return into the world and transform into action the knowledge and experience he has gained. The following diagram of the main factors of meditation will speak for itself.

FACTORS OF MEDITATION

PRELIMINARIES: Co-ordination and harmonization of body and mind, in secluded and quiet surroundings: in a beautiful spot in nature or in a shrine-room, set apart for meditation.
Complete mental and bodily relaxation through meditative posture (*āsana*) Conscious attitude: sense-awareness, openmindedness, receptivity.

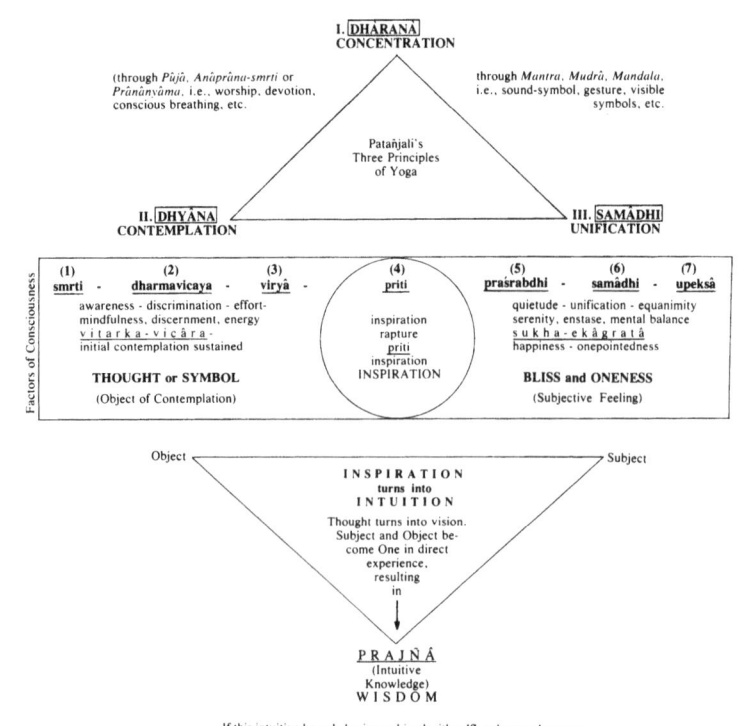

I. DHĀRAṆĀ
CONCENTRATION

(through *Pūjā, Anāprāna-smṛti* or *Prāṇāyāma*, i.e., worship, devotion, conscious breathing, etc.

through *Mantra, Mudrā, Mandala*, i.e., sound-symbol, gesture, visible symbols, etc.

Patañjali's
Three Principles
of Yoga

II. DHYĀNA
CONTEMPLATION

III. SAMĀDHI
UNIFICATION

Factors of Consciousness

(1)	(2)	(3)	(4)	(5)	(6)	(7)
smṛti	dharmavicaya	viryā	prīti	praśrabdhi	samādhi	upekṣā
awareness - discrimination - effort-mindfulness, discernment, energy vitarka - vicāra - initial contemplation sustained			inspiration rapture prīti inspiration	quietude - unification - equanimity serenity, enstase, mental balance sukha - ekāgratā happiness - onepointedness		
THOUGHT or SYMBOL (Object of Contemplation)			INSPIRATION	BLISS and ONENESS (Subjective Feeling)		

Object ← → Subject

**INSPIRATION
turns into
INTUITION**

Thought turns into vision.
Subject and Object become One in direct experience, resulting in

↓

PRAJÑĀ
(Intuitive
Knowledge)
WISDOM

If this intuitive knowledge is combined with selfless love and compassion (*maitrī* & *karuṇī*), it will lead to perfect enlightenment (*samyak-sambodhi*).

References and Notes

[1] *Crystal Mirror* IV, tr. by H. V. Guenther, Dharma Publishing, Berkeley, 1975.
[2] These were none other than replicas of the original centers (*cakras*) with their corresponding colors and elements (earth, water, fire, air, etc.) taken over from the ancient system of *cakra-yoga*, whose actual meaning had been forgotten by the time these exercises were adopted by the Theravādins.

7

THE DEVOTIONAL ATTITUDE IN MEDITATION AND PRAYER

EVERY RELIGION recognizes a highest value, a *summum bonum*. Theistic religions call it God; nontheistic religions call it Tao, Nirvāna, Sammāsambodhi (Perfect Enlightenment), etc. In theistic religions, prayer has been defined as a communion or a dialogue with God; in nontheistic religions, prayer could be defined as a state of intense longing for the highest state of perfection or completeness, the realization of perfect Enlightenment.

Prayer in its widest sense is "a direction of the heart" (Rilke) and presupposes a mental or spiritual polarity, either between man and God, or between the finite and the infinite, the individual and the universal, the imperfect and the perfect, etc. In Christianity, Judaism, and Islam the individual human pole is conceived as the soul, the divine pole as the Creator; in Hinduism as *jīvātman* and *brahman* (or paramātman); in Buddhism as the limited, mundane self-consciousness and the potential universal consciousness, which is latent in every sentient being and can be experienced and realized in its totality in the state of enlightenment.

Prayer thus arises from a state of creative tension between the human and the divine, the consciousness of incompleteness (or imperfection) and the ideal of completeness (or perfection), between the present state of ignorance or delusion and the longed-for, future state of liberation: the awakening from the illusion of separateness to the wholeness of life.

What here appears to us as "future," however, is something that is ever-existing, ever-present in our universal depth-consciousness (*ālaya-vijñāna*), which modern psychology has rediscovered only now, though greatly misunderstood by conceiving it as an enemy of reason and the source of uncontrollable drives and emotions and calling it "the Unconscious"[1] in order to subordinate it all the more to the limited surface consciousness, which identifies itself with the ephemeral interests of its momentary individual existence, thus losing the connection with its origin, the living source of power.

In prayer, however, we turn back to that source and reestablish its connection with the individual, focalized surface consciousness, so that the tension between the surface and depth, like the tension of a cord, produces a pure sound, a higher vibration of the spirit. It is not the object of prayer to eliminate this tension, but to transform it into a creative force by establishing a meaningful, harmonious cooperation between the two apparently contradictory, but in reality complementary, poles. Thus prayer becomes a source of strength and certainty, and not merely a sedative or a tranquilizer. The inner peace that comes from prayer is due to the establishment of a balance between the forces of our individual consciousness and the vast potentialities of our depth-consciousness, in which the experiences of a beginningless past are stored and through which we participate in that greater life that encompasses the universe and connects it with every living being.

Prayer—and in a higher degree meditation (of which prayer is only the first step)—is the *consciously directed* approach toward this vast storehouse of experience, which modern psychology merely observes in its passively accepted, functional effects on our subconscious mind (as in dreams and archetypal symbols) as if it were driven by irresistible forces.

> Common experience looks on the idea that we are pushed about by such inner drives as unreal and artificial! What meaning can it have, we say, for men whose lives are dedicated to the pursuit of knowledge or the creation of beauty or the service of their fellows? What place in it is there for devotion and sacrifice and that endless striving for truth and human betterment which ever has distinguished man at his best? . . . Men seem not to be pushed into the finest things they do but to follow the urgent call of something that draws them on through hardship and un-

certainty and discouragement to the attainment of a high desire.[2]

This conception has the advantage over present psychological orthodoxy in that its attitude is forward, *toward* a goal to be reached, and not back to the push and drive of circumstance, and is thus of harmony with the common verdict of experience.[3]

Prayer, being a "direction of the heart" (i.e. of the inner center of a human being which participates equally in his individual consciousness and in his superindividual depth-consciousness, and thus of his intuition, and not merely of his surface consciousness), is therefore a positive and active approach to the hidden treasury of universal experience. It does not blindly take hold of experience contents that happen to well up, but have no bearing on its intuited aim, like a man who descends without a light into a dark storeroom in the cellar of his house, aimlessly taking hold of what comes into his hands.

Prayer is indeed the lamp that enables us to discover in the vastness of the treasurehouse the very items needed or essential on our spiritual way toward completeness. Instead of dragging the fragmentary glimpses of contents of the depth-consciousness into the glaring light of the intellect and submitting them to a deadly analysis, prayer turns our conscious mind inward and transforms the potential forces of the depth into active ones, because "making the unconscious conscious transforms the mere idea of the universality of man into the living experience of this universality." (Fromm) In other words, instead of raising the archetypal symbols and visions of the depth to the surface and subordinating them to conceptual thought and the trivialities of temporal aims and purposes, the focus of our individualized mind should turn inward in order to become aware of its universal source and make use of its immense potentialities in the pursuance of ultimate completeness and perfect enlightenment.

Prayer as a means toward this aim would defeat its own purpose if it was the expression of selfish desires or exclusively concerned with our own individual welfare. Moreover, the Buddhist neither believes in separate egohood (or an unchangeable individual soul-monad that has to be "saved" and preserved for eternity) nor looks upon the Buddha as a God who fulfills his wishes. To him the Buddha is the model of the complete or perfect man who has become conscious of his universality, realized the divine within himself, and has thus become a light to others.

If, therefore, the Buddhist bows down before the image of the Buddha, he does not ask anything of him, he does not pray *to* him, but gives vent to his feelings of veneration in the same way in which he would show his respect and love to his living religious teacher or Guru, in whose footsteps he is determined to follow in order to make the teachings a living reality within himself. The formula which he utters during the act of veneration before the image or symbol of the Enlightened One (like a statue, a stūpa, a reliquary, the Bodhi-tree, or whatever helps him to bring the noble figure of the Buddha before his mind), consists of the words:

"I take my refuge in the Enlightened One;

"I take my refuge in the Teaching" (the Sacred Law, taught by all Enlightened Ones);

"I take my refuge in the Community (of those who have realized the Teaching)."

In Tibet this formula is preceded by the words: "I take my refuge in the Guru" because the Guru is the living representative, the mouthpiece of the Buddha, the transmitter and the embodiment of the Buddha's Teaching, who kindles the flame of faith in the disciple and inspires him to follow in the footsteps of those who have realized the Sacred Teaching (*dharma*), and have become members of the Community of Saints (*sangha*).

The first step of devotion and prayer in Buddhism, therefore, consists in the expression of veneration, loyalty, and gratitude toward the Teacher, the living Guru as well as the Buddha who speaks through him. And just as the person of the Guru is conceived as a link in the continuity of spiritual transmission of Buddha Śākyamuni's teaching, in the same way Buddha Śākyamuni is only one link in the infinite chain of Enlightened Ones. Thus the term "Guru" comprises the complete chain of spiritual teachers who passed on the living tradition through millenia from generation to generation, and similarly the term "Buddha" includes the totality of all the Enlightened Ones that preceded him or that have followed him.

Thus, in Mahāyāna tradition, the historical personality of Śākyamuni-Buddha recedes behind the universal figure of the

Perfect Enlightened One, the symbol of the Complete Man who has realized his divine nature. Instead of worshiping a God beyond all human conception, enthroned in a realm of metaphysical abstractions and generalizations, the Buddhist strives after the realization of those divine properties which have been demonstrated by innumerable saints and Enlightened Ones. He tries to realize them in his own heart, in his own mind, and in his own life.

The thought that a god should have created the world with all its evil, its suffering, its imperfections, stupidity and cruelty, appears to him as a kind of blasphemy of the very idea of God as the embodiment of perfection. For him it is not a god who is responsible for the evil and imperfection of the world, because the world that we experience is the creation of our own ignorance, our own cravings and passions. That imperfection should come out of perfection and completeness seems to contradict all reason, while the opposite appears more likely to the Buddhist. The experiences of life and the example of those who attained enlightenment have taught him that from a state of imperfection, perfection can be achieved, and the sufferings resulting from our passions are the very forces that lead toward liberation.

But while the Buddhist respects the idea of a Creator-God, he believes in the divine principle in man, the inborn spark of light (*bodhi-citta*) embodied in his consciousness as a yearning toward perfection, toward completeness, toward Enlightenment. To put it paradoxically, it is not God who creates man, but man who creates God in his image, i.e. the idea of the divine aim within himself, which he realizes in the fires of suffering from which compassion, understanding, love, and wisdom are born.

The unfoldment of individual life in the universe has no other aim apparently but to become conscious of its own divine essence, and since this process goes on continuously, it represents a perpetual birth of God or, to put it into Buddhist terminology, the continuous arising of Enlightened Beings, in each of whom the totality of the universe becomes conscious.

These Enlightened Ones are what the Mahāyāna calls "the infinite number of Buddhas" or—insofar as they are experienced as actively influencing the development of humanity— "the infinite number of Bodhisattvas." The latter represent the active forces emanating from those who have attained the highest state of consciousness, inspiring and furthering all those who are striving for liberation. This is represented pictorially by the aura of the meditating Buddha, which is filled with small replicas of the Buddha, symbolizing the infinite number of Bodhisattvas, who in myriad forms appear for the welfare of all living and suffering beings. Though they manifest themselves in innumerable individual forms, they are one in spirit.

We had described the first step of Buddhist prayer as an expression of veneration and gratitude toward the great Enlightened Ones, who taught the way of liberation to humanity by word and deed. As an example of the profound devotion which fills the Buddhist Sādhaka, I may quote here some passages from Śāntideva's *"Bodhicaryāvatāra,"* which describes the awakening of the inner light, or the practice of the Bodhisattvas on the way toward enlightenment (hence the Tibetan title: *Byang-chub-sems-dpahi-spyod-pa*).

> In order to take possession of the pearl of enlightenment, I worship the Tathāgatas and also the faultless jewel of the doctrine, as well as the spiritual sons of the Enlightened Ones, the oceans of virtue.
>
> Whatever there may be found in this world: flowers, fruits, vegetables, and life-giving waters; the mountains of precious stone, the forest-solitudes for meditation, the creepers adorned with beautiful, radiant blossoms, the trees whose twigs are bent under the burden of delicious fruit, the perfumes and scents from the world of gods, the miraculous trees, the jewel-trees, the lovely ponds of lotus-flowers, echoing with the sweet song of swans, the wild-growing plants as well as those of the fields: everything that is suitable as an offering and all that is contained in the infinity of space and does not belong to anybody; I collect all this in my mind and offer it to the Perfect Ones and their spiritual sons (the Bodhisattvas).
>
> I am without merits and, therefore, very poor. I have nothing else for their worship. May, therefore, the Perfect Ones, who have no other thought but the welfare of others, may they accept this for my sake.

The next step is the complete self-surrender and change of heart in the awareness of our faults and weaknesses.

> Wholely and without reserve I dedicate myself to the Enlightened Ones and their spiritual sons: Take pos-

session of me, exalted beings! Filled with humility I offer myself as your servant. Having become your property, I have nothing more to fear in this world. I will do only what is helpful to other beings. I will give up my former wrong-doing and not commit further misdeeds. Due to hatred and infatuation I have committed many wrong deeds. I did not realize that I am only a traveller, passing through this world. Day and night, without cessation, vitality decreases and death approaches. This very day, therefore, I will take my refuge in the great and powerful protectors of the world. From the bottom of my heart I take my refuge in the doctrine—and likewise in the multitude of Bodhisattvas. With folded hands I implore the Perfect Enlightened Ones in all the regions of the universe: may they kindle the light of truth for all those who on account of their delusion would otherwise fall into the abyss of misery.

After the devotee has thus opened himself to the Enlightened Ones and has offered himself to them as "an instrument of their peace" (compare the beautiful and universal prayer of St. Francis of Assisi,[4] which could have been spoken by Śāntideva or any devout Buddhist), he renounces the fruits of his good deeds and instead of being concerned for his "own salvation," he vows to dedicate himself to the welfare of all living beings. In other words, he will share the sufferings of his fellow beings in order to inspire and assist them on their way toward liberation rather than rest blissfully on the pedestal of his virtues, enjoying for himself the fruits of his good deeds.

It is in this spirit that he utters the vow:

Whatever merit I may have obtained, may I become thereby the soother of every pain for all living beings. The merits which I have acquired in all my rebirths through thoughts, words and deeds, all this I am giving away without regard to myself, in order to realize the salvation of all living beings. Nirvāna means to give up everything; and my heart desires Nirvāna. If I must give up everything, is it not better to give everything to living beings? I have dedicated myself to the welfare of all living beings; may they beat me and abuse me and cover me with dust. May they play with my body and make me an object of their ridicule. I have abandoned my body to them; why should I worry about it? Those who abuse me, or others who treat me badly, or those who jeer at me, may they all attain enlightenment.

Who would not be reminded here of Christ's words: "Love your enemies, bless them that curse you, do good to them that hate you, and pray for them which despitefully use you and persecute you"? Every true Buddhist who hears these words will be convinced that he who spoke them was one of the great Bodhisattvas, one of the enlightened helpers of humanity, to whom he pays respect in his daily devotions when he remembers the Enlightened Ones of the past and pays respect to those of the present and the future.[5]

The cultivation of an attitude of loving kindness and the conscious penetration of the world with compassionate thoughts and a loving heart, "like a mother who protects her child with her own life," has been called by the Buddha a "divine state," literally a "dwelling in God" (*brahma-vihāra*). Herewith he has at the same time given a perfect definition of what he considers "divine." The love of which he speaks here is far more than humanitarian good will, into which some Western interpreters have tried to dilute the Maitrī (Pāli: *mettā*) of the Buddha, though the above mentioned quotation, which defines maitrī as the spontaneous and selfless love of a mother, should have taught them a deeper understanding.

Also the other constituents of this "divine state," which naturally flow from this boundless love (and which, on account of their boundlessness, are also called "illimitables"), are compassion (*karuṇā*) and sympathetic joy (*muditā*), i.e. the sharing of others' sorrow and joy and, finally, that state of equanimity (*upekṣā*) which is unaffected by one's own sufferings or successes.

One of the greatest misunderstandings concerning the spiritual and emotional attitude of Buddhism is due to the wrong interpretation of the term *upekṣā* (Pāli: *upekkhā*). The current, purely negative rendering of this important term as "indifference" has repeatedly led to the opinion (especially on the part of Christian theologians) that love, compassion, and the sharing of happiness with others, are only preparatory steps for the attainment of complete indifference, which thus would seem to be the highest aim and the culmination of Buddhist ethics. The fact that *upekṣā* is placed at the end of these "divine states" has led to the conclusion that, to the Buddhist, love and compassion are only convenient means for his own salvation and that therefore they are not the outcome of true altruism and of equal value as the similar qualities in Christianity.

In reality the opposite is true: as love is not lessened by compassion but actually finds its fulfillment in these qualities, *upekṣā* does not extinguish the preceding attitudes. In fact, only a man who is not shaken by other people's enmity or favors, who is indifferent toward his own gain or loss, but not toward that of others, is capable of showing equal sympathy to all beings. Not only do love and compassion and the rejoicing in the happiness of other beings find their ultimate perfection in *upekṣā,* but we can equally say that *upekṣā* is the very foundation of these qualities, which the Enlightened Ones and those who follow in their footsteps cultivate and offer to the world, like the sun that shines for sinners and saints alike.

Thus *upekṣā,* in its highest aspect, is that unshakable steadfastness, that perfect mental and spiritual balance and equanimity in which neither indifference nor lukewarm emotions find a place, and in which the distinction between one's own self and that of others has disappeared. This has been beautifully expressed by Śāntideva in the firat *Kārikā* of his *Sikṣāsamuccaya:*

> Yadā mama pareṣāṃ ca bhayam duhkhaṃ ca na priyaṃ
> Tadāmanaḥ ko viseso yat taṃ rakṣāmi netaram?
> (If my neighbor, like myself, hates fear and pain,
> in what way, then, do I distinguish myself from others,
> that I should seek protection for myself and not for others?)

Here we come to the heart of the problem and to the chief motive of Buddhist prayer: it is love and compassion, based on the profound knowledge of the essential unity of life and the mutual relationship of all sentient beings. Just as the selfless love of a mother is not the outcome of an ethical demand or of a categorical imperative, but rests on the knowledge of the essential oneness of mother and child, in the same way the Buddhist attitude toward his fellow beings is the natural result of his innermost conviction.

This conviction is nurtured by experiences of meditation, of which prayer is the first step. In this sense we may call prayer a preliminary form of meditation. It uses words to guide the mind in a certain direction, and the further it proceeds, the fewer words it needs. Finally prayer becomes *mantra,* creative speech or word of power, that awakens the dormant forces of the soul, until the mind of the devotee dives into the ocean of his depth-consciousness (*ālaya-vigñāna*), where the reality of a greater life which connects him with all living beings and the very spirit of the Enlightened Ones, reveals itself through direct experience, beyond words and concepts.

Thus prayer in Buddhism is the path of devotion (*bhaktimarga*)—first to the Guru and the Enlightened Ones (through *śaraṇa-gamana, vandanā* and *pūjā*), then to all living and suffering beings (*maitrī-bhāvanā*) through the Bodhisattva vows of perfect self-dedication (*pranidhāna*)—that ends in the light of knowledge. For he who wants to partake of the light must first open himself. Prayer is an act of opening heart and mind; and while we open ourselves, we not only allow the light to enter, but we make the first breach in the walls of our self-created prison, which has separated us from our fellow beings. Thus, in the same measure in which the light streams in and makes us recognize our true universal nature connecting us with all that exists in the infinity of space and time, our love and compassion for all living and suffering beings wells up and streams out from us like a mighty current that embraces the whole world. In this way prayer becomes an act of devotion in a twofold way: to the forces of the light (*bodhi*) and to our fellow beings (maitrī, karupā). The forces of the light, however, are not an abstract ideal but a living reality, embodied in those great teachers of humanity whom we venerate as the Enlightened Ones.

The more intensely we can put ourselves into their presence, the more alive they become in our consciousness, the deeper we feel for them in response to their love, in admiration of their deeds, and in gratitude for their teachings, the greater is their power to act upon us. But in order to experience their presence, we require visible symbols in which the highest qualities of the enlightened mind are expressed and through which at the same time our deepest feelings are aroused.

Such symbols are the various representations of the Buddha-figure, which not merely depict a particular historical personality, but are the outcome of the integrated religious experience of innumerable generations of devotees. Thus the image is not an object of veneration (i.e. the Buddhist does not pray to the image) but a means to experience the presence of the Enlightened Ones, the reality of his aim. Instead of merely worshipping our ideal or praying to the Enlightened Ones—as if they were something outside ourselves—we must ourselves *become* our ideal, identify ourselves with it, in order to be able to *live* it also in our outward activities and in our daily life. An ideal becomes an effective, active force only when it is felt and experienced as an ever-present reality, as is the case in the higher states of meditative experience (*dhyāna*) or inner vision. Thus the outer, material image, and likewise the *pūjā*-ritual and the liturgy in congregational worship—in which prayer becomes an act of joint devotion and self-dedication—is only the beginning and the preparation for the unfoldment of inner vision in meditation in which the devotee becomes one with his ideal. In the gestures (*mudrā*) and actions (such as bowing down, offering lights, water, and flowers, etc.) of ritual worship (*pūjā*), our thoughts and emotions are made visible as a means of guiding and concentrating the mind upon the aim of the sacred path. We may call it a dramatized form of meditation: meditation put into action and rendered visible and audible. Through the parallelism of body, mind, and speech, the coordination of movement, thought, and word, the harmony of feeling, creative imagination, visualization, and verbal expression, we achieve a unity of all the functions of our conscious being, which not only affects the surface of our personality—namely our senses and our intellect—but equally the deeper regions of our mind. In the regular performance of such ritual worship the very foundations of our being are slowly but certainly transformed and made receptive for the inner light.

References and Notes

[1] "Since long it is no more a secret, that the venerable root-concept of modern psychology 'the Unconscious' is a rather uncritical and obscure concept," says Medard Boss in his *Indienfahrt eines Psychiaters*, p. 19.
"The present-day psychological terminology which postulates an 'Unconscious' in contrast to consciousness, becomes thereby guilty of a falsification of fundamental psycho-somatic facts. This terminology and the subsequently wrongly structurized phenomena are a typical example for

the faulty conclusions which arise from a radically applied dualism."
(Jean Gebser: *Ursprung und Gegenwart*, Vol. I, p. 327.)
"The modern mind suffers from the odd prejudice that consciousness is a purely superficial outgrowth of reality, and that the more fundamental the power, principle or substance becomes, the more blind and unconscious it must be." (Alan W. Watts: *The Supreme Identity*, p. 56.)
"In Freud's view the unconscious is essentially the seat of irrationality. In Jung's thinking the meaning seems to be almost reversed; the unconscious is essentially the seat of the deepest sources of wisdom, while the conscious is the intellectual part of the personality." (Erich Fromm in *Zen Buddhism and Psychoanalysis*, p. 96.)
[2] *The Biology of the Spirit*, Edmund W. Sinnott, p. 88.
[3] Ibid., p. 90.
[4] Lord, make me an instrument of Thy peace.
That where there is hatred, I may bring love;
That where there is wrong, I may bring the spirit of forgiveness;
That where there is error, I may bring truth;
That where there is doubt, I may bring faith;
That where there is despair, I may bring hope;
And where there are shadows, I may bring Thy light;
That where there is sadness, I may bring joy.
Lord, grant that I may seek rather to comfort than to be comforted.
To understand than to be understood; to love than to be loved;
For it is by giving that one receiveth,
It is by self-forgetting that one finds,
It is by forgiving that one is forgiven;
It is by dying that one awakens to eternal life.

[5] Ye ca buddhā atītā ca   The Enlightened Ones of the past
Ye ca buddhā anāgatā   The Enlightened Ones of the future
Paccuppaña ca ye buddhā   The Enlightened Ones of the present
Ahaṃ vandāmi sabbadā   I worship them at all times.

PART IV

ART AND MEDITATION

1

THE WELL OF LIFE

IN OUR INNERMOST BEING there is an incessant going and coming of forms and sounds, visions and voices, reverberating with unheard melodies and with the voices of beings born and unborn. It is the meeting place of the whole world. But it is great only if it is open and ready either to accept the world or to give it up.

It is not immutability that makes our soul great, but its faculty of transformation which enables us to resound with the tunes of all spheres of the universe. The rivers of life unite in the deep and hidden well of our being and flow through it.

The wise one knows how to listen to those melodies, how to watch those visions, how to feel those vibrations, and how to be carried by the great stream into the infinite.

In order to hear he must be silent; in order to see he must close his eyes to the external forms; in order to feel the cosmic rhythm he must quiet his breath and master his heart; and in order to be carried by the eternal stream he must give up his selfish desires. The creative artist will realize his visions in his works of art, the holy one in his life.

All of us could be creative if we would think less of the doings and achievements of our mundane life, of our personality and our ambitions—if we thought more of the hidden forces and faculties within ourselves. We make programs with our brain instead of using the ever present forces of our heart. We cheat ourselves with our coarse plans and trivial aims. We do not see what is nearest to us, we do not hear the whispering voices of our heart because of the noise of our own words. Our eyes are blinded by the glaring colors of daylight. Our restless life takes away our breath, our insatiable desires make our heart palpitate and cause our blood to race through the veins. Thus we do not hear the sound of other spheres, do not see the great visions, do not feel the mysterious vibrations—and the eternal stream flows past us into the infinite from whence it came.

Fortunately for us, there arise from time to time Great Ones, exalted leaders of humanity, explorers of the human spirit and of the eternal laws of the universe, who, by their noble example, shake us from lethargy and free us of our vain activities and blind desires. They inspire us by their profound wisdom and great compassion, by the sublime beauty of their works, deeds, and their very lives, and open our eyes to the realities within and without ourselves.

Then, again, we become aware that the deepest mysteries are manifested in this our physical world, our bodily existence revealed before our very eyes even in the "material" forms of things, if only we have found the center of our inner world, the primordial source within ourselves.

The hidden way that leads to this source is the path of meditation and absorption, and the vessel in which the water of life is brought up to the surface is art. The vessel may have many shapes: words, songs, forms and colors, signs and symbols, dreams and visions, or material creations.

Those who remain at the source are wise, those who return again to the world, in order to share the precious elixir with others, are the creative minds; but those who themselves become the vessels and give themselves to the world, are the All-Compassionate Ones, the Liberators of humanity, the Enlightened Ones.

2

PARALLELISM BETWEEN ART AND MEDITATION

ART AND MEDITATION are creative states of the human mind, both are nourished by the same source, but it may seem that they are moving in different directions: art toward the realm of the sensuous and outward manifestation, meditation toward inner realization and integration of forms and sense-impressions. But this difference pertains only to secondary factors, not to the essential nature of art and meditation.

Meditation is neither pure abstraction nor negation of form except in its ultimate illimitable stages. It means the perfect concentration of the mind and the elimination of all unessential features of the subject in question, until we are fully conscious of it by experiencing reality in a particular aspect or from a particular angle of vision.

Art proceeds in a similar way: while using the forms of the external world, it does not try to imitate nature, but to reveal a higher reality by omitting all accidentals, thus raising the visible form to the value of a symbol, expressing a direct experience of life.

The same experience may be gained by the process of meditation. But instead of creating a formal (objectively existing) expression, it leaves a subjective impression, thus acting as a character-forming agent, besides enriching and refining the consciousness of the meditator.

The highest or most intense form of meditation or perfect absorption, which has no particular subject, may be described as the attainment of a spiritual space-experience or "vacuum" in which the universal forces of our deepest center can manifest themselves. In this sense meditation can be called the art of arousing within ourselves a creative attitude, a state of intuitive receptivity.

The artist, on the other hand, who has the gift, or who by continuous training has achieved the faculty of expressing such intuitive experience, crystallizes his inner vision into visible, audible, or tangible forms by reversing the meditative process into a process of materialization. But this presupposes that the artist has first attained that intuitive state. This may be conditioned either by external stimuli or by the genius of the artist or by spiritual training. Often all these factors may work together: the beauty of nature or the impression of a human face, or an illuminating thought may act as a stimulus to arouse the dormant genius; and as a result of conscious concentration on this intuition the experience takes definite shape and finally materializes in the creation of a work of art.

Thus the creation of art does not move exclusively in the opposite direction from meditation, as it might appear to a superficial observer seeing only its formal expression. It moves in the direction of meditation as well, namely in the state of conception. Art and meditation compensate, penetrate, and create each other.

The importance of art and its relationship to meditation

is not yet exhausted with the aspect of its origination. The effect of a work of art, the experience to which it leads the beholder, is equally important. The artist himself may not care about the effect of his work. For him the process of creating is the only thing that really matters. But the primary influence of art in the life of humanity and as part of human civilization is its power to inspire all those who open themselves to it. Great works of art have had a more lasting impact on humanity than have mighty empires and even ancient religions, which have been survived only by their art-creations. The language of art speaks to us across the millenniums, even after all other languages of the time have fallen into oblivion.

The enjoyment of art is an act of re-creation, or rather of creation in the reverse direction, toward the source of inspiration. It is an act of absorption, in which we liberate ourselves from our small self in the creative experience of a greater universe and the interrelationship of all life.

> Thus art means the ever renewed concentric attack and the breaking through of selfhood towards infinity, the complete extinction of limitation by endless and as such uninterrupted turns of radiations and inhalations; it means the condensation of the universe to a microcosmic focus and ever again the establishment of a magic balance between soul and universe. The object of art is the condensation of all inconceivable streams, forces, and effects of the universe upon the plane of human understanding and experience; it is the projection of psychic emotion into the infinite. The self dissolved and transformed into the whole— in which case emptiness signifies the complete nonresistance—means the dissolution of the one into the other, the passionless acceptance of the world into the liberated, i.e., unlimited soul.[1]

Here art and religious life meet in a sphere of consciousness where no such distinction exists. Therefore, wherever religion is a living force, there it finds its natural expression in art; in fact, it becomes art itself, just as art in its highest attainments becomes religion. Art is the measure for the living quality of a religion.

The most perfect combination of art and religious life has been realized in past millenniums when Buddhist monks and mystics materialized their visions in sculptures and paintings, hymns and architecture, philosophy and poetry, and carried the message of a new civilization all over Asia.

The contemplation of the beautiful, according to the Buddha's own teaching, makes us free from all selfish concerns; it lifts us to a plane of perfect harmony and happiness; it creates a foretaste of ultimate liberation, thus encouraging us to strive on toward Realization. Realization, however, means the discovery of reality within ourselves and thus the reality of ourselves as a focal point of universal forces which stream through us like the light of the sun through a focalizing lens. The rays of light are not arrested there or in the focus; they do not become the property of the lens. The lens only serves to focalize them, to reunite them in the point-like image of the sun, and thus to integrate their power, even to incandescence. In the same way the human individual serves to focalize the qualities and forces of the universe, until they become conscious to the degree of "incandescence," in which moment the flash of inspiration or the flame of enlightenment springs up, and man becomes conscious of his universality, which is another way of saying that the universe becomes conscious of itself.

The truly beautiful is at the same time the truly meaningful, insofar as it establishes an intimate relationship of man, not only with his surroundings or the world in which he lives, but also with something that goes beyond his momentary existence as a particular or "separate" being. It is this which enables the contemplative as well as the artist to enter into spiritual relation with the hills and rivers, trees and rocks, human beings and animals, gods and demons. The beautiful does not even exclude the terrible, as we may see from the powerful representations of terrifying forces in Tibetan thangkas.

The contemplative artists of the East "became absorbed in themselves, or in a waterfall, or a landscape, a human face, according to what they wanted to represent, until they had become one with their object, and then they created it from within, unconcerned by all outer forms. Inner collectedness seemed to these artists to be more important than external training. And, surely, the completely 'inward' individual stands above reason, for its laws live within his mind... The rhythm of Far Eastern drawing it not of rational origin: it is an inner rhythm, like that of music."[2] (Keyserling)

Art as the manifestation of the truly beautiful (i.e. of inner truth) and the purity of inner vision is, therefore, the greatest creative power. Even the imperfection of this our world can be a stimulus for this creativeness, because "true beauty can be discovered only by one who mentally completes the incomplete." Buddhists value art as a meditative practice, as Yoga, because the dynamic nature of their philosophy lays more stress upon the process through which perfection is sought than upon perfection itself. "The virility of life and art lay in its possibilities of growth."[3]

Thus, Buddhist meditation inspired the art of Central Asia and the Far East with new ideals, as it had previously done in the country of its origin. The execution of a work of art was regarded in itself as an act of creative meditation, and the enjoyment of art, the contemplation of the artist's creation, became part of the spiritual training, without which nobody could claim to be really cultured. "The followers of Zen aimed at direct communion with the inner nature of things, regarding their outward accessories only as impediments to a clear perception of Truth. It was this love of the Abstract that led the Zen to prefer black and white sketches to the elaborately coloured paintings of the classic Buddhist school."[4]

It is not the subject of a work of art that decides its value; rather, it is the inspirational impetus, the spontaneity of inner experience, with which it has been created and which it arouses and reproduces in the beholder. But the faculty of responding to the inner meaning of such works of art has to be cultivated in the same measure as the faculty of creating them. Just as the artist has to master the material and the tools with which he creates, so the one who wants to enjoy art has to prepare and to tune the instrument of spiritual receptivity in order to achieve that profound resonance which is possible only if the mind has been emptied of all distracting thoughts and petty cares (in this sense *śūnyatā* may be called a perfect state of resonance).

Tibetan religious art goes even one step further. The beholder is not only expected to reexperience the vision of the artist by absorbing it in every detail, but to re-create it in his own mind and fill it with life until it takes on a reality of its own and stands before his inner vision as if it were projected into space. But unlike the artist's work that has become and remains an independently existing material object, separated from the artist, the meditator has to reabsorb his vision by reversing the creative process and integrating it into the essence of his own mind. This frees him from the attachment to his own creations and from the illusion of a separate reality of subject and object.

References and Notes

[1] Karl With: *Bali.*
[2] Count Herman Keyserling: *Travel Diary of a Philosopher.*
[3] Okakura Kakuzo: *The Book of Tea.*
[4] *Ibid.*

3

THE PROBLEM OF SUBJECT AND OBJECT

OUR HANDS CAN ONLY TOUCH or grasp things in our closest surroundings. Likewise, words can only grasp or convey truths of a very limited value, namely those "which are of the nature of information, that can be added to our stock of knowledge from the outside. But there are other truths, of the nature of inspiration, which cannot be used to swell the number of our accomplishments. These latter are not like food, but are rather the appetite itself, that can only be strengthened by inducing harmony in our bodily functions." Tagore, in this connection, says that religion is such a truth, and we can add that art in the highest sense represents truth in the same measure. "It establishes the right centre for life's activities, giving them an eternal meaning; maintaining the true standard of value for the objects of our striving; inspires in us the spirit of renunciation which is the spirit of humanity. It cannot be doled out in regular measure, nor administered through the academic machinery of education. It must come immediate from the burning flame of spiritual life."[1]

To keep this flame burning we have to keep alive the spirit of inquiry, which means that we ought not to look upon as final any solution presented to our mind. We ought to use thinking in order to become conscious of the unthinkable, to keep our mind open to ever new experiences and to be aware of the enigmatic character of the world and of our own existence. Then everything will become significant, because we shall look upon everything as if we had never seen it before, under complete omission of all former mental associations which we generally term knowledge.

The longer we can abstain from seeing things habitually, the more profoundly we shall be conscious of their true nature, which goes beyond concepts and definitions. Habit kills intuition, because it prevents living experience. Therefore thinking, after having grown to the point where existential or metaphysical problems appear, must not become paralyzed by intellectual solutions, abstract concepts, and generalizations. It should be transformed into a dynamic mental attitude which pursues problems to the very limit of logical thought and human reason, where words turn into paradoxes and a new language of symbols is born. Those who try to solve those paradoxes logically or to explain symbols on the intellectual level, lose themselves in an inextricable labyrinth. But those who open themselves to the new language of signs and symbols and baffling paradoxes will find that even the most significant thing can become a revelation, and that in truth "the external world is nothing but the inner world in a state of mystery." (Novalis) To penetrate this mystery, man must give up his egohood, because only by this complete spiritual renunciation of all concepts of "I" and "mine" is he able to overcome all his artificial limitations and inner hindrances.

In order to produce such a state of mind the Buddhists of the Far East invented special exercises of meditation, in which the methodical concentration on so-called "koans" played an important role. The koan is a problem in the form of a short—mostly paradoxical—question or statement, which cannot be answered or explained in words, but stirs up the mind and baffles the intellect in such a way that the insufficiency of reasoning becomes obvious and another way out has to be found. The pressure increases until by a sudden "explosion" thinker and thought are fused in a flash of profound insight into the nature of reality. This is called Satori.

To illustrate the difference between this state of mind and the ordinary consciousness, a Zen Master says: "When you have Satori you are able to reveal a palatial mansion made of precious stones on a single blade of grass; but when you have no Satori a palatial mansion itself is concealed behind a simple blade of grass."

In daily life our habitual concepts take the place of a blade of grass; they are hiding the living world from our mind. They are one-sided and partial though they may be true to the ordinary intellect. A poet may give us an apparently exaggerated account of an event and may yet be nearer to truth than someone who accurately describes facts. Why is that so? Because he does not pretend to be objective but takes the liberty of being entirely subjective in expressing truthfully how he has experienced the event. This unbiased subjectivity is the privilege of the genius and the child. Therefore we say that the child's tongue reveals the truth. But truth is generally suppressed in the later stages of life by the judging, measuring, dissecting, self-motivated intellect which divides the world into what it regards as good or bad, favorable or unfavorable, according to preconceived aims and objects. An unbiased and therefore true subjectivity can be regained and appreciated only by the attainment of a higher level of consciousness, in which the relationship between subject and object is no longer seen as that between two separate entities or mutually exclusive opposites, but as two sides of the same process of conscious awareness and actuality.

Therefore Goethe could say: "The highest works of art are those which possess the highest truth, but no trace of reality." Here we have a perfect koan in the form of an apparently paradoxical statement. The paradox consists in putting truth and reality in opposition to each other, in contrast to the common belief that truth and reality are synonymous. This forces us to think anew and to reconsider our position in order to understand the meaning of Goethe's words. What he means by "truth" is obviously more than the ordinary concept of reality. Truth in this context is that which expresses the highest validity for human existence, a value that can be experienced and verified only in the human individual, in contrast to the world of material facts, whose apparent substantiality misleads people to regard it as an independently existing objective reality.

Ouspensky deals with the same problem when he says: "Objective knowledge does not study facts but *only the perception of facts*. Subjective knowledge studies the *facts*—the facts of consciousness—the only real facts. Thus objective knowledge has to do with the unreal, with the reflected, the imaginary world: subjective knowledge has to do with the real world."[2]

Here arises the question of what we call real. The original meaning of this word is "thingish," because it is derived from the Latis *res*, which simply means *thing*. It is thus derived from an ancient static world-conception, which agrees neither with our present scientific understanding of the world nor with the dynamic world view of Buddhism nor the attitude of modern psychology or art. Reality is no more identified with substance but with action and interaction, dynamic relationship, actuality. Therefore reality cannot be anything in itself but only in relationship to something or to everything else. This makes the concept of anything absolute, or the abstract term "the Absolute," not only superfluous but meaningless, because bereft of any experience content.

The further philosophy moves away from human experience, the more it is estranged from life and moves in a sterile world of abstract concepts. It is this tendency of progressing intellectualization and conceptualization which has smothered the interest in philosophy in our time, while psychology with its emphasis on human experience has taken the place of philosophy and partly even of religion. Unless art becomes again the expression of genuinely individual experience— irrespective of whether it is abstract or concrete, realistic or surrealistic in form—it will become more and more dehumanized and estranged from life and in merely accidental patterns or arbitrary constructions without inspiration.

References and Notes

[1] Rabindranath Tagore: *Sādhanā*.
[2] Ouspensky: *Tertium Organum*.

4

ABSTRACT ART

IN ORDER TO ESCAPE THE DANGER of losing the essential value of art by submitting it to the external forms of nature, the artist again and again has to break these forms and to extract their intrinsic value. He has to abstract, literally: to pull off the cloak of concrete phenomena and habitual associations which divert the attention and mislead the mind toward the surface, until they have become pure manifestations of his experience. This does not mean that the artist violates the forms of things and nature by treating them arbitrarily. On the contrary, those forms cease to be merely exponents of static things deriving their meaning from realities outside of themselves (and of ourselves). They become the embodiment of movement which expresses their own nature as well as our corresponding feeling, because both are movement: in its least perceptible state, as on the physical plane, we call this extension; on the psychic plane feeling, or, if more intensified, emotion. The emotional quality is connected with the active, more aggressive nature of color (radiation) and sound (vibration). The perceptual side of feeling is more connected with two- and three-dimensional forms. They are nearer to the intellect because their perception demands clear spatial definition. Painting which contains form and color in equal value combines both sides of human experience—the mental as well as the emotional—and is therefore specially suited to the development of abstract art.

It is important to be quite clear about the meaning of this term, because there are people who think that abstract art is allegorical representation of abstract concepts. Even in cases where such concepts endeavor to find a formulation of something that lies in the direction of what art tries to express, there is a fundamental difference of procedure and emphasis. Abstract concepts are attained by logical operations, following analytical and deductive methods by which they lose life and reality in the same measure in which the operation proceeds. Abstract art, on the other hand, proceeds in the inductive and constructive way, by emphasizing and developing essential features; all secondary factors are suppressed if not entirely eliminated, so that the life hidden beneath the surface becomes intensified and more real to our consciousness.

Thus the term "abstract" is more related to the effect than to the process of artistic creation. It is not so much concerned with the attitude of the artist as with that of the beholder; what he will notice first is the absence of those concrete or so-called natural forms to which he is accustomed. The more he tries to find parallels for them the less he will be able to grasp the spirit of abstract art, because it does not take the roundabout way through the objects of the external, optical world, but creates compositions of form and color which in their totality reproduce a certain state of mind and experience.

The closest example, I imagine, is music, because it is the least imitative or descriptive of all forms of art. Nobody would ever ask what a single tone means. Not even a melody could be explained or described in words. We can say only that such and such feelings are aroused by it.

The same is the case with abstract painting. We cannot ask what a single color or a single shape means. One could ask this only if color and form were something different from what they are. It would, however, be wrong to conclude that they have no meaning. On the contrary, it is because of the profundity of their nature, the many-sidedness of their character, that we cannot define them in any exclusive way. It is only the composition as a whole that gives a particular, though not explainable, significance to them. Thus abstract paintings are just as real as a landscape or the shape of a human being. They imitate nothing, they do not depend on any superimposed idea; they speak for themselves, like a song which, even without words, carries its meaning within its own melody and rhythm. If words are added, they may emphasize its mood or its feeling content.

Just as a human face is the expression of a certain stage in the development of an individual, an abstract picture represents a certain mental or emotional stage in the development of an artist. After some time, when he looks back on his work, he may be able to understand its meaning and the state of mind from which it arose, but during the time of its creation his work is too much part of himself to see it objectively. And even if he could, he would not be able to explain it any more than one can explain one's own face, though one may see it in the mirror.

If a painting could be explained or described adequately by any other medium, it would not be necessary to express it through color and form. Words can only hint in the direction of a certain experience or idea which served as a starting point for the creation of the work, and thus help the beholder to find an adequate approach.

"Words are only like the pointing finger, showing one where to locate the moon," a Buddhist Patriarch once said. But we must not look at the finger if we want to see the moon.

5

SYMBOLISM OF ELEMENTARY FORMS AND COLORS

EVEN THE SIMPLEST FORM OR COLOR is a symbol revealing the nature of the primordial reality of the universe and the structure of the human psyche in which this universal reality is mirrored. In fact, if the structure of our consciousness did not correspond to that of the universe and its laws, we should not be aware of either the universe or the laws that govern it. "The same organizing forces that have created nature in all its forms, are responsible for the structure of our soul, and likewise for our capacity to think."[1] The forms in which nature reveals itself are symbols insofar as they express aspects of reality which cannot be limited by definitions and fixed concepts but which transmit a direct, flashlike experience disclosing a new meaning on each level of consciousness.

The visible world appears to us in an inexhaustible variety and multitude of forms and colors. And yet, this our world is confined to three essential forms and three essential colors. Even with the greatest imagination we cannot conceive of more than these six elements of formal representation. This fact is an important indication of an inner order pervading the multiplicity of outer phenomena. Once we are conscious of it, we begin to feel that these fundamental forms are the key to the understanding of our three-dimensional world and the nature of our own mind.

The fact that these forms express only a certain aspect of reality, namely that which corresponds to our state of existence (i.e. to our plane of consciousness), does not make them less significant, since our consciousness itself is a product of the totality of universal forces. The possibility or capacity to experience higher dimensions does not make the lower ones less real or less important. A consciousness bound to the third dimension may not be able to experience the next higher one, but it doubtless has the faculty to be aware of the first and second dimension.

The three essential forms are: the cube, the cylinder, and the sphere.

The cube and the sphere represent the two extremes: the former is composed of plane surfaces, the latter of a surface that is curved equally in all directions.

The cylinder takes the middle place as the mediator between the completely plane and the completely curved surface, being neither the one nor the other, but possessing properties of both: it is curved in one direction and straight in another direction (namely parallel to its axis).

If we imagine these three stereometrical bodies in relationship to a supporting plane, we find the following facts: the sphere touches a plane in a point, the cylinder in a straight line, the cube in a surface. From the standpoint of movability this means that the sphere can move (roll) in all directions, the cylinder in one direction, the cube in no direction. The cube, therefore, represents immovability.

However, this purely superficial observation is far from exhausting the nature of these forms, though it shows that even the surface of a body cannot be called a secondary property, because without it we could not speak of a form or a body (even in the abstract sense): it is the very limitation that makes the form possible. An intellectual definition, however, for an entirely different reason, is not able to exhaust the meaning of these forms.

It is not the external mobility of the bodies in their materialized forms, but the process of their origination from an inner center or form-principle, which implies an inner law of directedness and self-limitation. Here we touch upon the most profound principle of all form, where form and no-form, form and "emptiness," potentiality and actuality, are involved simultaneously in the process of an incommensurable and mysterious act of becoming, which we call "life."

This, however, can never be observed from the outside but only experienced within ourselves as dimensions or possibilities of movement, as expansion or growth of our own "consciousness-body." And in this experience, in which we no longer identify forms with objects of the external world, but rather identify ourselves with the forms, the seer becomes one with his vision, as often described in mystic scriptures.

In such a case the spheric form is no more the imitation of a seen object, or the orb of a heavenly body, or the imaginary form of an atom, but the essence of all that is alive, organic, moving and, at the same time, resting in itself, perfect and germ-like potential. The cubic forms are not reminiscences of architectural structures, but represent the power of resistance, of immobility, the rigidity of all inorganic forms, 'the inertia of matter, and also the principles of stability, solidity, of steadfastness and, last but not least, the principle of materialization.

Each of the three fundamental forms can be projected to a point. In this way we derive from the cube the pyramid; from the cylinder the cone; and from the sphere the spheric cone. Each of these secondary forms expresses the qualities of the form from which it originated, plus the active qualities of directedness and one-pointedness. There is something more definite, more aggressive (direction), more positive in these pointed forms. The relationship between cube and pyramid, cylinder and cone, sphere and spheric cone, is like that between female and male respectively.

In this sense we may call pyramid, cone, and spheric cone active forms in contradistinction to their "female," passive counterparts (from which they were born). But we have to bear in mind that the terms "active" and "passive" in relationship to male and female qualities can be used only in a very relative sense. Passivity as a characteristic of the female attitude, for instance, does not exclude activity within the particular realm of female properties.

Female activity is activity by way of reproduction and transformation, while male activity is activity by way of intensification or direction. Female activity is inwardly centered, male activity is outward-directed. While female passivity is a positive attitude, namely that of receptivity, latent creativeness or potentiality, male passivity is merely an absence or a lesser degree of action, and therefore negative.

Though the preponderance of male or female properties determines the sex in the higher forms of organic life, each individual possesses simultaneously male and female qualities. The higher the state of spiritual development, the greater is the conscious interpenetration of male and female properties. The greatest artists, poets, and thinkers are able to express with equal perfection the psyche of man and woman, which means that they are able to experience the male and the female within themselves. The saint, the holy one, i.e. the one who has become whole or complete, has polarized the male and the female within himself and attained a state of perfect harmony.

A fundamental modification in meaning and value of pure form-elements arises with the addition of colors, which not only determine the emotional atmosphere of a pictorial representation or its inner vision, but open a new dimension. While the three Euclidian dimensions of space with which we are familiar represent three outwardly directed movements, colors and tonal values (attention may be drawn to the double meaning of "tonal," which can be related to colors as well as to music) are inwardly directed and thus create a space in which things exist not only side by side but also within each other, penetrating each other, and yet not dissolving or annihilating each other.

Color and sound (music) are direct expressions of psychic experiences which cannot be grasped, defined, or expressed by the intellect. While pure abstract forms initially appeal to the intellect, colors appeal first and foremost to feeling. The intellect defines and limits; the same is done by form. Color, however, gives us the warmth of life, of feeling, of emotion and all the indescribable nuances of experience, which the intellect is not able to express or to define. Therefore, the virtue of form is clarity; the virtue of color is depth. From the intellect we demand clarity, consistency, logic, distinction; we demand the same of form. From feeling we demand depth; the same applies to color.[2]

Thus, color reveals something that has to do with the inner nature or emotional value of form, and this is all the more so to the extent that we keep away from a mere imitation of externally visible objects and create exclusively from our inner vision or our meditative experience.

Here the question arises whether any definite relation exists between fundamental forms and colors beyond our subjective attitude or experience.

If we consider that the universe—as it is reflected in our human consciousness—is composed of three fundamental forms and three fundamental colors, and that the forms as well as the colors develop into pairs of opposites which condition and compensate each other like the positive and the negative poles of a magnet, or like the active and passive properties of the male and the female, then it is hard to believe that this parallelism is a mere accident. For my part I am convinced that both express the structure of our three-dimensional world by which they are conditioned, that they represent the same harmony in different dimensions, and the hence there *is* a definite relationship between colors and forms. This relationship may be expressed in different ways, according to the standpoint of the individual, but this changes only the key-note, not the melody. Even a different rhythm, according to the individual temperament and experience, would not destroy that melody.

Let us reiterate some simple facts.

The three fundamental or primary colors, from which all other colors can be developed (but which themselves cannot be further reduced) are blue, red, and yellow.

For each of these colors a complementary color can be found, being the product of a combination of the remaining two primary colors. Thus, the combination of blue and red produces the complementary color of yellow, namely violet. The combination of red and yellow produces the complementary color of blue, namely orange. The combination of yellow and blue produces the complementary color of red, namely green.

If the primary color is active, then the secondary, complementary, color is passive. Active colors are red, yellow, and orange; green, violet, and blue are passive colors. There are sufficient physiological and psychological reasons for this division which we need not repeat here. But in addition to these there are many different kinds and degrees of activity and passivity which can be experienced by those who are sensitive to colors, though one may also find an intellectual approach by means of comparisons and associations quite apart from scientific methods of investigation.

If we compare the activity of the two primary, active colors, red and yellow, we find the same difference as between fire and light, between material and immaterial, or between emotional and intellectual activity. The activity of fire is felt more intensely and even bodily;[3] the activity of light is radiation comparable to the activity of consciousness.

Orange, which unites red and yellow, combines both these qualities: warmth and light; in the human sphere: feeling and knowledge, the highest form of spiritual activity which we associate with the saint or an Enlightened One. This color, therefore, is used all over the world to characterize the aura of a saint. It is likewise the color of the sun and of gold, both symbols of divine qualities, of highest value, spiritual power and incorruptibility.

The complementary color of orange is blue, the only passive primary color. The passivity of blue, however, is of a very positive nature, a quality of cosmic potentiality, not to be confounded with the vegetative passivity of green. Blue, especially deep blue, is associated with the depth and purity of space, the unity and infinity of the universe, the potential, primordial ground of all that exists. Therefore, it is the symbol of the metaphysical emptiness or plenum-void (*śūnyatā*) in Buddhism and of Vishnu and Krishna, the divine embodiments of universal reality, in Hinduism. The significance of blue in Christian symbology is shown in its association with the Madonna, the Universal Mother, whose all-embracing universality is symbolized by the deep blue color of her mantle, in contrast to her inner garment, which reveals a deep red, expressing the warmth of motherly love.

Red and green are primarily colors of bodily nearness, of life in its warm-blooded as well as in its vegetative aspects. They represent creative forces, both in the inorganic as well as in the organic physical world. On the psychic level they represent feeling (emotion, passionate desire or aspiration, ecstasy) and vital harmony (peacefulness, non-violence, adaptability). According to the preponderance of the one or the other of its components (yellow and blue) green can approach a highly spiritualized or profoundly mystic expression. However, in the present context we want to confine ourselves only to the fundamental principles and possible guidelines in the meaning and mutual relationship of colors and their corresponding abstract stereometic forms. We have to bear in mind that we are not dealing with purely scientifically determined relationships or interpretations, but with an approach that is equally dependent on intuitional, and therefore mainly subjective, evaluations.

The third passive color, violet, is perhaps the most difficult, because the most complicated and protean color (it shares this protean character with the sphere). It combines the most intensely active color (red) with the most passive (blue). It contains an enormous inner tension, a tendency of transformation (the Shiva-aspect in Hinduism), even of dissolution, of inner movement and struggle. It is significant that this color is the latest to appear in art. It was unknown to primitive man and not even used by the early Greeks. In Christian symbolism it is the color of spiritual suffering, of Passion.

The sphere, resting completely in itself (blue) and at the same time having the greatest mobility (red) is, therefore, in a position similar to violet among the colors. Consequently the spheric cone, as the active counterpart of the sphere, assumes the position of the active complementary color of violet, namely yellow.

The cylinder in its capacity of a virtually infinite axis of stability, comparable to a unifying cosmic law, corresponds to the stability and restful unity of blue. The mediating position of the cylinder between the two other form-principles emphasizes its central and unity-creating character; this takes its active shape in the cone, to which orange, the active complementary color of blue corresponds.

The physical activity of the pyramid corresponds to the physical activity of red, while the inertness and resistance of the cube, in which movement is only thinkable as extension, is related to the physical passivity of green.

It goes without saying that the parallelism between forms and colors, (which for me was the subject of a meditative experience and took shape in three abstract compositions), does not exhaust the relations between forms and colors; in fact, it is only one of the innumerable aspects of cosmic reality which has as many facets as there are conscious individuals.

The first of these "cosmic abstracts" represents the urge toward creation or material existence, the craving for form, the first stage of materialization. I have, therefore, called it "BECOMING" (the principle of Brahma, the manifestor of the universe). Cubic and pyramidal forms crystallize out of each other. In the foreground a cube is seen, containing a sphere as a germ; in the upper left corner the background opens and allows a view into the next stage of form-development, indicated by a cone. The colors of the cubic forms are different shades of green, those of the pyramids, various shades of red. The sphere is deep violet and the cone orange against light blue.

Orange and blue are the governing colors of the next picture. Only the cubic forms in the foreground, a reminiscence of the first composition, are in green and red hues. With the exception of these forms the picture is composed of bodies with curved surfaces: blue cylinders, most of them ending in orange-colored cones. Warm yellow reflections vibrate in the blue, while the orange deepens into bluish shadings. The centralizing tendency in the cones culminate in the background, in which dark blue cylindrical columns meet in a central sphere. The middle column, which is about twice as thick as the others, emphasizes the axis.

Thus the picture grows from an unrestrained form-desire into the centralization and stabilization of the law, which regulates the growth, the composition, and the relationship of forms. I, therefore, call this picture and the psychocosmic state it expresses, "BEING"—the principle of VISHNU, the embodiment of the universal LAW.

It occurred to me long after I had painted these meditation pictures, that Vishnu, according to Hindu tradition, is represented in blue color (as also Krishna and Rama, his most prominent incarnations or Avatars) and that the conical Shikara-towers are mainly associated with Vishnu-temples (which originated in the north of India), while the hemispheric cupola is mainly associated with the Shiva-temples (prevailing in the south). In the case of Brahma, the square shape is emphasized by the four entrances to his temple, his four heads, and his four-sided pillar. His color is red, because he is originally the fire-god. "From the flaming Tapas (the cosmic heat, which manifests itself in man as the psychic heat (Tibetan: Tummo), the flame of inspiration) order and truth were born," according to the Rigveda.

Vishnu is the preserver of the world, the world-preserving Law, the cosmic order, the unifying and directing principle in a world of diversity, the center of life, the illuminator, the sun-god. In his last-mentioned capacity, orange, as the color of the sun, and gold, the sun-metal, belongs to his symbols. The Law is the resting axis around which the world revolves. The cylindrical form represents the ideal axis, in fact, an infinite axis (since the cylinder by its own nature has no beginning and no end) and, as such, stability. Also, as we have seen, it takes the central and mediating place between the bodies with completely planed surfaces and those with completely curved surfaces (i.e., curved toward all sides). In this connection we may also point out the tremendous importance of the column in Egyptian and Greek temples, as well as in many other related civilizations. The column was not merely a functional part of the architecture, like a mere prop or support for the roof, but had a divine dignity in itself, independent of functional or space-creating properties. The column was more an expression of the plastic arts, like sculpture, in which mass and form, rather than the surrounding space, are the primary elements. This is particularly evident in ancient Egyptian temples, where each column is a monumental sculpture in itself, dwarfing and almost negating the space around it as a negligible or secondary byproduct. Each column is a divine symbol of power and directedness, of law and harmony, measure and stability, embodying the principles of creative life and growth beyond human conception, awe-inspiring and uplifting. Even single columns, left standing after the destruction of those ancient temples (not only in Egypt, but also in Greece, Rome, and similar places of antiquity) effect us as awe-inspiring monuments, whose inexplicable fascination is felt even by those who are unaware or unmindful of their original meaning and their sacred origin.

To return to our picture: the dark violet sphere in the upper center of the composition points toward the third stage in the development of forms, which is the subject of the third picture.

In the foreground we find again the suggestion of the previous stages in their characteristic colors. But predominant are the spheric forms which finally swing out into a rhythmic movement in which form and space interpenetrate and create each other. It is the transformation of form into rhythm, and of movement into space. It represents the disintegration and liberation of matter into energy, the liberation of form into the unformed, the overcoming of stagnation by breaking down the limitations, the victory of life through—or over—death. I, therefore, call this picture "DISSOLUTION AND INTEGRATION" or the principle of Shiva, the Transformer.

He is the Lord of Dance, who destroys the world in his ecstatic dance—a destruction which is not negative, but which removes the hindrances of accumulated form and matter, of stagnating karma, of frozen law, of principles that have overgrown life and try to suffocate it (so to say "principles for their own sake"), of coagulation, of torpor. He is the destroyer of the world of illusion, uniting in himself asceticism and ecstasy, concentration and activity, integration and dynamic intensity.

The profound connection between the idea of transformation and the sphere becomes apparent also in the symbolism of the Buddhist Stupa (which later on developed into the forms of the Dagoba, the Pagoda, and the Chorten) in which the hemisphere represented the elements of spiritual transformation and the complete removal of the above-mentioned hindrances on the way toward enlightenment. The origins of the Stupa, which originally symbolized the Buddha's Parinirvāna, can be traced back to the prehistoric tumuli and the cult of the dead, based on the faith in immortality. The hemispheric shape of the tumulus survives in the domes of Shiva temples.

The color of the spheres in our last picture is a dark red-violet, while the spheric cones emanating from them appear in an oscillating greenish yellow against a deep purple background.

The experience of this threefold Cosmic Meditation resulted in three poems which reflect the stages of Manifestation, Universal Law, and Liberation, corresponding to the principles of Brahma, Vishnu, and Shiva, or to the states of Becoming, Being, and Dissolving. These states are reenacted in every Tantric Buddhist meditation, which begins with the productive state (Sanskrit: *sriṣṭi-krama*; Tibetan: *skyed-rim*), in which certain aspects of the inner world, in form of archetypal symbols, are manifested and visualized, and finally—after having realized the universal law inherent in them—dissolved and reintegrated into the plenum-Void from which they sprang. This process of reintegration is known as *laya-krama* in Sanskrit and as *rdzogs-rim* in Tibetan. Without this liberating process the crystallized and solidified forms of our objectified imagination and world-conception would finally imprison us in a deadly jungle of frozen phantoms, a *samsāric* world of delusion, in which the waters of life had ceased to flow and had turned into a stagnant pool.

References and Notes

[1] Werner Heisenberg: *Der Teil und das Ganze.*

[2] These distinct qualities of form and color are made use of and are the basic means of realization in Tibetan Tantric systems of meditation, in which guided imagination in the form of visualization of archetypal symbols combines the clarity of form with the depth of metaphysical and emotional color-experience.

[3] It is interesting to note that red is the first color to be observed or to act upon awakening color-sense of children and primitive man.

6

COSMIC MEDITATION

I

BECOMING
(BRAHMA: THE POWER OF MANIFESTATION)

Breakers roar in rocky clefts,
Mountains of water roll against the cliffs,
Form follows form, craving to be,
Yet swallowing each other, merciless.

Will towards form, urging into existence,
Vibrates in crystals and piles rock on rock.
It makes the mountains grow into the sky,
And on their crumbling dust the jungles rise.

Life's thirst creates the beings' form
Ceaselessly longing, growing, pressing on:
An ecstasy of joy and pain, bursting into existence
And thundering in vain against the adamantine
    mountains of eternity.

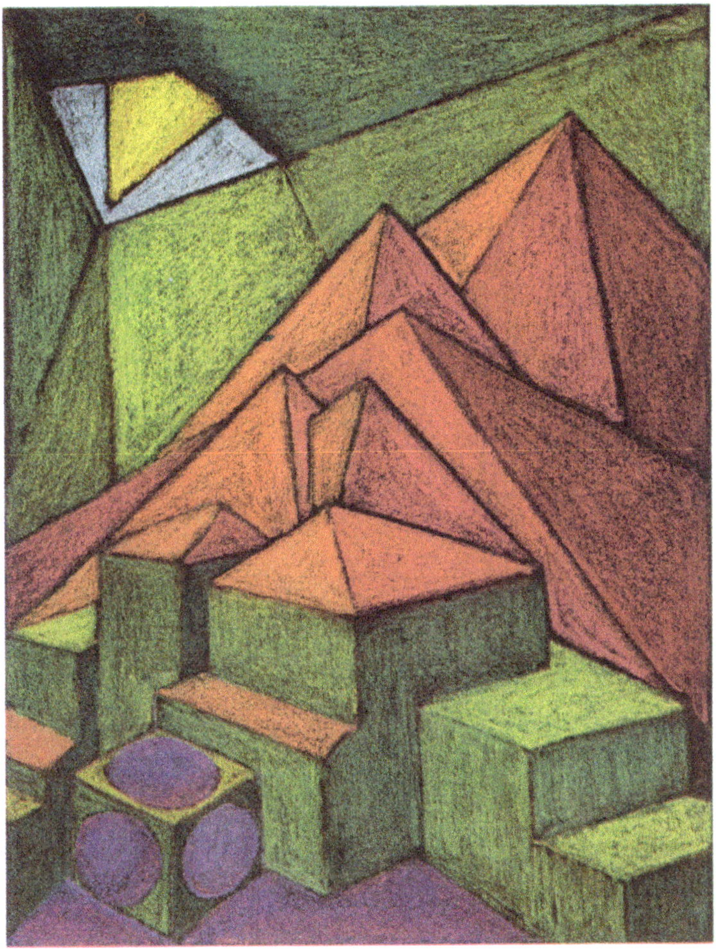

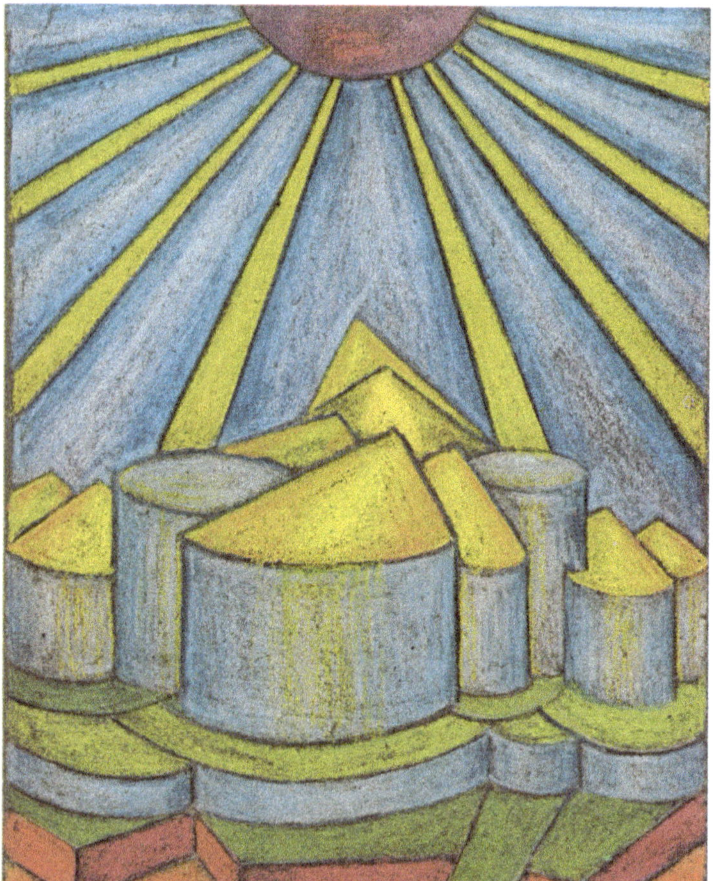

II
BEING
(VISHNU: THE POWER OF STABILIZATION)

As twin suns swing around
    an invisible point in space,
And as the orbit of their course
    creates their center ever new,
So cosmic law is formed
    by the pendular swinging
Between becoming and dissolving.

Imperceptible,
    because omnipresent;
Inconceivable,
    because all-embracing.
Omnipresent embracing creation:
Ever uniting—
    but never completing the world.

III

DISSOLVING

(SHIVA: THE POWER OF TRANSFORMATION)

SHIVA!
 Thou storming destroyer of the world!
 Thou transforming transformer!

Thou, who giveth and taketh within one breath:
 Release me from myself!
 Dissolve the form into freedom:
 Undo this life earth-rooted,
 Undo this life of craving,
 Undo this life of clinging!

Deliver me from the death of stagnation
  to the storm of life:
 The storm that uproots all craving,
 The storm that defies all clinging.
 The storm that breaks down what resists!

Deliver me from a life that negates death,
 O thou eternal transformer
 Thou dancing liberator of the Universe!

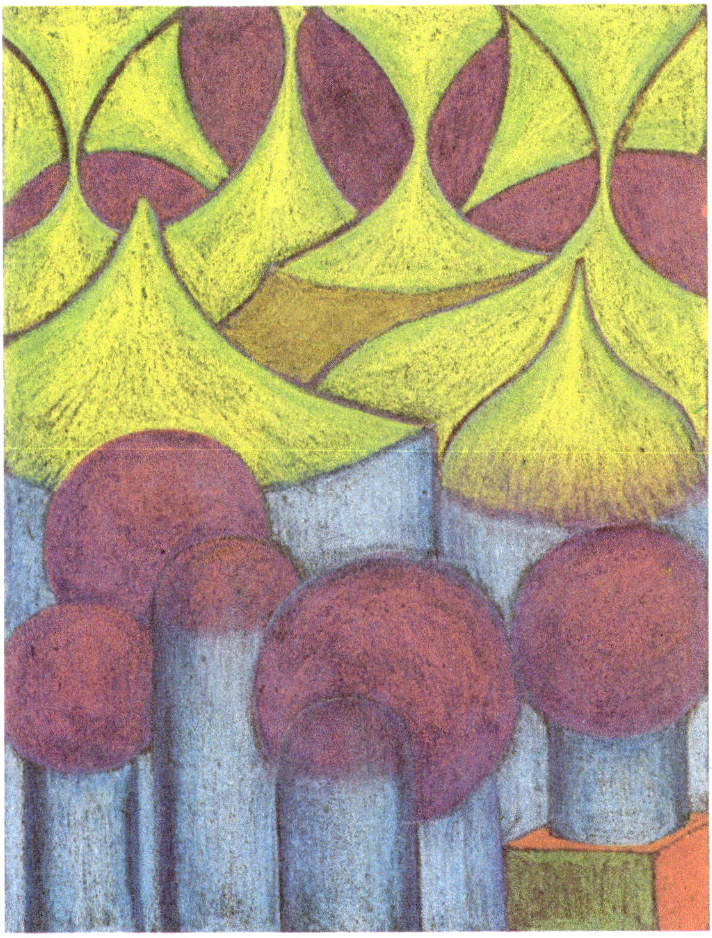

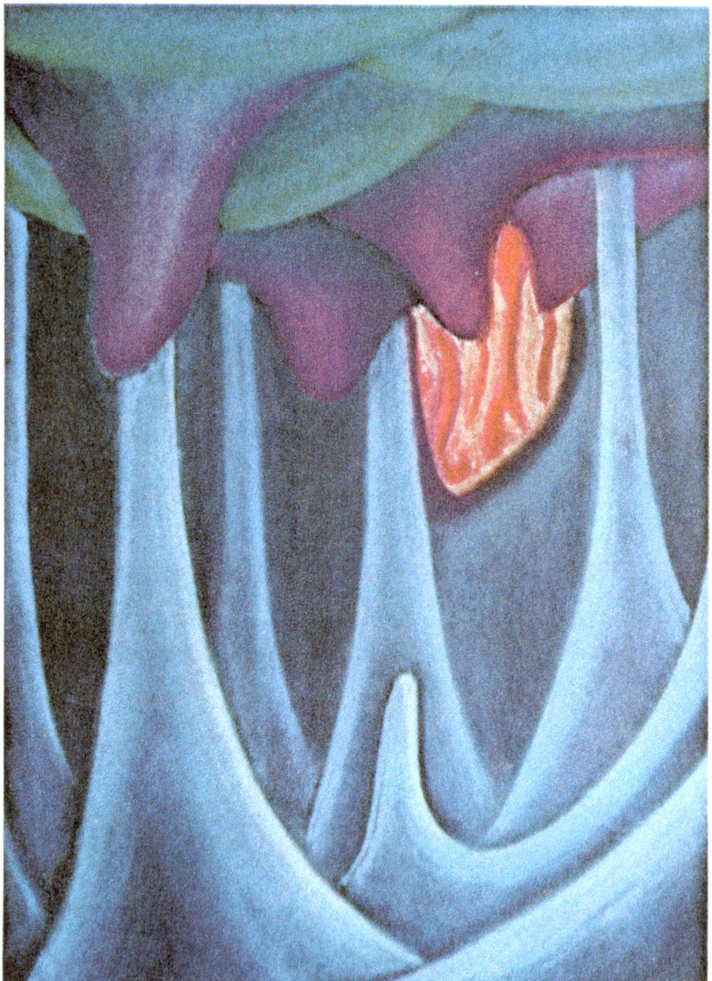

I

TURNING INWARDS

(The first Stage of Absorption)

The last reflections
    of a burning world
Pierce through
    the narrow gate of senses.
Within, however,
    grows an invisible space,
Expanding steadily
    the more the flames recede.

And from the ground
    that trembles still and heaves,
Responding to the
    outer world's commotion,
Columns are shooting up
    with shining crystal stems,
Their heads unfolding chalice-like
    into a vaulted ceiling.

II

UNIFICATION

(The Second Stage of Absorption)

The senses' gates are closed,
 the flames have disappeared,

And yet a wondrous radiance
 fills the inner space,

Reflected from
 the ever-changing walls,

Which seem to widen
 and to swing apart,

Uniting in their forceful
 all-embracing sweep

The hidden depths,
 the arches high above.

The depth, however,
 like a tranquil sea

Is filled with liquid light,
 vibrating and serene.

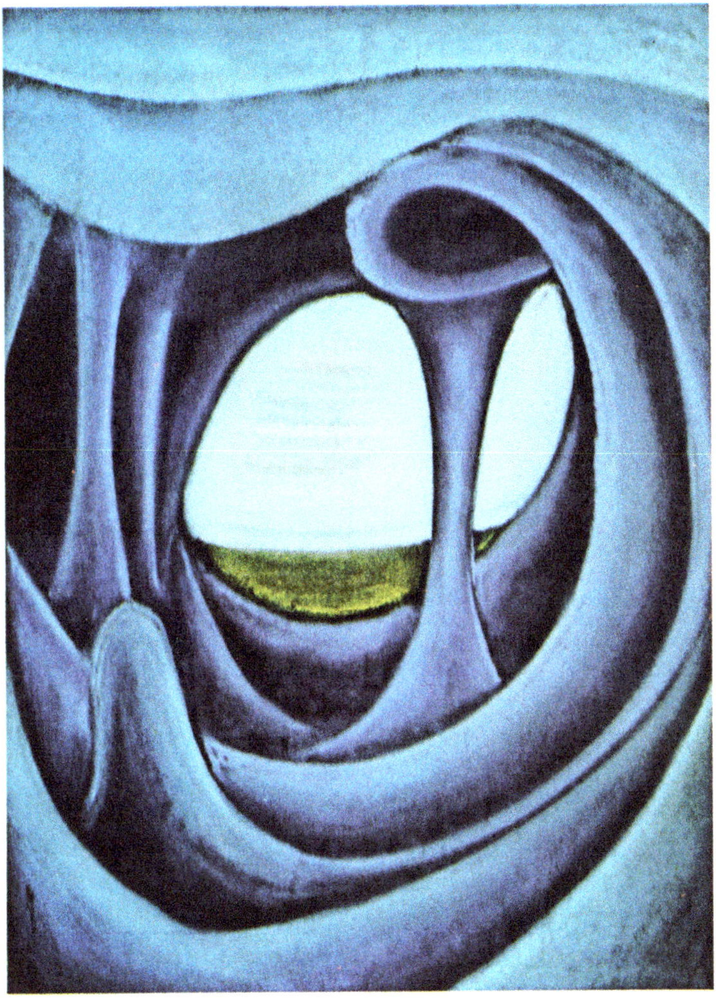

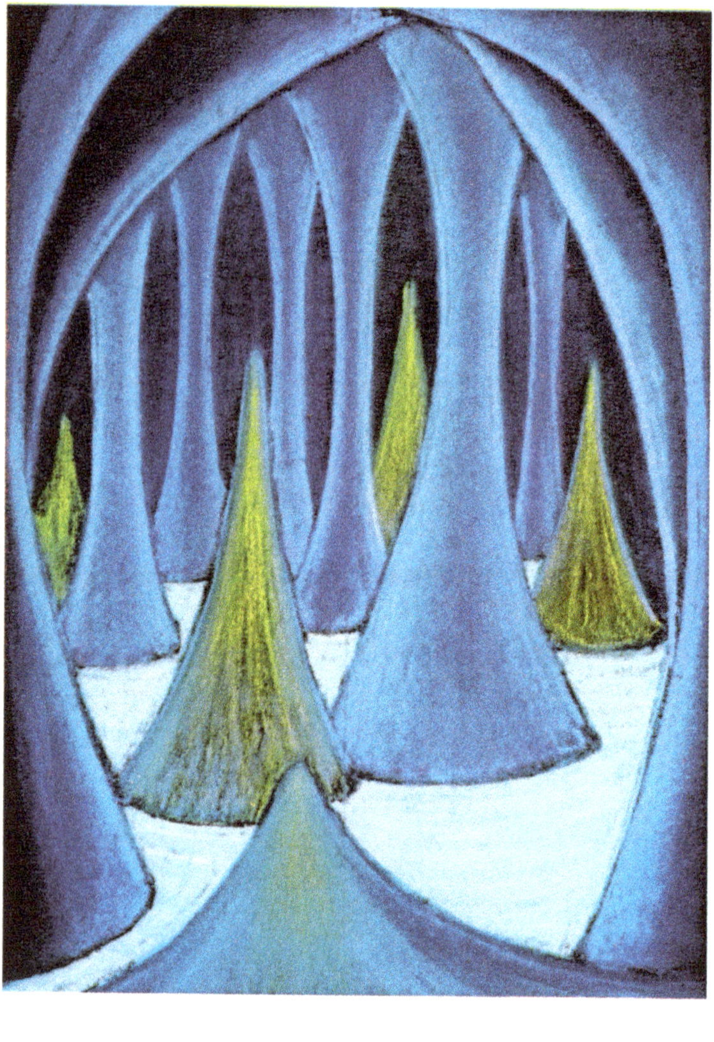

III

BIRTH OF HAPPINESS

(The Third Stage of Absorption)

From the tranquillity
    of this deep inner sea

The golden sprouts
    of happiness arise,

They grow and swell,
    burst forth in boundless joy,

Filling and penetrating
    space and living form,

Until they merge
    in highest ecstasy

Into an all-consuming
    wave of bliss,

That carries us
    beyond all earthly stress,

And leaves no room
    for feelings, words or thoughts.

IV

SAMADHI

(The Fourth Stage of Absorption)

The flood subsides;
> the ecstasy of joy
Ebbs off into a clear
> transparent pool
Of deep serenity
> that holds the central realm
Of our inmost being
> like a magic spell.

The waves die down,
> their circles come to rest
Like final chords
> of a symphonic score.
Sound dies away—
> and silence becomes sound;
Light radiates
> from the transparent gound.

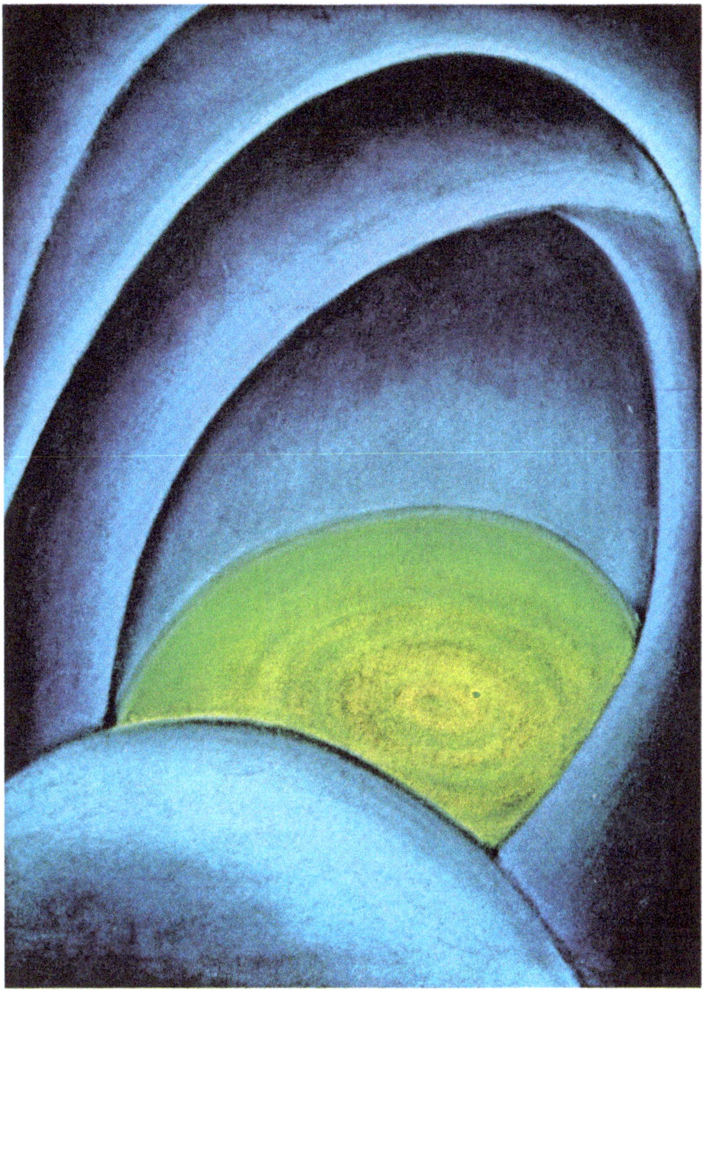

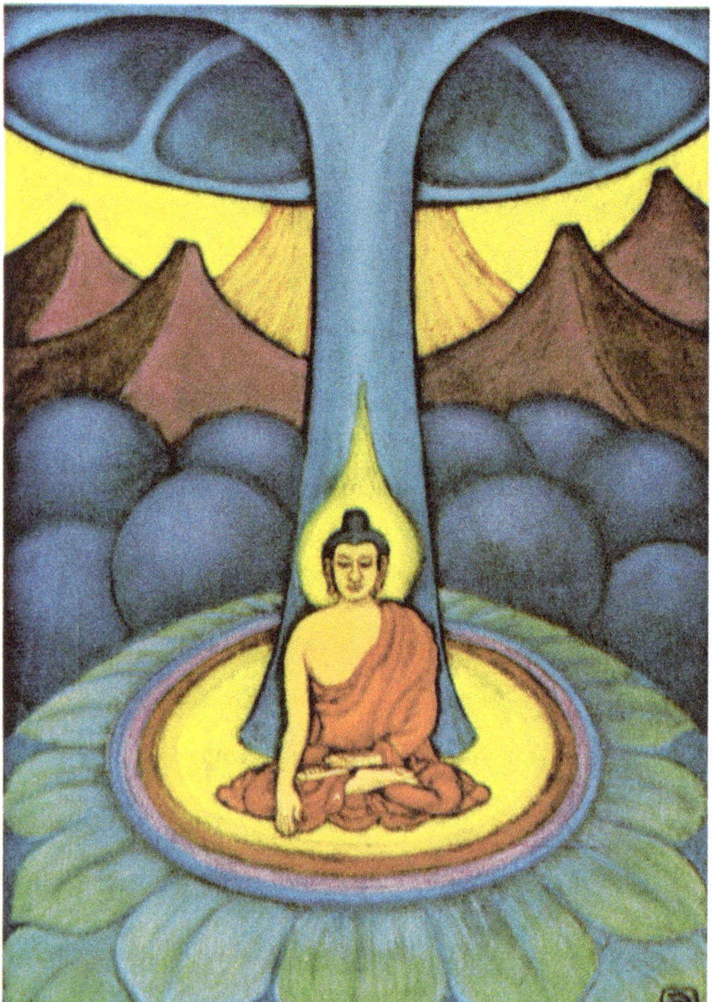

MAṆḌALA
The Sacred Circle

When entering the realm of inner vision,
We must create a threefold sacred circle,
Composed of purity, of strength and knowledge
Surrounding us like a protective wall.

The purity of heart creates the lotus-circle;
The adamantine scepters form the second ring:
The power-circle of determined will and higher aims;
The third one is the ring of wisdom-flames.

The threefold magic circle thus unfolded,
Grows with the depth of our heart's vibration,
Grows with the strength of inner penetration,
Grows with the wisdom that knows life and death.

But only when this world becomes a magic circle,
In which each point can be a living centre:
Then we surmount the cause of all illusion,
The riddles of rebirth, of death and dissolution.

Then nothing remains rigid, self-contained;
No point coagulates into a finite 'I',
Each being in the others is enshrined,
And in the smallest lives infinity.

Then we shall see released to higher norm
This world as essence of the highest mind,
Which, formless though, creates and moves all form,
Inspires and transmutes it, ever unconfined.

PART V

CONTEMPLATIVE THOUGHTS

1

IMPERMANENCE AND IMMORTALITY

WHY IS THERE SUCH A DIFFERENCE between the knowledge that is acquired through life and the knowledge that is transmitted to us through others? Why is it that those who have been educated in the thoughts of great thinkers are often still very far from being wise?

It is because experience means participation of our whole being, and this is more than a merely objective and unconcerned observation. The contemplation of food does not still our hunger; we must eat, digest, and assimilate. Similarly, every real experience means an incorporation and assimilation of something essential.

The indifferent, unfeeling, untouched individual, who does not allow either things or living beings to enter his heart, is as little capable of real experience as he who allows everything to take possession of him and who is merely the slave of the outer world or of circumstances over which he has no control.

The first one excludes himself, the second one loses himself. The first one is comparable to a person who dies of thirst at the bank of a river, because he refuses to drink from it; the second one is like a man who throws himself into the river and is drowned.

Life means giving and taking: exchange, transformation. It is breathing in and breathing out. It is not the taking possession of anything, but a taking part in everything that comes in touch with us. It is neither a state of possession nor of being possessed, neither a clinging to the objects of our experience nor a state of indifference, but the middle way, the way of transformation.

We are transformed by what we accept. We transform what we have accepted by assimilating it. We are transformed by the act of giving, and we contribute to the transformation of others by what we are giving.

He who opposes this process of transformation will die the slow death of rigidity; he will be expelled and rejected from all that lives, like dead matter from a living organism. Death is a deficiency of the faculty of transformation.

This faculty is fundamentally different from decay or mere transiency, in the sense of unqualified or arbitrary change. Decay is the dissolution of that which has ceased to be an organic unity, a system of harmonious relations within its specific limits and with the world in which it functions.

Transformation, however, is not arbitrary change, or change governed by chance, but change governed by law, according to the inherent nature of the object in question. There are many categories of law operating on different levels, as for instance:

> the law of causality, proceeding in a strictly linear fashion, operating in physics beyond the nuclear level;
> the law of Dependent Origination or relative causality, characterized by irreversibility, operating in the realm of biology, in the realm of living organisms;
> the law of association, based on affinities, operating in the realm of psychology;
> the law of simultaneity or synchronicity, operating in universal space;
> the law of transformation, operating in time.

In other words, the categories of law stretch from the most universal to the most individual; from the general laws of inorganic matter to the particular (and more intricate) laws of organic life and individual self-expression; from the realm of necessity to the realm of freedom, because freedom is not lawlessness, but the possibility of self-expression or self-realization within the framework of universal laws. Self-realization, however, can never consist in egocentricity, exclusivity, or individual separateness, but only in a higher degree of responsiveness and creative activity, in a dynamic exchange of vital and spiritual forces.

> Our self to live must go through a continual change and growth of form, which may be termed a continual death and a continual life going on at the same time. It is really courting death when we refuse to accept death; when we wish to give the form of the self some fixed changelessness; when the self feels no impulse which urges it to grow out of itself; when it treats its

limits as final and acts accordingly.[1]

Thus, transformation contains both change and stability, plurality and unity, movement and constancy. It has the nature of life, namely, to connect organically the polar opposites, the stumbling-blocks of logic, and to unite them in an all-embracing rhythm.

Rhythm and direction represent the stability of movement, a movement that never follows a straight line (which exists only in mathematics, i.e., in abstract thought, but not in life). Therefore the logic of the brain is different from the logic of life.

If we want to have stability, we can find it only within ourselves, namely, as the stability of our inner direction (toward the center, toward enlightenment). This is not the stability of inertia, but the stability of a dynamic movement. Therefore the Buddhist symbol of the "stream" which one enters as soon as one has found that inner direction, and hence the designation of "stream-winner" (Pāli: *Sotapan*) for one who has entered the path toward liberation. Whether this movement comes to a standstill when the center is reached, or whether it is transformed into another, higher kind of movement, is of no importance; in either case the individual limitations, the cause of all our problems, would have ceased to exist. At any rate, the inner stability and integrity of one who has found his inner center is infinitely greater than that of a world experienced by unenlightened and spiritually undirected individuals, a world that Buddhists and Hindus alike characterize as *samsāra*.

It is this samsāric world which has to be overcome and which is, as certain schools put it, an illusory world. This is not a negation of the reality of the world, but only of wrong values derived from or applied to a distorted reality. Values can be produced only by the determination or attitude of a conscious mind. There are no self-existent values, but only values in relationship to spiritual aims or to practical necessities of life or individual circumstances. It is, therefore, impossible to ascribe values to nature or to the world as such. The world as such is neither good nor bad; it produces criminals as well as saints, ignorance as well as wisdom, fools as well as Enlightened Ones. One may say that the number of fools is out of proportion to the number of the Enlightened, but this means that one mistakes quantity for quality. The human body is built up of millions and millions of living cells and is inhabited by further millions of minute living organisms; and yet, there is only one human mind to justify this immense organization. Likewise, the existence of one enlightened consciousness cannot be outweighed by millions of unenlightened individuals. One wise man means more than a thousand fools.

So it all depends on what we make out of the material which we call the world or our surroundings. Out of the same clay, beautiful and ugly, useful and useless, things can be made. The quality depends on the potter, not on the clay. Similarly, it is not because there is something wrong with the world that we suffer, but because there is something wrong with us. We do not suffer, for instance, because everything is impermanent, but because we cling to impermanent things. If we did not cling to them, we should not mind their impermanence.

We enjoy a waterfall or a cloud-formation in spite of its impermanence; the changing forms heighten our delight. We admire the fleeting and fragile beauty of a flower, and we appreciate it all the more because of its uniqueness, its momentariness, its unrepeatable individuality. It is precious because it is a unique expression of life, based on all that has been, and thus incorporating in its individual form the immensity of the universe. This is why the Buddha's last gesture in holding up a flower, when asked by Subhuti to reveal the quintessence of his teaching, was the most profound sermon he ever preached—without uttering one word!

A high degree of culture and insight are required to experience the eternal in transient forms, to see the timeless harmony in the momentariness of phenomena, to feel the infinite rhythm that pervades even the most insignificant expression of life.

It is the deadly sameness of machine-made things and of a life governed by technology which perverts the mind and kills the spirit. Infinite variety is the hallmark of the creative genius; sameness the hallmark of mediocrity and decadence. The symbol of the machine is the wheel. The machine-wheel is the symbol of *Samsāra,* of ever-recurring birth and death, of the inescapable law of existence. (It may be of interest to note that no wheel was known in Tibet before the Chinese takeover; and the people were happy, even in the face of hardships. Now the wheel has come to Tibet, and with it slavery for those who have fallen under its sway.)

But there is another wheel, an invisible one, which does not revolve, but which radiates and pervades every form of life. It is the Dharma-Cakra, and he who realizes it, realizes his universality and the infinite relationship of all things and forms of appearance, without denying their relative existence and value.

We live in a world of impermanence and instability, because we are blinded by tiny fragments to which we cling under the influence of unreasonable desires; and thus blinded we lose the great connections and inner relations which give meaning and harmony to the flux of life. If we could see the whole picture, the totality and completeness of relations, we would be able to see things and beings in their proper perspective. The change or movement—which until then could be conceived only under the negative aspect of impermanence (as the principle of destruction)—would reveal a consistency of rhythm, a stability of direction and a continuity of organic development and spiritual unfoldment which could restore to our world and life a higher order of permanence and value than ever conceived by intellectual abstractions and speculations.

We accept the unity of a thing in space, though it extends in various dimensions with various aspects and proportions. But we doubt a similar unity if it is extended in time (which is merely another dimension), where it likewise shows various aspects and properties, developing according to its inherent nature.

> Our intellect . . . grasps this ultimate truth about things slowly, laboriously and piecemeal. It sees but one thing (and one aspect of it) at a time, and so always brings a feeling of incompleteness and limitation. But we have occasional moments of insight when something presented to our imagination will from its own character or from some exalted mood of our own, seem like a perfect and perfectly comprehended universe in miniature.[2]

This is what the great mystics of all times and the greatest of artists have experienced. But while the latter can only achieve it in their most creative moments, the former, due to their complete inner detachment and their fundamentally changed spiritual outlook, have been able to dwell more or less permanently in this state. For them the impermanent world of ordinary mortals has disappeared, though they may live with them and extend to them their loving kindness, because they have found the central harmony and never can lose the conception of totality in that of the individual. They are the Siddhas who have achieved the magic power that transforms *Samsāra* into *Nirvāna*. They are the saints and sages who attained enlightenment.

References and Notes
[1] Rabindranath Tagore: *Sādhana*.
[2] E. F. Carrit: *What Is Beauty?* p. 29.

2

THE CONQUEST OF DEATH

SINCE WHAT WE CALL DEATH is not a direct experience but only a concept deduced from the observation of external happenings, the conquest of death depends on the overcoming of the concept. This, however, cannot be achieved by the intellect, the very originator and playground of conceptual thought, but only by regaining a state of unprejudiced, direct experience.

In other words, the conceptualization of our individuality or our individual existence creates the impression of a permanent ego. The conceptualization of change (which we generally see only under the negative aspect of impermanence, in contrast to our imagined ego) creates the idea of death. Neither death nor ego can be experienced. They are opposite ends of the same concept. Their characteristic mark, like that of every concept, is abstraction and limitation or the artificial establishment of boundaries.

If death were something real, we could experience it. But as long as we are able to experience anything, we are not dead. If we could observe the process of dying or the moment of death, we would have proved that death does not destroy the experiencing subject and that, therefore, death is not what we have assumed it to be.

Therefore, if death is something which actually cannot be

experienced, why should we be afraid of it? We would not be afraid of an illness which we know could not befall us. If, nevertheless, we fear death, this only proves how much we are under the dominance of the intellect.

A typical property of our intellect is its striving after objectivity. This is justified and useful as long as we are dealing with objects or things, i.e. with something that is limited, delineated, circumscribed, and defined conceptually. But this objectivity fails us whenever we are concerned with questions of vital importance—questions concerning the very essence of man and the deeper meaning of individual existence. The only way out of this dilemma is to replace the intellectual attitude of objectivity by subjective experience.

The problem of immortality, or the conquest of death, is not objective but is purely subjective and, therefore, can be solved only by direct inner experience. From the objective point of view we can speak only of the cessation of bodily functions and the decay of the physical organs that made them possible. But what happened to the forces that built and maintained them is quite another question. Unless we become conscious of them by turning our attention inward, we shall not be able to solve the problem; it actually has arisen because of the screen which we have created between our peripheral surface consciousness and our universal depth consciousness.

In animals and children of tender age this screen has not yet been formed. Although we cannot return to the state of innocence in which the concept of death does not exist, we can rise above the point of view of the average man, who is delivered unto death because he believes in it—who does not realize that the conquest of death is within his reach. By recognizing the illusoriness of a separate and change-resisting ego and accepting the law of transformation as the very nature of life and spiritual growth, we destroy the presupposition on which the concept of death is based.

The annihilation of the ego-illusion, however, is in no way identical with the annihilation of individuality or of individual continuity. On the contrary, it is just the elimination of this impeding and narrowing illusion which makes it possible for us to see beyond the limits of our momentary selfhood—the focal point of our universally conditioned personality—and to recognize the connections with previous and possible future forms of life.

In Tibet there is a well-known spiritual exercise for those who are initiated into the teachings of the Bardo Thödol. This is a method of penetrating into the deeper layers of the human psyche, into which consciousness retreats at the moment of physical death, and thus anticipating spiritually the experience of the transition from one form of life to another. It is not a matter of becoming conscious of the past or of the future, of remembering former lives or of trying to have prescience of the future. It is something far more important: the conscious direction of our psychic forces at the moment in which the bodily functions cease (or the conscious projection of these forces in a similar state during meditation), in which the influence of bodily functions is reduced to a minimum, if not altogether eliminated.

By observing and obeying the laws of nature, man has succeeded in mastering its forces. By observing and obeying the laws of the spirit, man will become the master of spiritual reality. This reality does not run counter to the laws of nature, it is not opposed to them nor does it break them; it includes them and goes beyond them, just as the third dimension contains the first and second without abolishing or violating the laws of either.

For thousands of years people have argued whether man is immortal or whether his physical death is the end. Here the most important point has been overlooked, namely that immortality and its opposites are not facts of nature, but depend upon ourselves. Immortality does not mean preserving the status quo in regard to either our body or our mind; nor does mortality mean the annihilation of all that caused body and mind to come into existence.

Man is mortal as long as he tries to hang on to his present state of mind and body, as long as he does not endeavor to rise above his present condition, i.e. the state of his present ignorance, his contentment with the irrelevant and partial phenomena of his existence. Immortality is not a gift of nature or of a god: it has to be acquired.

The terrible idea of eternal damnation (which seems to be incompatible with the idea of a benevolent God) has perhaps its unconscious origin in the correct notion that the individual who has not found his true inner center and the connection with the universal and timeless foundation of his deepest being, is indeed a prey to transiency and deprives himself of his immortality. For immortality does not consist in the preservation of our ego or our limited personality, but in the awareness of that great flow of reality in which our present life is only a fleeting moment. In this knowledge lies the liberation from death leading to the experience and realization of immortality.

3

THE MYSTERY OF LIFE

THE AVERAGE MAN BELIEVES in the reality of his own individual life and of the world revealed by his senses.

The thinker is disappointed when he discovers that life has no greater reality than a dream.

The wise one, however, though he is conscious of the illusory character of human life, transforms the illusory forms and perishable materials into exponents of the imperishable by seeing them as symbols of a reality far surpassing the limits of individual life and intellectual understanding.

To know that a statue has been made of ordinary clay or stone does not give us any clue to the nature of the statue or to its meaning or value as a work of art. In the same way, the analysis of the human individual—his body, his psychic properties, his mental functions or psychological factors—does not bring us nearer to the meaning of his existence or his essential nature.

Even if we think that individual life is illusory and, because of its impermanence, its sufferings and limitations, of little value, this should not prevent us from making it into a work of art, from giving it beauty and dignity by converting it into an instrument of highest spiritual achievements and a structure of inner and outer harmony. Life has no meaning in itself, but only the meaning we give it. Like the clay in the artist's hand, we may convert it into a divine form or merely into a vessel of temporary utility.

If Confucius says that it is not truth that makes man great, but man that makes truth great, we may modify this by saying: it is not life that makes man great, but man that makes life great. Because life is everywhere; but only if it is centered in an individual focus does it gain the power and the capacity to become conscious of its supraindividual, all-embracing nature.

This is the great paradox of the mind: individualization is necessary in order that it may become conscious of its universality. Individuality, however, requires a continual process of molting, of dissolving and reconstituting itself, of liquifying and reintegrating its constituents and thus preventing their ossification and the consequent destruction of their original functions. The process of dying is essential to individuality; it liberates from the accumulated incrustations of the past and prevents spiritual death—the death of stagnation and rigidity which separates the individual from his primordial and universal origin.

To make life great, we must not try to hold on to any of its momentary aspects. Even the functions of our body teach us this by reflecting the laws of life. Everything that we try to hold on to, be it air or food, turns into poison. Exhalation and elimination are as important as inhalation and the intake of food. Similarly the process of dying is as important for life as the process of being born. It is only because we identify the process of dying with the dissolution of the body, without recognizing the simultaneous process of spiritual regeneration, that we arrive at our one-sided and negative conception of death.

In the fact of dying the deepest mystery of life is revealed. The necessity of physical death stands in direct relationship to the vitality of creative spirit, for which no single form can suffice forever.

Only he who has realized that birth and death are only the two sides of the same process, and that they occur simultaneously in every moment of life—comparable to the ever-present functions of inhalation and exhalation—only such a one will comprehend that death is not the negation of life but one of its functions which can be separated from it as little as can birth.

Plutarch said that in the moment of physical death the soul has the same experiences as the initiates of the great mysteries. The initiates go through the portals of death and rebirth in the act of initiation and thus know about the inseparable oneness of both in the stream of life.

This mystery has been known in Tibet up to our days and

was passed on in the teachings and symbols of what is known as *The Tibetan Book of the Dead*. This book is far more than an instruction for those who are dying or near death; nor is it merely a mass for the dead or a guide through the realm of death. Its real title is *The Liberation from the Intermediate State through Hearing* [the Truth].

The Intermediate State (Tib.: "bar-do"), however, is not only the state between the physical death and the physical rebirth, but relates to every moment of our life. Because the life of an unenlightened person is nothing but such an intermediate state, which has no greater reality than the experiences of a dream or of other illusory and time-conditioned states of the mind. The word "illusory," as we use it here, is meant to denote a state that is real only in a limited sense, but is not a mere hallucination.

Those, however, who have listened not only with their ears but with their heart and their whole mind, thus having realized already in their present life the profound teachings of the Bardo Thödol, have wakened from the illusory intermediate state and have entered the state of recognizing a deeper reality. They have become masters of life and death. In Tibet they were called "Tulkus," i.e. those whose bodies (Tib.: "sKu") are conscious projections or creations of their minds, in contrast to the ordinary man, whose body is the product of unconscious drives and inclinations (which are the subject of modern psychoanalysis).

Such "Tulkus" (my own Guru was one of them) have been called by Westerners "Living Buddhas," an entirely misleading term just as are most of the things that have been reported about Tibet by superficial travelers or gullible storytellers. "Sprul" (pron. *tul*) is the creative power of the mind, and he who is able to utilize and to direct this power is called a Tulku. However, not all who claim to be Tulkus are so in fact.

If the spiritual perversion and brutal force of our machine civilization should ever extinguish the living tradition of the Bardo Thödol and the spiritual culture that was handed down to us from ancient Tibet, humanity would be deprived of its last connection with the great mysteries of prehistoric times.

But here the question arises: How are we able to keep alive a tradition or a spiritual culture that has been handed down to us not only from the past but from a people whose language and customs, whose mental, historical, and environmental background are so different from that of modern man who, under the influence of Western science, has developed an entirely different outlook on life? Are not all cultural forms and traditions equally subject to the laws of transformation, of death and rebirth, if they are to survive? Was not the Tibetan religious tradition in danger of suffocating in its own scholasticism and in the unquestioned acceptance and blind faith in its constitutional forms and rituals, whose original meanings had been forgotten? Is it not, therefore, our first duty to rediscover the spirit behind the forms of Tibetan tradition and the original meaning of sacred symbols and rituals before we try to take them over like lifeless relics of a dead past? This would be their final death and our own spiritual emasculation.

Experience has taught us that cultivated plants degenerate when sown again and again in the same soil, and that this degeneration can be prevented either by rotation of crops on the same soil or by getting seeds or seedlings of the same type grown in a different soil and under different climatic conditions.

The same seems to be true in spiritual life. Religious or spiritual traditions tend to degenerate if they are kept too long in the same soil, i.e. without fresh stimuli, without exchange with or access to other forms of thought and temperament.

Buddhism disappeared from the soil of India, while it grew and flourished in many other countries of Asia. The same happened in Ceylon, where Buddhism was preserved as in an air-tight compartment, in one of its oldest forms and under ideal conditions. Nevertheless, it degenerated to such an extent that it became almost extinct, and the Sangha had to be reintroduced from Burma and Siam.

Christianity would have remained an unimportant Jewish sect had it remained confined to Palestine! By being transplanted to the countries of the West and by coming in contact with Greek and Roman thought and civilization, it grew in vigor and breadth of outlook, and finally became a world-religion.

Taoism, being confined to China for thousands of years, degenerated into a system of magic rituals and lost all influence upon the modern Chinese mind as a philosophy of life, while in many Western scholars and thinkers the teachings of

Lao-tse caused a profound reaction and gave rise to a substantial and influential literature which may in the future play an important role in the spiritual development of humanity.

The same may be said of the great spiritual treasures preserved in Tibet. Modern Tibetans worship them with sincere faith and devotion, but they are not able to revive them. Fresh blood, a new beginning, a spiritual awakening are necessary in order to bring forth a new blossom on the tree of this ancient tradition. Spiritual things—like all living organisms—are alive only as long as they grow. The moment they stop growing, they deteriorate and die of stagnation. To take over the forms of the past or of a tradition in which one has not grown up is not possible unless one has experienced the reality of those inner forces of the human spirit from which they grew. The human spirit, however, is to be understood as that which is common to all human beings: the deepest center of our consciousness. Unless we are able to dive into this center, we cannot reexperience or relive the organic growth that led to the creation of those archetypal symbols and forms which to our intellect have merely a historical or aesthetic significance.

4

THE DANGER OF WORDS

IN THE LANKĀVATĀRA SŪTRA it is said: "May every disciple take care not to cling to words, as if they were a perfect expression of the meaning; because truth is not in the letters. When a man points to something with the finger, the tip of the finger may be mistaken for the thing pointed at. In the same way the ignorant and simple-minded are like children, incapable of giving up the idea that in the finger-tip of words the actual meaning is contained."

Words are misleading, not only if they describe the same thing in different ways, but even more so if the same expression is used in different contexts with different meanings and for different purposes. The negative attitude which orthodox Buddhists take toward various forms of Hinduism is generally based on a lack of knowledge concerning the other religious system (and vice-versa) or on the naive supposition that equal words have equal meanings, or that statements which contradict in their verbal expression certain formulations of Buddhist philosophy, must necessarily exclude each other. Such a purely scholastic attitude gives more importance to the surface meaning of words than to the underlying religious experience.

Keyserling, in his *Travel Diary of a Philosopher*, has correctly observed that the Westerner "advances from thought, inducing, deducing, differentiating, integrating; the Indian advances from condition to condition. The former rises higher and higher in the domain of abstractions, from particular to general concepts, from these to ideas, and so forth; the latter changes continuously the form of his consciousness. He has, of course, objectified what he has experienced on various planes, and he has done so in conceptual forms; and these concepts are often found identical with ours, as far as the words go. The Indians also speak of the Absolute. But whereas this concept means a certain stage of abstraction for us, it means to the Indian rendering objective an experienced subjective condition. It is, therefore, not a question of identity but of incommensurability. Ātman is not a rational idea to the Indian, but the description of an attainable level of consciousness; purusha is not the soul of an imagined world but a principle of experience, and so on."

It is, therefore, a childish undertaking to place the ātman-experience of the Upanishads on the same level as the naive concept of an individual "I" (or ego), which the Buddha rightly rejects in his anattā-teaching. The way of the Upanishads and the way of the Buddha differ in many aspects; and people who stop halfway may find themselves in opposite positions, like two travelers who, starting from the same place, move around the globe in opposite directions. The spot at which they arrive is the same, though they may not find the same word for it, because their words are conditioned by their experiences.

If we meet a man who, by his actions and character, his spiritual maturity and integrity, convinces us that he has attained complete liberation (this was the case, according to all human evidence, with Ramana Maharshi, the great Indian saint of our time) would it not be foolish to refuse recognition to such a man only because he used a terminology different from ours?

It was the special merit of the Buddha to find a way and a formulation of truth which was so universal that men of different races and cultures could accept and realize them. This merit is in no way minimized by admitting that, even before the advent of the Buddha, great saints and sages had gained the highest realization, and that likewise, after the passing away of the Buddha, there were many who on the same way, or even on totally different ones, attained the same noble aim.

The greatest danger threatening Buddhism—as all other religions—is the dogmatism of small sects which imagine themselves to be the sole proprietors of the pure doctrine and who believe that their way is the only way. The more sincerely we try to understand others, the better we learn to understand ourselves. The awe before all that is great is the root of all that is great in ourselves.

He who possesses this awe, this profound reverence, has at the same time respect for the living form and the inherent law of each spiritual way and the symbols in which they are expressed. There can be no greater sin against the spirit than the leveling of all values by arbitrarily mixing and confusing spiritual forms of expression. They are as little exchangeable as the limbs and organs of different individuals, because they are the products of organic growth and not just part of a lifeless mechanism.

As little as it is physically possible to walk at the same time on two or more different roads, it is impossible to follow at the same time different paths of spiritual practice. We may be able to recognize the justification and meaningfulness of each way, but we must choose for ourselves which way we want to tread, and we must consistently follow it to its end if we wish to reach its aim. He who turns back halfway in order to try another way, has to begin again from the very beginning, and the oftener we repeat such experiments, the less we have a chance of getting anywhere. This should not prevent us from investigating various ways and making ourselves acquainted with different religions, philosophies, and spiritual practices. In fact, the knowledge of different ways may help us to find and to recognize our own way with greater clarity.

5

ETERNITY AND INFINITY

ETERNITY AND INFINITY in the spiritual or religious sense are not mathematical values but experiences common to all men who have reached a certain spiritual maturity, and most of all to the great leaders of humanity in the fields of culture and religion. Only those who do not live out of their own abundance—the uncreative, mediocre, and unimaginative—deny the reality of such experiences; and since they have not known them, they find satisfaction in their intellectual dissection and devaluation.

Those who see in the Buddha's denunciation of the belief in eternity (*sassata-ditthi*) a negation of eternal values, or who interpret his *anattā* doctrine as "soullessness," have not yet understood what Buddhism means. The Buddha never denied the eternal in man, but only the mistaken idea that it is identical with his ego or his limited personality. This is what *anattā* (non-ego) means. But just as the Buddha denounced the belief in an eternal ego, he rejected the belief in the annihilation of the human being at the time of death (*uccheda-ditthi*).

The question is not whether we are finite or infinite, mortal or immortal, but whether we identify ourselves with the infinite and imperishable or with the finite and ephemeral. This is the leit motif of all Indian thought, the common basis of Indian religiosity, which also the Buddha recognized as self-evident, without having to put it into so many words.

The impermanence of the world of birth and death (*samsāra*) stands in contrast to the imperishable, all-embracing consciousness of enlightenment, in which the state of *nirvāna*, the liberation from the delusion of egohood, is realized. We are not dealing here with a dualistic conception of the universe, but with one and the same reality, seen under two different viewpoints: the ego-conditioned on the one side, the ego-free on the other.

It is completely misleading, therefore, to declare that Buddhism regards life as meaningless. One can arrive at such a conclusion only if one denies the metaphysical background of Buddhism. This denial springs from a lack of historical knowledge or from a one-sided intellectual analysis of traditional concepts, torn from their origin and from their continued connections with religious experience.

Because the Buddha emphasized the practical aspects of religious life, avoiding philosophical speculations and theories, as well as unfounded and fanciful beliefs in supernatural phenomena, he did not live in a spiritual vacuum in which nothing existed beyond the given facts of our empirical world. His teaching rises from the very foundations of a metaphysical, non-Vedic tradition,[1] probably of pre-Aryan origin, which recognized neither castes (*varna*) nor sacrifices (*yajña*) and insisted on the sacredness of life (*ahimsa*). This tradition was represented by the nontheistic systems of Yoga and Sāmkhya, as well as by Jainism and the groups of wandering ascetics or Śramanas, all of whom made the individual's own effort (*śrama*) and responsibility (*śila*) the basis of their religious life. This presupposed a universal and moral world order (*dharma*), the law of action and reaction (*karma*), the continuity and mutual relationship of all forms of life in the cycles of births and deaths (*samsāra*), and the liberation from these ever-recurring cycles through higher knowledge (*prajñā*) and the at-one-ment, in which all ego-bound limitations are dissolved. The latter is the realization of the anattā-doctrine of the Buddha, which is neither a denial of the human soul (psyche), nor of that higher reality on which it is based and which is realized in the experience of enlightenment.

To equate the denial of an unchangeable, eternally limited and separate "I" with a denial of the eternal in man, and thus to represent Buddhism as the doctrine of "soullessness," is the misconception of those for whom the teaching of the Buddha is not a religious experience, but merely a system of intellectual concepts which at best serves as a foundation for the establishment of a puritanical morality. We may arrive at such a system on the basis of a strictly scholarly analysis; but any such purely analytical procedure will end in mere negations.

D. T. Suzuki, one of the greatest Buddhist scholars of our time, has characterized the danger of this method in vivid words: "I began with the analytic method," he said in an essay, published some years ago. "This analysis ends in negation; it is the annihilation of desires, the dissolution of all existing objects. We must go beyond this into synthesis. Through the synthetic method, all that we have killed, dissected and reduced to mere lifelessness, will be revived and re-awakened. The analysis has transformed the living object into a corpse. The corpse must be revived and its resurrection must be effected through synthesis. This is the great affirmation, the highest affirmation. To say, there is no 'I,' there is no Ātman—that is not enough. We must go one step further and say that there is an Ātman; however, that this Ātman does not exist on the plane of the relative, but on that of the absolute. When the dissected elements of nothingness have been reconstructed, then we have the real truth. The integrating method does not replace the analytical, but we must reconstruct what we have destroyed."

Our egocentricity, our overestimation of ourselves and the feeling—or, indeed, our conviction—of having a separate existence, will in no way be lessened by the idea that there is no "I in itself" or that we are only an aggregate of various qualities, forces, and substances. On the contrary, the more we are convinced of it, the more uninhibited, unscrupulous, and selfish we shall be in our actions, which in this case are nothing but "the rolling on of empty functions and phenomena." Though we have then thrown the self out of the front door (namely our intellect), it returns with doubled strength through the backdoor (our subconsciousness), because of the skepticism which does not recognize any higher values and to which "nothing is worth an effort."

If the mere conviction of the nonexistence of an Ātman or an "I" or an immortal soul were sufficient to overcome egoism, all materialists—who believe only in the reality of the senseworld or in the results of a purely analytic-deductive science and a universe of unconscious, mechanically interacting forces —would be the ideal Buddhists.

There is only one way to overcome our egocentricity, our ego-limitation, and that is the positive way of the knowledge that we are the exponents of something greater and worthier than a mere complex of individual drives, subconscious chain-reactions, "dynamic-energetic quantas," or other meaningless processes, functions, and "aggregates of existence." It is the living way of experience that teaches us: the more we emphasize our imaginary selfhood and try to uphold it against all other forms of life, the less we can partake of the freedom and completeness of our true nature, which is realized in the experience of our universality in the state of enlightenment (*bodhi*).

Meaningful creation and self-realization are thinkable only in a universe permeated by a higher consciousness. The more the individual becomes conscious of the universe within and outside himself and of his profound relationship with all that lives (and what could be excluded from it?), the less he will believe in the importance or reality of his own ego and of his own separate existence.

Thus we may summarize:
He who lives only on the physical level perishes with his body. He who lives only in the realm of egocentric thought and feeling, will be tossed about on the ocean of worldly existence (*saṃsāra*) as a victim of the power of Karma, a slave to his deeds and desires. But he who realizes the totality and completeness of his true being in the fire of inspiration and selfless devotion, and has thus become perfectly transparent and luminous (i.e., enlightened), he alone has won true immortality.

References and Notes

[1] Cf. *Brahmanism, Buddhism and Hinduism* by Prof. Lalmani Joshi, The Wheel Publication, No. 150/51, Kandy (Sri Lanka), 1972.

6
ANALYSIS AND SYNTHESIS

TRUTH AND FACTS are two different things. A fact may be entirely different from truth or reality. Reality is infinite relationship, truth its synthesized recognition. Facts are momentary, single aspects; fragments detached from their organic or general connections.

That the human body consists of cells is a fact. Yet it is impossible to gain an idea of what a human being is or looks like by contemplating the cells. The nature of the cells and the essential nature of a human being are two entirely different things. A cell is more than the sum of its atoms, and man is more than the sum of his cells.

The microscope may be a thousand times superior to the human eye, both in its objectivity and its accurateness. Nevertheless, the illusory image of the human body perceived by our eyes conveys more of the true nature of man than all microscopic facts and scientific details.

The whole is more than the sum of its parts. The part receives its meaning from the whole, but not vice-versa. If we detach the individual from his relations to the totality of the universe, he will be reduced to a meaningless illusion, a nonentity. If we see him in relationship to the whole universe, he becomes an exponent of cosmic reality (the Ātman of the Upanishads). And if he becomes fully conscious of it, he becomes an Enlightened One, a Buddha.

Because the potential universality of the human consciousness was confused with the illusory I-consciousness, the Buddha was compelled to replace the ātman-idea by that of the anātman, the non-ego.

The naive mechanistic materialism of a Nagasena, which compares the human being with the lifeless parts of a cart, would certainly not have been approved by a Buddha. The comparison leaves out what is most essential: the organic composition and mutual relationship of the different parts of the cart and the human body (of which the latter have been arbitrarily, i.e., conceptually, separated) and the vital, creative force of the mind which has brought them into existence. Neither the different parts of the cart, nor the way in which they were joined together, come into existence without the creativity of the imaginative, planning mind. And likewise no human body can develop without an organizing vital force which, according to Buddhist psychology, depends on the directive principle of our depth-consciousness.

An analysis based on the arbitrary dissection of what organically belongs together, and which leaves out of consideration the creative principle of all that is alive (whether we call it a spiritual or potentially conscious or psychic force, or whether we regard it as an unconscious current of vital energy or the like) is a conscious falsification of reality, from which no true knowledge can arise. Even the most materialistic minded modern scientist has a deeper insight into the nature of the psychophysical organism of man than the monkish authors of many of those ancient and revered Buddhist texts, in which the human body is reviled and represented as a bag full of uncleanliness, a collection of repulsive details, the contemplation of which is intended to create disgust and contempt. Even if one should succeed in this way to alienate oneself from the body, it would have no spiritual value. It would not lead to a deeper understanding of our corporeality or solve the problem of our body-mind relationship. It would merely lead to a negation of the fundamental facts of life and to spiritual self-mutilation. Any meditation based on contempt for the body is in no way better than one that leads to the opposite attitude: the exaggerated attachment to the body. Aversion is as great a hindrance to liberation as attachment. The way of the Buddha avoids both extremes and overcomes them in the only possible positive way: the way of knowledge, of profound insight into the true nature of things, which is nothing else than our own true nature. Knowledge, however, does not fall into our lap if we just sit and wait; it has to be patiently acquired through life's experience and an ever wakeful awareness without preconceived judgments. And this is the first step in meditation. This does not preclude spontaneous flashes of intuition; on the contrary: only in the stillness of an open, receptive mind can the intuitive qualities of our mind be developed and cultivated.

As long as we really understand—in its whole depth—that it is the mind that creates the body, there will be no place for an arbitrary dissection of the human body by way of a purely conceptual or intellectual analysis or mere verbalization of its functions. This is the method used in certain meditative practices which try to dissociate the body from the experiencing subject, as if it were a mere mechanical device that had nothing to do with the observer. He who has realized the profound relationship between mind and body will not be deceived by such superficial observations but will enlarge his vision to an awareness of the totality of that spiritual dynamism in which the visible becomes the symbol and the final exponent of the invisible. One may perhaps usefully quote Alan Watts on this subject:

> It is increasingly clear to those who study ecology, sociology, biology, and even physics, that the individual organism is not what it usually feels itself to be:

a bag of skin stretched around bones, muscles, and other organs as the temporary vehicle of a distinct and particular self or ego. The sensation of oneself as a separate center of consciousness and will, confronting an external world in which one is an alien and intelligent fluke, is quite clearly a hallucination. It bears no resemblance to man, or any other organism, described in the above-named sciences, all of which see beings, events, and things as processes which, however clearly distinguishable, are inseparable from the processes which surround them and constitute their environment.

The scientist is therefore bound to recognize that what he is describing is not a solitary organism but a vast and theoretically limitless field of relationships which he calls (rather clumsily) the organism-environment. This is not merely a deterministic situation in which the organism responds like a puppet to environmental influences. It is rather that they are two aspects, or poles, of a single process. They transact mutually, almost like the left and right sides of a moving snake.[1]

Every analysis must be preceded by a synthesis, i.e., by the understanding of the greater universal background of each single phenomenon and its infinite relationship with all other phenomena. This is better insurance against the megalomania of a separate egohood than endless analytic dissections of the human body and mind into their functions and material components.

Therefore all great Tantric meditations of Tibetan Buddhism anticipate the universal aim, the great mystic synthesis, i.e. the ideal Buddhahood; and only after they have identified the meditator with the goal do they leave him to the appropriate meditative methods and individual experiences.

Just as the archer concentrates on his aim and becomes one with it in order to hit the mark with certainty, so the meditator must first identify himself with the aim and feel one with it. This gives impetus and direction to his striving. Then, whatever his ways and methods—whether creative or discriminating, emotional or intellectual, synthesizing or analyzing, imaginative or discursive—he will always proceed toward his aim. He will neither get lost in the desert of discrimination and dissection, nor cling to the products of his imagination. The latter danger is avoided by the process of integration and dissolution of all spiritually created forms and perceptions.

The demonstration of the mind's capacity to create a world and to dissolve it again, demonstrates better than any intellectual analysis the true nature of all phenomena and the senselessness of all craving and clinging.

The analysis which dissects the building materials will never reveal the true nature of the building, because the idea is earlier than the building. The idea of the architect, and not the form or nature of the stones, decides the shape of the building.

The building cannot be understood from the nature of the stones and, therefore, an analysis can be meaningful only in connection with a synthesis. In such a case the analysis becomes a meaningful discernment of interrelated elements instead of an arbitrary separation of organically grown or developed details. It will be the establishment of living relations instead of a collection of dead concepts. Only if the "neither-identity-nor-nonidentity" principle is adhered to in the analysis can it remain within the realm of reality.

References and Notes

[1] Foreword to *The Ecstatic Adventure,* ed. by Ralph Netgnes; New York: The Macmillan Company, 1968.

7

INDIVIDUALITY AND UNIVERSALITY

FORCE AS SUCH IS NOT CREATIVE. Only when force finds resistance can it become creative. Therefore, the universal requires the individual and the divine requires the human in order to realize itself. The greater the tension or the distance between these two poles, the greater the creative impetus or the power of realization.

The danger in the West lies in the overemphasis on the this-worldly pole of individuality, of egocentric activity, of self-assertion and willpower. The danger in the East lies in the overemphasis of the universal pole, the metaphysical, the negation of the value of individuality, which leads to a passive dissolution in a formless unity. Both attitudes contradict the innermost law of existence, the one by denying universality, the other by depriving individuality of its value. The latter would actually contradict the idea of a divine (or divinely evolved) universe—one of the basic beliefs of the East—because it would amount to the accusation that the godhead had meaninglessly created individual forms and beings.

The overemphasis on unity is as great a fault as the overemphasis on duality or plurality. If we conceive duality as the irreconcilable opposition of two independent and mutually exclusive principles, and not as the necessary polarity of two mutually complementary aspects of reality or of a higher unity—or if we cling only to one side, under complete exclusion or negation of the other—then, indeed, we suffer under a serious illusion. If we try to deny the fact of polarity (imagining that reality consists only in unity) then we simply close our eyes to the most evident reality.

As a man who is bereft of his senses, due to intoxicating drugs or drink, imagines himself to live in a state of perfect oneness and harmony with the world because his individuality, his power of discernment, and his feeling of responsibility have been deadened, so those who believe themselves to have attained the highest state of divine union in subconscious or unconscious trance-states, only deceive themselves. Unless they are capable of integrating the experience of universality into their normal individual consciousness and of realizing it in their daily life, they have attained nothing worth striving for. Only when the universal has become conscious and realized in the individual has the state of enlightenment and liberation been reached.

To a god the finite would be as great a necessity as the infinite is to man, because only the finite gives meaning to the infinite. Only a man of spiritual maturity and deep insight is capable of appreciating the true value of the finite in the uniqueness of its momentary appearance. This is why only the greatest among us are capable of understanding the simple things of life in their true depth and significance. We may be reminded here of a great poet's saying: "In the smallest you may find a master, whom the deepest in you can never satisfy." (R. M. Rilke)

The undeveloped human being strives after the finite for the sake of his own profit.

The thinker strives after the infinite for the sake of his freedom.

The Knowing One returns to the finite for the sake of his infinite love.

The Knowing One, however, is the Bodhisattva, the being in whom the light has become radiant.

A Fairytale About God

> When God had become conscious of his omniscience, he suddenly felt terribly bored because, whatever happened, he knew the outcome. There was no more any surprise; there was nothing that was not known beforehand. There was no expectation, no sense of accomplishment, no joy—only the deadening routine of a mechanical sequence of foreseeable events. The world had become a predeterminable (if not predetermined) mechanism.
>
> It was then that God relinquished his omniscience and descended into the world, into the ever-changing rounds of life and death, joy and suffering, wrapped in the mystery of his own being.
>
> But he retained in every form into which he descended, a spark of limited knowledge that would guide him through the endless labyrinth of the world and his infinite incarnations.
>
> And now the world changed for him into a gigantic stage, on which a soul-stirring—nay, a soul-creating—drama was being performed: a drama in which every actor was the creator and performer of his or her role, and in which all roles combine in one universal mystery play.
>
> Sometimes an actor got lost in his role and forgot his relationship to and position in the play as a whole, until sharp pangs of suffering awakened the spark of knowledge within him and brought him back to the recognition of the significance of the play and of his own role.
>
> And finally his knowledge became wisdom, which is not omniscience but the faculty of seeing the in-

finite in the finite, the universal in the individual, and of creating out of an infinite variety of phenomena an all-encompassing harmony.

Wisdom is the outcome of creative spontaneity, which gives meaning and depth to our existence. The creative impulse in man is the very essence of the divine. The uncreative man, even though he may believe in a God, has no part in him. The creative man is the instrument, nay, the living exponent of divine power, divine spirit. The world is in a continuous state of creation, of becoming, and therefore in a continuous state of destruction of all that has been created and has become rigid and lifeless.

We must create God anew daily (or whatever expresses the deepest reality within ourselves) because the God of yesterday is dead and becomes a fetish, a mere concept. This is the meaning of the Tantric meditative practice (*sādhana*) in which the divine presence is ever re-created in luminous images and archetypal symbols, until the mind and body of the devotee are transformed into the visible and tangible expression of Buddhahood.

In a poem, "The Thoughts and No-Thoughts of Mu-Shin," Christmas Humphreys gave expression to a very similar idea about God as symbolized in our fairytale:

> The God I know is no Saviour.
> Rather he cries out to be saved,
> for he is my fellow men in their totality
> and the life that is not yet man.
> This is the God I serve, who of my service
> will be given power to save.

8
THE EXPERIENCE OF AWE AND THE SENSE OF WONDER

IT IS NOT OUR BUSINESS to explain the world, but to give it meaning. The same holds true with regard to the mysteries of life and of consciousness. All that can be explained loses therewith its infinity and becomes circumscribed, limited, finite—and becomes a "thing"! Thingness is the opposite of aliveness, of all that is conscious and whose nature, in its inner freedom and autonomous movement, consists of its very unpredictability.

"Reality is not a fixed condition, but a magnitude capable of various degrees of intensification," as Martin Buber has said. Therefore: "It is the glorious paradox of our existence that all conceivability of the world is only the footstool of its inconceivability."

People who try to explain everything in the world, kill everything. Spiritual life cannot exist without the recognition of and awe before the ultimate mystery. A mystery can be experienced and yet remain inexplicable. It is not a mystery because it is something hidden and unknowable, but because it is too great for words. Do we not find something similar in great works of art, which likewise can be experienced but not explained, though they stand before our eyes in all clarity and distinctiveness?

The feeling of awe and the sense of wonder arise from the recognition of the deep mystery that surrounds us everywhere, and this feeling deepens as our knowledge grows. The greatest scientists are nearest to the greatest mystics. It was Einstein who said: "The most beautiful and most profound emotion we can experience is the sensation of the mystical. It is the source of all true science. He to whom this emotion is a stranger, who can no longer wonder and stand rapt in awe, is as good as dead."

The feeling of awe and wonder which seizes us in moments of intuitive insight grows in strength and depth the more our knowledge extends. It makes us humble in the realization that indeed our knowledge is only "the footstool of the inconceivability of the world." The less we know, the more certain we are in our explanations; the more we know, the more we realize our limitations.

Those, however, who arbitrarily assign a "purpose" to the universe deprive it therewith of its universality in time and space. The same applies to all concepts concerning the divine as an absolute and omnipotent power. The moment we ascribe "purposes" to it, i.e., limited motives and actions, we destroy the very premise on which our concept is based. It is for this reason that the Buddha abstained from making any assertions about God.

Those who see in God the sole actor, without whose will nothing can happen, only try to escape their own responsibility and make God the scapegoat for all their failings and limitations. So long as we have not realized the divine nature within ourselves in the universality of our deepest consciousness, we cannot relinquish our individual responsibility.

Though all the qualities of butter are contained in the milk, we cannot speak of the presence of butter before we have churned the milk. In a similar way we cannot speak of our consciousness as being divine—in spite of having the totality of the universe as its base—as long as we have not freed it from its individual obscurations and attachments.

This requires a sincere spiritual effort, a "churning of the mind"—which in Buddhism is symbolized by "setting in motion the Wheel of the Law" (*dharma-cakra pravartana*), i.e. by activating and vivifying or awakening the universal law within ourselves—until we become conscious of the spiritual order governing the universe.

This law can be summarized negatively as nonlimitation, non-ego-ness; positively as the all-relatedness of each individual being. This all-relatedness, however, is not merely the relationship between the individual and an abstract whole (as the sum total of an infinite number of parts), but represents the organic connection of every single being with all that exists and is alive, because each individual form is a unique expression of the whole.

Uniqueness is the empirical focus of universality; momentariness or uniqueness in time ("onceness") the vehicle of eternity; and, therefore, the complete and direct awareness of the unique moment in the infinity of time and space and the eternity of life is the highest achievement of meditation, which ultimately means the realization of solidarity with all living beings.

An experience which is not yet limited by preconceived ideas has all the qualities of infinity; similarly, the absence of time in an experience which is thus free from arbitrary associations has the quality of eternity. The smallest unit of time is equal to its longest imaginable duration. Both are outside of measurable time, outside of empirical time; strictly speaking they are "not-time"; they are timeless.

Meditation "opens the mind of man to the greatest mystery that takes place daily and hourly; it widens the heart so that it may feel the eternity of time and the infinity of space in every throb; it gives us a life within the world as if we were moving about in paradise; and all these spiritual deeds take place without any refuge into a doctrine, but by the simple and direct holding fast to the truth which dwells in our innermost being." (D. T. Suzuki)

What opens the mind to the great mystery of life, to the infinite within (not behind) the finite, to the eternal within the ephemeral, is that "sense of wonder" which Socrates called the feeling of a philosopher and the beginning of philosophy. It is the switching over of our mind from the old grooves of our habitual thought to a new unimpeded way of thinking and feeling, unimpeded by the prejudice of egocentricity, or by the duality of such contradictory concepts as being and not-being, self and not-self, eternity and noneternity, oneness and otherness, existence and nonexistence. These are the grooves in which the mind is caught and kept imprisoned, so that it can never take a new direction and never get a glimpse of the great mystery of nonduality, which in the philosophical language of Mahāyāna Buddhism is *śūnyatā* (the emptiness of all conceptual positions) and which, exactly as Socrates's sense of wonder, opens new, unheard-of dimensions of consciousness and spiritual exploration.

This sense of wonder is what gives depth to our experience or vision of the world; it is the spiritual dimension of depth, the indispensable space for the unfoldment and growth of our mind. It is the background without which the experience of freedom would not be possible; it is the psychic breathing space without which our soul would suffocate. It is the starting point of every spiritual activity, the "conditio sine qua non" of all inner movement and creative emotion, the liquifier and dissolver of all that is cramped, hardened, or coagulated within us.

We need a spiritual rebirth to see the world with new eyes, without the prejudices and worn-out associations which have accumulated like a crust around the source of living experience. That which has hardened into a fixed form already belongs to the realm of death, and if we identify ourselves with it we are delivering ourselves unto death.

Instead of realizing the elements of immortality which lie in the very process of becoming, we cling to its external forms, to its material byproducts, and thus we block the living stream which connects us with the universe. Lao-tse expresses a similar idea when he compares man to a low valley through which rivers flow, or to a channel of universal forces. A river or a channel has two functions: that of receiving and that of giving, but not that of keeping. He who tries to keep life or any of its gifts to himself thereby loses both. The ego closes the channel and converts it into an evil-smelling pool, a breeding ground of death and decay.

Therefore, there is no illusion more dangerous, more inimical to life, than the illusion of the ego; no illness deadlier than the illness of craving and clinging. Wisdom does not consist in the accumulation of abstract knowledge or a collection of facts, but in the openness, the receptivity of the spirit which is born from the sense of wonder, while ignorance—real ignorance—is characterized by the absence of it.

Charles Morgan, through the mouth of one of his unforgettable characters (in his novel *The Fountain*) discusses this idea in the following words:

> I supposed that ignorance was what chiefly separated the mortal from the immortal state, and I believed that death would be a door to secrets—that after it everything would be made plain. Nor do I suggest now that the greater knowledge and understanding are not attained to in the immortal state; but that they are the distinguishing essence of God I no longer believe. What I have hitherto called omniscience is better thought of as infinite power of wonder. Knowledge is static, a stone in the stream itself—in common men a trickle clouded by doubt, in poets and saints a sparkling rivulet, in God a mighty river, bearing the whole commerce of the divine mind. Is it not true

that, even on earth, as knowledge increases, wonder deepens?

And it is equally true, we may add, that knowledge decreases or loses in importance if the sense of wonder has disappeared. People who have lost this faculty are empty and shallow, and their teachings are platitudes in spite of their scientific vocabulary and their pseudophilosophical detachment which sails under the flag of logic and objectivity. A philosophy or religion which tries to deprive man of his inborn sense of wonder by attempting to explain everything or by rejecting everything that cannot be explained, is nothing but an artificial construction of the intellect, and as such it will never be able to influence or to direct life, but will only impede it. It is a blind alley, a river that disappears in the sand. For it is not the business of philosophy, nor that of religion, to explain the world, but to give it depth and meaning and—most important of all—to clarify man's position in it.

It goes without saying that the sense of wonder is not to be confused with a belief in miracles or obscure mysticism—a mixture of sensationalism and emotionality—but is based on the acknowledgment of a reality which surpasses the realm of logic and has nothing in common with metaphysical speculation. In fact, it is precisely the awe of the inexpressible which prevents those who have experienced it from discussing it in words and from indulging in speculations. They content themselves with hinting at it, and they do so with the help of similes, symbols, and paradoxes, because these are the only forms which defy the dissecting knife of the intellect and the petrifying effect of dogmatic thought.

The sense of wonder is based on the admission that our intellect is a limited and finite instrument of information and expression, reserved for specific practical uses, but not fit to represent the completeness of our being. It is the profound respect for a mystery which may be known but never revealed because it is too great to be shown in its completeness, too closely interwoven to be taken apart, too subtle and immaterial to be exposed to the glaring light of the day. It was respect for the mystery and wonder of ultimate things which made Tibetan sādhakas refrain from speaking about their deepest experiences and practices to the uninitiated, not because there was anything secret in their practice, but because the very attempt to put it into words destroyed or misinterpreted the subtle quality of the actual experience. By conceptually objectifying an intimately subjective experience, we create a barrier between the experiencer and the experience and thus destroy the inseparable unity created by the inspirational climax of the meditational process. This is why even Tantric sādhana-texts confine themselves to a mere skeleton of terse injunctions and instructions which can be understood only after adequate preparation and initiation by the Guru. In translating and indiscriminately publishing such texts to satisfy the curiosity of a public that is not only unfamiliar with their spiritual background, but totally lacking in religious experience and reverence for an ancient tradition, we only create more misconceptions and mislead those who believe they can follow such instructions on their own or blindly use mantras into which they have not been initiated.

Some dreams stand out more clearly than any experience of our waking mind, but dissolve into meaningless details the moment we try to tell them or to describe them objectively. It is as if all that is describable is nonessential. Objectivation and objectivity separate the object from the experiencing subject. But in all cases of real knowledge, of immediate or spontaneous perception, the unity of subject and object is so complete that any separation is equal to a destruction of its vital essence. The closer our relationship to something, the less we can demonstrate it or talk about it. This is why Goethe could say: "The highest works of art are those which have the highest truth but no trace of [objective] reality."

Only those who understand the depth of these words, can appreciate the real significance of religious art which—especially in the Tibetan tradition— reflects a reality of spiritual experience that reveals to the sensitive mind far more than do all learned treatises and scholastic scriptures. It is here that we come in direct touch with a reality which may baffle our intellect, but which fills us with that sense of wonder which opens the way to the inner sanctuary of our mind, to the heart of the great mystery of life and death, and beyond into the Plenum-Void of Inner Space from which we derive our conception of an outer universe that we mistake for the only genuine reality. In other words, our reality is our own creation, the creation of our senses as well as of our mind (i.e.

the mental activity, interpreting our sense-impressions and feelings); and both depend on the level and the dimension of our present state of consciousness.

9

CONTEMPLATIVE ZEN MEDITATION AND THE INTELLECTUAL ATTITUDE OF OUR TIME

ALTHOUGH ZEN, the contemplative Buddhism of the Far East, is a way toward the overcoming of our limited intellectual attitudes, we must first have developed the capacity of thinking and the faculty of discrimination before we can really appreciate and practice it. One cannot go beyond an intellect which one has never developed and mastered, or which, in other words, one has never acquired or possessed in this sense. It is a common phenomenon that precisely those who are lacking in intellectual qualities are the most vociferous in condemning them. The intellect, however, is as necessary for the overcoming of mere emotionality and spiritual confusion as intuition is necessary for the overcoming of intellectual limitations and conceptual abstractions.

The intellect that stops halfway is the greatest hindrance to spiritual progress. The intellect that goes to the very limit of its capacity in the full understanding of its own nature and limitations is a valuable help in spiritual life. It acts like the rudder of a ship. But as the rudder can work only as long as the ship is moving and is powerless if there is no propulsive force, so the intellect can function adequately only if moved by the force of inner experience—in other words, as long as the individual progresses mentally or spiritually by moving beyond his present condition or striving beyond himself. Only where such movement exists is it possible for the intellect to fulfill its legitimate functions, namely to create order, to discriminate, to select critically, and to maintain a consistent direction toward the solution of a practical or mental problem or the attainment of a desired aim.

Those who live only in their emotions are like a rudderless ship; the merely intellectual—but aimless—individual is like a ship without a driving force, whose rudder does not find the necessary resistence to act upon and, therefore, exhausts itself in useless movements without any effect. Applied to the human condition, this results in empty activities and spiritual stagnation. On the other hand, a man whose intellect stops halfway, incapable of pursuing a subject or problem to its last possible conclusion, or who regards the problem only in a partial or one-sided way, is like a helmsman who moves the steering-wheel in only one direction and whose ship, therefore, runs in circles.

The remedy for this, however, is not to throw the intellect overboard, but to use it in a fuller, less limited way by freeing it from the ruts of habit and allowing it to proceed to the very limits of its capacity, where words and thoughts cease and where intuition replaces conceptual reasoning. By freeing ourselves from habitual thought-patterns, we break the monotony of a deadly cycle and put ourselves in relationship to all that exists; then we find the courage for the leap over the chasm that separates us from the completeness and universality of our true nature. This is the main purport of Zen, and this is the point where its apparent irrationality comes into play.

It is a strange paradox that Zen, in spite of its irrationality, appeals more to the intellectual than to the nonintellectual. In Japan, Zen was more or less the privilege of the Samurai, the ruling class, whose higher standard of education and discipline played a great part in the historical development and practice of Zen. On the other hand it must be admitted that underneath the apparent irrationality of Zen there is a solid basis of rationality; Zen does not depend on any belief in dogmas, rituals, or traditional thought, but relies on direct experience and unprejudiced observation. Experience, however, is the common ground from which both science and mysticism arise. The only difference between these two realms of experience is that the truth of science is objectively verifiable, while that of mystic experience can be verified only subjectively.

The fact that Zen does not accept preconceived ideas, opinions, dogmas, and articles of faith, keeping aloof from all that popularly goes under the name of religion, has greatly impressed the scientific and antireligious attitude of modern

Westerners. The extremely individualistic method of Zen impresses the intellectual, while the appreciation of beauty and nature attracts the artistic mind.

But just because Zen meets modern taste and mentality halfway, there is a certain danger of superficiality; people take over outer forms of Zen without doing justice to their inner meaning. As long as paradoxes help us to free our mind from habitual ways of thinking and shake us out of conventional ruts and solidified dogmas, they fulfill a useful and wholesome purpose. If, however, playing with paradoxes becomes a kind of intellectual game, it leads nowhere except to a cynical destruction of all values. The latter, however, was never intended by genuine Zen. In this respect it is completely different from the modern intellectual attitude which thinks itself superior because of its freedom from religious beliefs and traditional values. The intrinsic value of man and of all living beings, however humble they may be, is implicit in Zen; each form of life is looked upon as a unique exponent of a consciousness that pervades and embraces the whole universe.

The attitude of Zen is, therefore, neither agnostic nor libertinistic, like that of modern man who has lost faith in himself and in the world. On the contrary, the attitude of Zen rests on the deep conviction of a universal law (*dharma*) and the meaningfulness of all that exists (not to be confused with the "purpose" of a teleological system), in which the individual experience is as important as the abstract law, the impermanent as significant as the eternal. The eternal can be experienced only in the present moment, the infinite only in the finite, the universal only in the individual.

"It is through conscious individual existence," says Sri Aurobindo, "that the developing consciousness becomes organized and capable to awaken into its own reality. The tremendous significance of individual being which increases in the measure in which it rises in the order of the world, is the most remarkable and important fact of the universe, which began without individuality in an undifferentiated state of nescience. This significance can only be justified if the self as individual is not less real than the self as cosmic being or spirit and if both are forces of eternity.... Only in this way we can explain the necessity for the origination of something individual ... and the discovery of itself as a precondition of the cosmic self and consciousness and of the highest reality."

The unconventionality of Zen Buddhism exists against the background of a profound metaphysical tradition which is so alive that it can renounce conventional concepts. Zen's rejection of religious dogmas and formulated beliefs does not spring from a skeptical attitude, but from an indescribable certainty, born from inner experience of reality.

We "believe" in things only when we are not certain of them. We do not "believe" in the existence of the sun; we see it, feel it, live in its light and warmth. In a similar way Zen does not doubt the values of religion and tradition, but only the methods by which they have been conventionalized. Zen wants to open a direct way toward those values and forces which are the living source of all culture, religion, and tradition.

If, however, people who have lost the connection with these forces and values try to use Zen methods in a spiritual vacuum, they will hardly get beyond intellectual jugglery and a superficial aestheticism. Then Zen will become an excuse to live as one always did, only giving different labels to the same actions: waywardness will be made into spontaneity, weakness into the principle of nonviolence, laziness into the ideal of nonaction, lack of logic into spiritual profundity, and emotionality into inspiration.

The practice of Zen can be successful only—and this applies to every spiritual discipline or method of meditation—if it proceeds from a truly religious attitude or a living tradition which recognizes those fundamental values which give depth and meaning to human existence.

10

RELIGION AND SCIENCE

SINCE THE MEANING AND THE SIGNIFICANCE of scientific "facts" depend on the context in which they are seen, on the premises from which the scientist starts, and on the general intellectual and cultural attitude of his time, "facts" may turn into the very opposite of what they were supposed to be originally. Science, therefore, could just as well be seen from the point of view of psychology.

Both religion and science strive after truth and can, therefore, exist side by side without contradicting each other and without impeding each other. But this does not mean that they can be amalgamated, because their essential difference is not so much in their aims and objects as in their methods. The method of scientific research is outwardly directed; that of religion, inwardly; and each of these methods can achieve its best results if it follows its own inherent laws. The nature of science consists in observation and deduction from sense data, i.e., perception and observation of physical processes. The nature of religion—as well as that of art—is based on intuition derived from psychic experience. Just as art does not require to prove the value of its creations by their accord with scientific observations (though such accord may happen to exist sometimes), religious truth does not depend on science (though it need not contradict it).

Science, due to its reliance on outer facts, always remains incomplete, fragmentary (though philosophy tries to fill in the gaps), while religion, like every true and spontaneous work of art, always represents something that is complete in itself because of its intuitive character, born from the experience of the oneness of man and his world or the essential universality of his being.

Science is the human endeavor to grow beyond nature.

Religion is the striving of man to grow beyond himself.

The mental attitude from which science springs is reflection. The attitude of religion is devotion. This does not mean that religion excludes reflection or that science excludes devotion. But reflection is not sufficient to create a religion, and devotion is not sufficient to create science: but the reverse is possible.

The fact that all religions agree in the denunciation of egoism is not due to supernatural revelation or to profound reflection or mental exertion, but lies in the very nature of religion. Devotion is the opposite of selfishness.

With this we arrive at the definition of the religious man. Religious individuals are not those who believe in a certain dogma or in the truth of certain teachings, or those who follow certain moral rules, but those who are filled with true devotion and act accordingly.

The function of religion is not to produce certain beliefs, ideas, and conventional morality; it is a spontaneous psychic tendency, inborn in man, a centrifugal spiritual force that acts as a counterweight and a balance against the natural centripetal force of egoism. In the animal the centripetal tendency is most prominent; in the saint the centrifugal; he gives himself without reserve and feels himself one with all. The average man occupies the middle position.

Religion, therefore, is not merely a means to an end, but something that carries its meaning in itself, just as does life. Indeed, religion is a spiritual form of life, an individual intensification of consciousness on a general human, if not cosmic, foundation. It is the nature of religion to release the individual from his sense of separateness, convert him into a social being, and raise him into a state of universal awareness.

Moral judgements such as "good" and "bad" have nothing to do with religion as such. Morality is only a secondary product of religion, but not its purpose. Moral people are often entirely irreligious, and immoral people may sometimes be astonishingly religious. To identify religion with morality is one of the most tragic errors of humanity. It degrades religion into a narrow-minded puritanism, until even the best of men lose faith in it. The Western antagonism against religion is due mainly to this error, which was made worse by confusing morality with sex.

Due to this puritanical attitude, primitive religions were looked down upon, though from the standpoint of religious intensity, of direct experience and sincere devotion, even the shamanism of the most primitive South Sea Islanders, or similar tribal traditions in remote parts of Asia or Africa, may be regarded as superior to many a modern form of secularized religion.

We may regard the customs and ideas of primitive peoples as naive; nevertheless a deep truth is hidden in an attitude that does not allow a single event of life to pass by without invoking the spirits of earth and heaven, of water and winds, of trees and mountains. We have neglected these for so long in our uninhibited exploitation of nature that now the very elements take revenge on us. How different an attitude in which "the whole nature is asked to give its blessings at the dawning of a new life or the departure of a soul," as Laurence Binyon says in his *Spirit of Man in Asian Art*.

> All nature is implored to be beneficent . . . to every undertaking that is concerned with the tilling of the fruitful earth or helps to build the social fabric centered in the life of the family. It is the credulous, popular side of what in the minds of poets, artists and philosophers, becomes a singular completeness of vision, a juster sense of man's place in the universe and of the relation of human life to the lives outside it, than has ever prevailed in the West.

It is indeed strange that what poets, thinkers, and artists—the actual creators of Western culture—have expressed in their greatest works is looked upon as primitive superstition when it is practiced and made into a living expression of religious faith by people who are still in close touch with nature.

Only a religion that is capable of giving meaning to our life and the world that surrounds us has value and the right to exist. To give meaning, however, does not consist in a superficial justification of all that exists, but always points beyond our individual limitations and sense-impressions, thus creating the dynamic element necessary to all life and to all genuine effort on our part.

However, the ethical attitude which grows from such a meaningful understanding of life differs from a morality of commands and prohibitions by being in conformity with our innermost convictions. It is not forced upon us; it is something that flows spontaneously from the depth of our being, in harmony with ourselves and the world in which we live. Thus, the higher the religion and the purer our devotion, the higher will be our ethical standard.

11

THE CREATIVE POWER OF THE MIND

WE COMPLAIN ABOUT the impermanence of the world and of our own corporeality as long as we do not know that we ourselves have created them. But he who knows that throughout eternity we have created our innumerable bodies and the worlds experienced through them, will bemoan the transiency of these creations as little as the singer will grieve over the vanishing notes of his song since he knows he can recreate them whenever he wishes.

Herein lies the secret of immortality: we are immortal not by holding on, but by letting go. Whatever we master, we need not cling to; we can always create it anew, thanks to the creative power of the sovereign spirit within us.

Do not the flowers awaken every spring? Nature is lavish due to its creative power. Only the uncreative mind clings to the solidified dregs of life.

The mere belief in an immortal soul, or the conviction that something in us survives death, does not make us immortal unless we know what it is that survives and that we are capable of identifying ourselves with it. Most human beings choose death instead of immortality by identifying themselves with that which is perishable and impermanent, by clinging stubbornly to the body or the momentary elements of the present personality, which they mistake for the soul or the essential form of life.

Differently expressed: immortality is within our reach but like a poor man who does not know that a treasure is hidden in his house, we are not able to make use of it. If we do not know of what immortality consists, it is as useless as a buried treasure—and even more so if we know that it exists and do not know where to search for it.

If a man dies and is reborn without recognizing the identity (or, more correctly, the connection) with his previous life, he truly has died, and will die again and again in the midst of all his immortality. As long as we cannot reestablish the connection between one life and another, our immortality remains a mere concept and never becomes a reality.

But why should we establish the connection between one life and another, instead of letting each of them rest in itself? With the same justification we might ask: why not let each day rest in itself and make every morning a new beginning?

The answer is simple: we would sink to the level of animal life by merely satisfying our physical needs or following our momentary moods and impulses without conscious connection with past activities and experiences or any purposeful direction of our individual existence. Our life and death would be entirely dependent on outer conditions. Perhaps we should be happier—as long as our physical needs were satisfied—but we should have to renounce all that we value most: our human nature and achievements, our cultural life, our spiritual aspirations—in short, each and every kind of meaningful activity or creative effort, or any endeavor to grow beyond our present state of knowledge and imperfection.

To live in the present "timeless" moment may be a valuable experience, but it does not solve the riddle of our existence. It is like wanting to hold onto the pause between two breaths and declaring it the only real state (the ultimate state of "emptiness"), while denying the value or the necessity of the other two functions of breathing, namely inhaling and exhaling. Emptiness has meaning only in conjunction with fullness or plentitude.

The importance of the present moment does not justify our denial of past and future. Without the past the present would have no meaning. There cannot be mind without memory or culture without history and tradition. But some of the self-appointed prophets of our time dispose of all these things by designating them as worthless because they are "conditioned."

But why should the fact that something is conditioned be regarded as negative or worthless? Why not recognize the fact that *there is nothing in the universe that is not conditioned,* in fact, that the world (and that relates to the world of the spirit as well as to the phenomenal world) is a system of infinite relations, an organic whole, in which every single part is related to and conditioned by all the others. On the lowest plane this conditioning appears as the law of cause and effect, in which causality is equal to determinism and [mechanical] necessity. But on the next higher planes of organic life (i.e., of self-perpetuating organisms) an element of individuality appears, and this causes the first breach in the principle of pure determinism and predictability. An element of chance (as we may call it) or of choice and, therefore, free will seems to be possible. But as long as an organism is not yet conscious of itself, it cannot make use of the chances which offer themselves. Consciousness (and not only consciousness, but reflective consciousness, aware not only of its surroundings, but of its own existence, that is, conscious of itself) is therefore the precondition of freedom of choice, the very foundation of all spiritual values and of all that gives meaning to life and justification to our existence.

Just as every instrument in an orchestra plays its own part in the general score, but finds its consummation and highest fulfillment in the perfect coordination and meaningful relationship of all the instruments of the orchestra, so every individual consciousness finds its consummation in a perfect relationship with the universe in all its variety of life-forms and individual forces which allow neither standstill nor stagnation.

But only he who knows the complete score can play his tune to perfection. This means that unless we reach the state of enlightenment or universal consciousness (in which the universe presents itself as the totality of our past, from which we sprang) unless we reach this ultimate state, we cannot find our highest fulfillment.

Those who refuse to play their part because they are unable or unwilling to "condition" themselves to the whole through practice and experience until they have reached that perfect "tuning in" will merely drop out of the orchestra in proud isolation and die a spiritual death. They are not heroes, merely failures, due to their incapacity to coordinate their individual movements with the greater rhythm of life. Because they hate change and try to hold onto the present, they deny the existence of time. They do not understand that melody means an unfoldment of movement in time, and that even the moments of silence, of apparent timelessness—the pauses within the melody—become meaningful through the unfolding movement in the eternal stream of time.

To separate timelessness (or the experience of eternity) from time, is like trying to play only the pauses of a symphony! The meaningfulness of the present moment, the complete experience of the present, without reference to past and future, does not invalidate the existence of memory or of the past or the future. Nor is it true that such an experience leaves no remembrance. On the contrary, such moments may be remembered for a lifetime as highlights of experience.

To despise creative thought and imagination because they are conditioned, is like discarding music because it moves in time—and more so, because timing and rhythm are essential elements of music. And yet, it is in music, more than in any other art-form, that we experience timelessness—a sense of being lifted out of time, out of ourselves, out of all limitations of our self-confined consciousness—in the most remarkable way.

To live only in the present may be a high achievement for one who has mastered the past; but not for those who merely want to forget the past because they are unable to face it and to transform it. Only he who has transformed the past by accepting it in its entirety as his universal foundation, and raising it into his present consciousness as an integral part of his individuality and life, can experience the fullness of the present moment in which the eternity of time or the timelessness of eternity can be realized, as the Buddha realized in the moment of his enlightenment. But to accomplish this we have to go the aeon-long way of the Buddha, the way of spiritual growth which, like the growth of all living things, unfolds in time.

We can accelerate this process if we make use of our previous and present experiences: this is the purpose and meaning of the faculty of remembrance— not the clinging to past memories, but the making use of them in the present. In this way memory is transformed into a sense of responsibility and a conscious dimension which gives us freedom of movement and the choice of direction.

Those, however, who live only in the present—and for the present—without having faced, mastered, and accepted their past, merely shun their responsibilities in the enjoyment of the moment, only to discover that they are not capable of remaining in this blissful state. They sink back all the more into a meaningless life, governed by clock-time activities and self-centered aims. The spontaneity of the moment is not a gift from heaven, but the outcome of lifelong practice and endeavor in the cultivation of insight and absorption in creative meditation.

It is here that the connection from one life to another becomes possible in the realization that the essentials of the past and their creative forces are still alive within our depth-consciousness. By recognizing these essentials, we are in a position to continue and to intensify our efforts toward self-realization in a consciously directed and meaningful way.

In speaking of the essentials of the past and their creative forces, it should be understood that we are not concerned with the accidentals in form of personal and emotionally related remembrances of former lives, but with the discovery of those laws that govern the continuity of consciousness, i.e., our spiritual heredity from one incarnation to another. Having realized this, we should not waste our time and effort in exploring or reviving the details of our past, but direct our energies toward the creation of a new spiritual body which determines our further life and our future rebirth. This inner body which grows in the steady cultivation of intense meditational practice is known as the "Diamond Body" (*vajra-kāya*) in Buddhist terminology, because its nature is indestructible and transparent, it is the realization of our Buddha-nature which sooner or later ripens into the state of perfect enlightenment.

12

RELATIVITY OF PERFECTION

LIGHT INCESSANTLY MOVES through the universe, but it becomes visible only when it meets resistance. In the same way consciousness becomes aware of itself only when there is resistance. If this resistance is impenetrable or insurmountable, it is felt as suffering; if it can be mastered, it is felt as joy.

Joy means the overcoming of resistance. This is why people climb mountains, endure self-imposed hardships, and engage in all kinds of adventure and sports. Life becomes worthless and unbearable if there is no resistance or if the obstacles we meet cannot be mastered.

But what about aesthetic pleasure—the happiness of solitude or that of samādhi in which there is apparently no resistance? However, these states cannot be attained without overcoming hindrances or without mastering our instruments of perception and knowledge.

This is why we cannot dwell indefinitely in the bliss of samādhi or in the enjoyment of beauty. As soon as effort ceases and we get accustomed to a certain condition, joy also ceases.

It is only in the movement toward perfection that perfection can be experienced. Only in the movement toward the infinite is infinity experienced. Infinity attained is no more infinity. In order to enjoy the blissful state of samādhi, we have to develop it again and again. In order to enjoy beauty, we have to create it within ourselves.

Thus there cannot even be aesthetic pleasure without creative effort; and as there is more creative effort in the artist than in the person who beholds a work of art, the joy of the former is more intense.

The way to samādhi is a continuous process of spiritual renunciation, a continuous giving up. To give up a thing means to be free from it, to be master of oneself and of one's decisions.

Freedom exists in the act of renunciation. In other words, it is the faculty of renunciation that gives us power over ourselves and the things of the world around us. Not the things that we renounce but the act of renunciation is what matters. Therefore even samādhi has temporarily to be renounced if we do not want to lose that faculty, because a faculty which is not constantly reacquired loses its power.

If renunciation is genuine, then things can no more enslave us, but we have become their masters and can use them without danger. Then we can fearlessly go from the unity of samādhi into the diversity of the world. After we have convinced ourselves that we can do without things, we have now to prove that we have no more reason to fear them—that we can accept and even create them without losing our independence, our inner liberty.

It is the way of the Buddha: starting with the renunciation of the world, culminating in the realization of enlightenment, and leading back into the world through compassion. It is like the threefold process of breathing: the inward movement of inhalation, the moment of stopping or motionlessness, and the outward movement of exhalation.

Both sides of this process are repeated in Tantric meditation as practiced in Tibet; only here the objects are first produced from the state of "perfect emptiness," and afterward they are reduced again to "emptiness." Here the state of Buddhahood or Enlightenment which lies between the two movements has been chosen as the starting-point.

But how can such a starting point be chosen if the state of Buddhahood has not yet been actually attained? The answer is: because it is only in the movement toward perfection (which, after an intricate process of spiritual purification, is here produced temporarily as a mental image or symbol) that perfection can be experienced.

Perfection is not an absolute value or a static condition, but the harmony of forces that can be established in every moment in which their movement is coordinated by the direction toward a common aim. In such a moment these forces form a "universal" group (the word "universal" taken in its literal sense: directed toward one point), a universe in miniature.

But the ideal point toward which these forces move must lie in the infinite and can never be reached by them; otherwise they would clash and merge into each other, i.e. their ideal differentiation which is balanced by the common direction would be destroyed, and their movement, without which life is impossible, would be stopped. Harmony needs differentiation as much as it needs unity. One tone alone cannot make music.

Thus we can say that perfection is possible at each stage of development, in each form of life. A human being who has properly developed all his human qualities can be called perfect, though there may be other beings who surpass humans in many respects. And in the same way we can say that an animal which possesses all the qualities of its kind is perfect; and similarly a plant or a crystal which expresses harmoniously the characteristics of its nature.

Thus perfection exists neither as an end at the top of a scale, nor as an absolute or fixed measurement, but as an infinitesimal moment of harmony in movement.

In self-conscious beings this harmony is generally disturbed by exaggerated egocentricity and a destructive type of intellectualism. Only one who has completely overcome the illusion of egohood and its concomitant evils, i.e., one who has attained enlightenment, is able to dwell permanently in a state of harmony, which ordinarily we are able to experience only for short moments.

Harmony establishes itself more or less permanently by an organic or unconscious process of continuous readjustment in forms of life in which the balance has not yet been upset by the hypertrophic growth of ego consciousness. A similar continuous readjustment takes place in those individuals who have conquered the ego and regained their spiritual balance.

The difference between the perfection of a flower or of an animal and the perfection of an Enlightened One is that the former is unconscious, while the latter is conscious of the harmony which he has established by creative effort, and in which he continues to dwell by virtue of his wisdom, which makes a relapse into the unbalanced state impossible.

PART VI

DIMENSIONS OF CONSCIOUSNESS

1

LOGIC AND SYMBOL IN THE MULTI-DIMENSIONAL CONCEPTION OF THE UNIVERSE

MATHEMATICS, ATOMIC PHYSICS AND DEPTH-PSYCHOLOGY have burst the frame of our habitual thinking and of our conception of the universe. They have produced such a bewildering amount of specialized knowledge and new theories that the layman is thrown into a state of helpless confusion, because the familiar rules and expressions of his language are incapable of adequately expressing or assimilating the results of these sciences without violating the very laws on which his thinking is based.

It is, therefore, necessary to develop a new kind of thinking, free from the dogmatism of our self-created laws which—though being useful and justified in a world of concrete objects and concepts—are not compatible with the laws of a universe that goes far beyond our sense-experience and thought-forms. As it is not possible to assimilate the universe to our mode of thinking (and by "universe" I do not only mean the data of the outer, but also those of the inner world, hidden in the depth of the human psyche), there is no other alternative than to accommodate our thinking to the facts of the universe by trying to create a more all-inclusive basis for our thinking by freeing it from the narrowness of a one-sided dogmatism. This can only be achieved by overcoming our one-dimensional logic which—while proceeding in a straight line towards any given object—cuts the world apart with the knife of its "Either-Or," in order to build from the lifeless pieces of a dissected world a merely conceptual and totally abstract universe.

From an interview with Prof. Heisenberg in Munich I gained the impression that modern atomic physics has outstripped our present mode of thinking to such an extent that the discrepancy between the consciousness of the average man, who uses the results of science, and the knowledge of the scientist, who makes them possible, is so great that this will become a great danger for Western civilization and therefore in the end a danger for mankind which becomes more and more identified with this civilization.

This discrepancy between the perfection and power of the means created from a higher dimension of knowledge and the level of consciousness of those using them, must in the end result in a schizophrenic civilization in which man no longer controls these means because he no longer understands the powers at his disposal, but is controlled by them. He then resembles the magician's disciple who is no longer able to hold in check the powers which he has conjured up, because he is not related to their nature, he does not really know them.

It is, therefore, the task of the leading scientists to build a bridge toward the level of comprehension in the average man, so that the latter gains a conscious access to that world (or that spiritual dimension) which science tries to open up for him. For only the man who has conquered, gained this world spiritually, whose consciousness has reached this stage of knowledge is capable of using sensibly the forces derived from it without misusing their power. Only such a one is entitled to use them.

But in order to build a bridge toward that stage of knowledge, first of all a new language is needed, not so much in the sense of a new vocabulary which is, in any case, taken over by the layman without much difficulty—but in the sense of a new way of thinking, an extended multidimensional logic which is as different from the classical Aristotelian logic as Euclidian geometry is from Einstein's theory of relativity.

The creation of such a way of thinking may be helped by a knowledge of Eastern logic, especially Indian thought. While Western logic moves in a straight line from a definite "point of view," an unambiguously defined premise, toward the object of thought or contemplation, the Eastern way of thinking rather consists in a circling round the object of contemplation. The Western "frontal attack" leads to a quicker and unambiguous result; but it is as unambiguous as it is one-sided.

The East gains by a constantly renewed "concentric attack," by moving in ever decreasing circles toward the object, a many-sided, i.e. multidimensional, impression formed from the sum-total or the integrating superimposition of single impressions from different points of view—until in the last, conceptually no longer intelligible, stage of this concentric approach, the experiencing subject becomes one with the object of contemplation. Out of this experience the symbol, the directing sign (comparable to the symbolic language of mathematics) and the self-transcending paradox is born.

The new language thus resembles more the language of the poets than that of conventional scientists; and therefore in atomic science an idiom has been evolved in which one—as Heisenberg demonstrated by the example of the mutually exclusive theories of waves and particles respectively—though describing the actual facts, uses *contradictory* images.

As it is impossible to find out exactly the spatial position and the speed belonging to the time-dimension of an elementary particle, at the same time, one has, as Heisenberg says, "to use in atomic physics two mutually *exclusive* ways of description which, however, also *complement* each other, so that only by playing with the different similes or images an adequate description of the event is finally achieved."

Bohr spoke, as Heisenberg mentioned in this connection, of a complementary relation of the two concepts of place and speed. "This fact of a complementary relation has also resulted in physicists being satisfied with an imprecise and symbolic language when talking about atomic events. They are only trying, like the poets, to conjure up by image and symbol in the listener's mind certain movements pointing in the intended direction without forcing him by an unambiguous formulation to follow precisely a certain train of thought."

In this way of thinking, therefore, it is not a matter of fixing the mind according to the system of classical logic, according to which two opposite statements cannot be true at the same time and according to which there is no third possibility—but to keep the mind moving, i.e. to change the viewpoint by letting it, as in Indian logic, circle round the object contemplated. This way would as little abolish conventional logic as the multidimensional logic of higher mathematics, but would apportion to each of these types of logic its own place. Between the dualistic Aristotelian logic, dominated by the law of contraries and the excluded third, and the logic of higher mathematics, a whole scale of systems of logic can be inserted.

As an example, the four propositions of Indian logic are here adduced:
1. is
2. is not

3. is and is not
4. neither is nor is not.

In other words, the four statements postulate:
1. Being (or "existence" of the object)
2. Not-being
3. Being as well as Not-being.
4. Neither Being nor Not-being.

The first two statements refer to the realm of concrete objects perceptible by the senses or through concepts, the realm of fixed entities, where we can speak of identity or non-identity. The third statement refers to the realm of relativity and corresponds to the stage of living-organic events. The fourth statement refers to the realm of transcendental experience, exceeding sense perception and concepts, because its objects are infinite and accessible only to intuition, i.e. to direct experience or the experiencing of higher dimensions.

We can understand only as much of the world as we have developed and realized within ourselves. As Plotinus (the Alexandrian philosopher of the third century of our era) wrote in his letters to Flaccus:

> Truth, therefore, is not the agreement of our apprehension of an external object with the object itself. It is the agreement of the mind with itself. Consciousness, therefore, is the whole basis of certainty. The mind is its own witness. Reason sees in itself that which is above itself and its source; and again, that which is below itself is still itself once more.
>
> Knowledge has three degrees—opinion, science, illumination. The means or instrument of the first is sense; of the second, dialectic; of the third, intuition. To the last I subordinate reason. It is absolute knowledge founded on the identity of the mind knowing with the object known.

Intuitive knowledge is free from partiality or dualism; it has overcome the extremes of stressing subject or object.

It is the vision of a world-synthesis, the experience of cosmic consciousness where the Infinite is realized not only conceptually but actually. Although there is in every one of the lower states of consciousness something present which leads or points towards the next stage, it is impossible to solve problems belonging to a higher dimension of consciousness from the point of view of a lower level of consciousness. This is why scientific problems cannot be solved from an egocentrically conditioned emotional point of view, or metaphysical problems or those of modern atomic or astro-physics lying beyond the realm of the finite, by using the laws of the world of three-dimensional experience or by a limited logic derived from it.

> If we desire to escape from the three-dimensional world and go farther, we must first of all work out the fundamental logical principle which would permit us to observe the relation of things in a world of many dimensions—seeing them in a certain reasonableness and not complete absurdity. If we enter there armed only with the principles of the logic of the three-dimensional world, these principles will drag us back, will not give us the chance to rise from the earth. (Ouspensky)

In this way each plane has its own laws and its own problems, and the methods helpful toward a solution in one case can become a hindrance in another. One of the main hindrances when considering multidimensional phenomena is the premise of a temporal-causal connection expressed in classical logic by the principle of "sufficient cause."

If we consider, instead of the sequence, the simultaneity of certain seemingly unconnected phenomena, we shall often be able to observe a parallelism, a coincidence of certain qualities, not causally or temporally conditioned, but rather giving the impression of a cross section of an organically connected whole. And conversely, we can observe in the sequence of certain events or experiences an "unfolding" in time of a structure of a higher dimension of reality which is independent from time and so-to-speak "pre-existent."

The relations between individual qualities and destinies and planetary constellations, as observed by astrology, are not necessarily causally conditioned, i.e. due to the "influences" of the respective planets, but may just as well, if not better, be explained as parallel events in our acausal synchronic situation.

The constellation of the stars, in this case, serves only as a system of co-ordination to define or characterize a certain situation. Such situations are undergoing a constant change and appear to us as causally conditioned phenomena happening in a time-sequence. By apprehending this time-sequence as real (i.e. effective) and the single moment as an impermanent, in itself unimportant link in the chain of causal events, we are fettered to the one-sided direction of an irreversible dimension of time, which progresses, as it were, horizontally, i.e. on the level (surface) of our individual consciousness, without realizing the vertical connections leading into the depths, perceptible in the state of "deep sleep," of the "timeless" moment in which the living organic oneness of the whole universe is present and concentrated as in a focus.

If we regard the horizontal as the direction of our time-space development (unfolding), then the vertical is the direction of our going within, toward the universal center of our being and thus the realization of the timeless presence of all potentialities of existence in the organic structure of the whole of the living universe. But while the horizontal probably—i.e. according to the laws of all movement in space—forms an infinitely large circle (which therefore appears as a straight line) or a spiral movement in which certain phases are repeated rhythmically (without ever being absolutely identical)—this is the regularity observable in all change—the vertical moves toward the motionless center of this circular movement, i.e. toward the timeless present inherent in all existence. This is what the poets call the "eternity of the moment" which can be experienced in the state of complete inwardness, i.e. when we turn within (instead of toward the outside world) toward the center of our own essence and being, such as happens during meditation and creative inspiration.

In an earlier work of mine[1] I have illustrated those two directions by a circular diagram in which the movement along the periphery represents the time-spatial development of the individual, and the movements vertical to it, toward the center, represent the increasing stages of inwardness. The more the inwardness progresses, i.e. the more we approach the inner center, the more universal becomes experience, and when reaching the center we realize the full range of our conscious being, the totality of universal consciousness.

Consciousness progresses in this fashion from limited to wider, from lower to higher dimensions, and each higher dimension includes the qualities of the lower, i.e. it incorporates them into a higher system of relations. Therefore the criterion of the consciousness or cognition of a higher dimension consists in the coordinated and simultaneous perception of several directions of movement within a wider unity, without destroying those individual features which had characterized the lower dimensions thus integrated.

It is important to stress this, for nothing would be more dangerous than a frivolous throwing overboard of the normal logical thinking appropriate to our world, in favor of seemingly profound paradoxes, as has become the fashion in some intellectual movements of our time (and not the least in modern art). Until we have achieved a clear cognition of the laws underlying our three-dimensional world it is useless to be occupied with a higher dimension (whose substructure is represented by those laws). We must first have reached the limits of our thinking before we are qualified to transcend them.

But until then we must make do with the symbols provided by language and the archetypes of consciousness; for such symbols have, as C. G. Jung says, the great advantage of being able to unite heterogeneous and incommensurable factors in one single image. This is true for the symbols of mathematics as well as for those of depth consciousness: on both roads can we progress towards the cognition of higher dimensions, and even now we can see that they largely complement one another.

References and Notes

[1] *The Psychological Attitude of Early Buddhist Philosophy*, Patna University 1937, Rider, London 1961.

2

THE CONCEPTION OF SPACE IN ANCIENT BUDDHIST ART AND THOUGHT

I

ACCORDING TO SPENGLER, the conception of infinite space is an exclusively Occidental idea, a creation of the "Faustic" consciousness, entirely foreign to Greeks and Romans, as well as to Indians and Egyptians. "What *'infinite space,'* this creative interpretation of the experience of depth by us people of the Occident, and by us alone, tries to express,—this kind of dimension, which the Greeks called the Nothing, and which we call the All,—saturates the world with a color, which neither the Greek or Roman, nor the Indian or the Egyptian soul had on its palette."[1]

India has produced quite a number of philosophical theories and definitions of space, a fact which in itself shows that the experience of space was strong enough to give rise to serious speculations, and to influence religious doctrines and practices to such an extent that it can hardly be said that Indians took a negative attitude toward the problem of space, as may have been the case with the ancient civilizations of the Mediterranean.

It cannot even be maintained seriously that the experience of the mere idea of "infinite space" is a peculiarly Western achievement or a characteristic of the "Faustic" soul or the "Faustic" consciousness, because the concept of the "infinity of space" is one of the fundamental ideas of Buddhism, which is all the more important as it derives its value not merely from philosophical considerations or intellectual speculations, but is based on direct spiritual experience, achieved by the systematic exploration of the human mind in the process of meditation.

The philosophical definitions which were evolved later on, though interesting in themselves, are of secondary importance in comparison to this experience. The infinity of space, which is frequently mentioned in the most ancient Pāli texts as ākāsanañcāyatana, has retained its importance all through the Buddhist literature up to the present day, and it was known as one of the higher states of yoga-experience even before the advent of Buddhism, as the Buddha himself acknowledges when describing the yoga-exercises of his brahmanical teachers.

The word ākāśa itself is significant, as it is derived from the root kās, "to shine." It implies an active, if not creative quality of space, something which is connected with movement, vibration or radiation (comparable to the former hypothesis of ether in physics). Even in the negative definition of the Sautrantikas, who denied the reality of space in contrast to other Schools of Buddhism, the idea of movement seems to have been instinctively associated with the concept of space, when they circumscribed it as the "non-existence of obstruction (or hindrances)."

The Theravādins, who neither maintained nor denied the reality of the outer world, confined themselves to the psychological—and thus necessarily subjective—standpoint, and therefore arrived at a conclusion very similar to that of Kant, who declared space to be an element or a property of our mind. They defined *ākāsa* as a permanent mental element (*niccapaññatti*), thus giving *ākāsa* a higher degree of (subjective) reality than matter, which is enumerated under the impermanent mental properties that have only a momentary phenomenal existence.

The Sarvāstivādins, on the other hand, believed in the objective existence of space, and classified it as one of the three unconditioned elements (*dharmas*) out of their list of 75 existing *dharmas*, of which 72 were conditioned, while the remaining two unconditioned elements were equivalents of *nirvāna*, namely the conscious (*pratisamkyā*) and the unconscious (*apratisamykā*) cessation of passion. Thus, space and *nirvāna* were the only lasting elements, and therefore a kind of higher reality. The fact that they could not be described in positive terms does not weaken their reality, because all positive qualities belonged to the world of conditioned elements, having no independent reality. The positive value which space had in the minds of early Buddhists could not have been demonstrated better than by its association with *nirvāna*.

We can observe a striking parallelism in the development of modern Western civilization, in which, according to Spengler, pure, active space appears as the essence of real being ("wahres Sein"). It is *being*, pure and simple. Objects of sense-perception, therefore, appear as facts of secondary value—we significantly speak of them as space-filling objects, thus assigning to them their relative rank—and with regard to the act of understanding and judging Nature, these sense-perceptions are felt as questionable, as appearance and hindrance which must be overcome if, as a philosopher or a physicist, one wants to discover the real essence of being. The Western skepsis never turned against space, but always against concrete things only. Space is the higher concept—force is only a less abstract expression for it—and mass appears only as its counter-concept, i.e., as that which exists *in* space.[2]

This is exactly what happened in the history of Buddhist philosophy. Its skepsis never turned against space, but always against concrete things, which we regarded as illusory and unreal, together with all the other sense-perceptions. This tendency reached its climax in Nāgārjuna's Śūnyavāda (the teaching that all things are "empty" (śūnya) of an unchangeable substance, and at the same time Buddhist universalism found its strongest expression.

The anthropocentric character of Buddhism turned more and more into a cosmic attitude. The human character of the historical Buddha gave place to innumerable Dhyāni-Buddhas and Bodhisattvas, who filled and penetrated the infinity of space in an ever-expanding movement.

Infinity is the key-note of the Mahāyāna, which, according to Mahāyāna-Śraddhotpada-Śāstra, is interpreted as three kinds of "immensities": The first immensity is its all-embracing wholeness (dharma-kāya), the second is its immensity of potentiality (sambhoga-kāya), the third is the immensity of its manifesting activities (nirmāna-kāya).

The Mahāyāna conceives of numberless world-systems, peopled by an infinite number of beings, existing in unlimited space, penetrated by gigantic forces. Even modern astronomy has not been able to paint a more comprehensive and gigantic picture of the world. The development of mathematics and of astronomical instruments gave an opportunity to the West to express its urge toward the infinite in mathematical magnitudes and symbols (and nowadays in space research and interplanetary travel).

In Mahāyāna literature a similar urge was expressed in the form of philosophical and metaphysical symbols (due to the exploration of "inner space" in meditational practices), to describe the immensity and multiplicity of worlds, spiritual forces, and beings. Among all these symbols, however, space had become the most important, and if it could be said that in the West since the days of the Renaissance the conception of God became more and more similar to the idea of pure, infinite space in the minds of all culturally important men,[3] then it may be said that for similar reasons the concepts of space (ākāśa) and nirvāna became ever more closely related, the more the ideal or the inner experience of infinity took possession of the Indian, especially the Buddhist mind.

But while the Western experience of space was increasingly concerned with the optical and mathematical definitions—so that an inner feeling turned into the observation of external, optical space—the Indian conception of space developed in the opposite direction. Instead of exploring visible space, they regarded it merely as a projection or an imperfect reflection or symbol of their inner experience, and consequently they dived into the center of their own being, into the depth of human consciousness, in which the whole infinite world is contained.

From this treasury or store-house of consciousness (*ālaya-vijñāna*) they drew their cosmic inspirations, their mystic visions and artistic creations. In these creations they did not try to imitate the world before their eyes, or things as they appeared, but the world which they knew within themselves. In their paintings they never tried to create the illusion of optical space and its "accidental" perspective, depending on the momentary standpoint of an individual observer.

> The painter thinks in pictures and when he paints them he shifts their stage from within his consciousness on to the other side of the limits of his body. He turns the figures around and also their whole setting so that they confront him. They have come out from his mind to be seen by his eye. The process of turning them round, turning the contents of his vision inside out, is however a later stage of his work. It presupposes the 'return' of his mind, at the moment of beholding the objective world as a manifestation of mind itself.[4]

Since the times of the Renaissance, Western paintings lead from the beholder into the illusory space of the picture; "with the Ajanta painter we look however into the opposite direction." His paintings seem to manifest their forms from a spaceless background toward the beholder. But this spacelessness applies only to the eye. The background is teeming with life, but with life in the making, from which forms come forth in unceasing streams, manifesting themselves as they come forward. The background is comparable to the dark space of the mother's womb, a space filled with growing life, crystallizing into forms, a state between chaos and cosmos, creative space, that can be felt or divinated, but not seen or defined in terms of three dimensions.

> While the painting as a whole appears to come forward with all its scenes in uninterrupted progression, the latter is closely bound together by the rhythms which play over the surface. The entire compact mass

of painting results from movement. Its space is charged with directions. The major direction is the forward movement and its origin is metaphysical.[5]

Directedness and movement are indeed the characteristics of the Buddhist space-experience, which has been more adequately described in terms of religious ideas and meditative practices. In the description of the four *brahma-viharas* or "divine states of mind," it is emphasized that one should radiate love, compassion, sympathetic joy, and peace, first in one direction, then in a second direction, likewise in a third and fourth direction, and equally to the regions above and below. Recognizing oneself everywhere and in everything, one should penetrate the whole world with love, compassion, joy, and equanimity, with a deep, all-embracing, unlimited mind, purified from ill-will and aversion. It is not sufficient to produce feelings of love and compassion, etc. within oneself; it is necessary to direct one's mind fully conscious toward each of the six directions of the universe, until the consciousness has become identified with the entire universe, filling out the infinity of space, so that no trace of egohood is left. The mind is regarded as an active center of force, radiating unceasingly; but force cannot be effective without direction, nor can consciousness be so without being focussed. Therefore each direction, each quarter of the universe has to be penetrated separately and made conscious, before an all-embracing space-consciousness becomes possible.

Thus space is "built up" in consciousness by movement and direction; it is a space that is felt and known, and of which external space is a mere symbol, a reflection, limited by the finite qualities of our eyes, our physical faculty of vision. In fact, what we see with our eyes is not space, but only a world of light-resisting objects which we interpret in terms of our inner space-consciousness. The fact that this inner space-consciousness was experienced or conceived in ancient India as a kind of radiation is proved by the term *ākāsa*, in which the faculties of "shining" or "radiating" are embodied. And as the paintings of Ajanta are "charged with directions" and held together by a rigid system of compartments or space-receptacles, so the space-experience of Buddhist meditation was saved from the chaotic vagueness of undefined feelings, emotions, and impressions, by creating a well-established structure of directions.

While in meditation space seems to expand in the same proportion in which the spiritual radiation penetrates the infinite, converting it into conscious space and thus uniting and re-absorbing it in the creative center of consciousness, the work of the painter, as represented by the art of Ajanta, appears to express a movement in the opposite direction.

> Aware of ourselves as experiencing the world, we turn back upon ourselves as the place which holds the world and there we behold it in a direction that does not lead away from us, but points back towards ourselves. We are stage and spectator of the world as we see and live it. There is nothing to lead us away into a distance outside ourselves and there is no room for nostalgia or perspective. There are no places to be gone to for they are all within us, seen, visualized and remembered. No time is lost, for it does not exist, to take us from the one to the next. Past and present events are there all together and nothing has happened which does not hold good, and nothing holds good that will not endure. Memory transmutes time with a rhythm of simultaneous sequences on the stage which we ourselves make up and behold.[5]

The close association of space and consciousness can also be seen from the fact that in the higher stages of absorption (*dhyāna*) the experience of the infinity of space (*ākāśanañcāyatana*) immediately leads to the experience of the infinity of consciousness *vijñānañcāyatana*). After the elimination of all thing- and form-ideas or representations, space is the direct and intuitive object of consciousness.

It has two properties: that of infinity and that of non-materiality ("no-thing-ness"). They condition each other like "above" and "below," "right" and "left," "positive" and "negative." Each of these two properties contains the germ of the other, can be the basis or starting-point for the experience of space. Without them there would be no such experience, because "space as such" cannot be the basis of consciousness.

The "infinity of space" (*ākāśanañcāyatana*) and "no-thing-ness" (*akiñcanyāyatana*) are thus of equal value as expressions of space-experience or as objects of intuitive consciousness. If, however, the consciousness of the infinity of space itself becomes an object of meditation, the experience of the infinity of consciousness (*vijñānañcāyatana*) arises. In other words: if infinity becomes conscious, it reveals the infinity of consciousness.

II

During an intuitive experience, consciousness entirely identifies itself with and merges into the object: if it is an infinite one, the consciousness also becomes infinite, unlimited. But only retrospectively does the consciousness become aware of its own boundlessness. In an analogous way the consciousness of emptiness, of the absence of all material or imagined "things," of "no-thing-ness," becomes the object of the consecutive stage of absorption, which consists just in the awareness of that "emptiness of consciousness," called "neither perception nor non-perception" or "ultimate limit of perception." All these states of absorption are not only in correlation through their common denominator, the concept and basic experience of space, but also by forming a process of progressive unification: from the differentiation of surface-consciousness to the oneness of depth-consciousness.

It is from this experience that the philosophical idea of śūnyatā drew its inspiration, and only on this basis does it become understandable. How was it possible that such an apparently negative and utterly abstract term could become the very center of Mahāyāna philosophy? Only the profound space-experience of meditation (dhyāna) could satisfy the inner urge for infinity (which the Buddhist shared with the followers of all other Indian religions as well as with the Western Aryan civilizations), and only a term which denoted the complete absence of "thing-ness" and limitation could adequately symbolize the inexpressible. If Spengler says that the "pure, infinite space represents the profoundest symbol of the Occidental soul," then it can be said that this is equally true with regard to the Indian soul.

The ways in which East and West realize the Infinite may be different, just as are the particular mood and "color" in which it is experienced. But this does not minimize the fact that both feel the same urge, a fact which appears all the more significant if we remember that for the Greeks, for instance, this urge for the Infinite was entirely foreign. We have already observed how, in painting, the space-experience of East and West developed in opposite directions, the one dealing with the conscious (inner) space of introspective meditation, the other with the visible space of the external world.

Yet, this does not mean that there are no points of contact in the space-conceptions of these otherwise so different civilizations. But we must not necessarily search for them in the same medium of expression.

Western civilization has found its most profound and unique expression in music, India in its introspective meditation (*dhyāna*). It is in these two realms, therefore, that we have to look for parallels or points of contact. Only here are comparisons possible.

In fact, Western music produces a kind of space-sensation which is as remote from visible space as is that which is experienced in states of deep absorption. It is a space-experience which cannot be experienced in terms of three dimensions, because it belongs to a higher order; it is as undefinable in words as are the highest experiences of *dhyāna,* or the ultimate reality of *śūnyatā.*

> The primordial feeling of a release, deliverance, dissolution of the soul in the infinite, a liberation from all material weight, which is aroused in the highest moments of our music, liberates also the depth-urge of the Faustic soul . . . .[6]

This depth-impulse (*Tiefendrang*) became apparent in the architecture of Gothic cathedrals (architecture has been called "frozen music") with their emphasis of direction, expressed by their interior space as a way leading to the holy of holies, the altar, as well as in their external structure pointing towards the Infinite, the symbol of immaterial, transcendental reality as the highest aim of spiritual life. In a progressive process of universalization, this depth-impulse was liberated from its one-sidedness, its exclusive one-pointedness, by the more immaterial medium of music, which took the place of architecture as the chief form of expression in the age of Baroque, opening up a new dimension of depth.

A similar process can be observed in the development of Buddhism, in which the feeling of direction, the spiritual depth-impulse, which was first emphasized in the idea of the "Way," the "Path," the "Stream," etc., became more and more universal by laying more stress upon the cosmic qualities of Buddhahood, and of consciousness in general, than on individual liberation, which appeared insignificant and selfish, if not impossible, in view of the close interrelatedness of all living beings—an interrelatedness which appeared all the more powerful and significant, the more the full meaning of the doctrine of *anātma* or *śūnyatā* revealed itself to the followers of the Middle Path.

Thus, while there was first the idea of an individual path, leading out and away from the world, the later idea aimed at transforming and finally liberating the world. Though both these tendencies existed side by side from the very beginning of Buddhism (the Bodhisattva-Ideal, as shown in the *Jātakas*, belongs to this ancient tradition), the emphasis was shifted from the individual toward a universal attitude. Architecturally the old Caitya Halls give expression to the idea of the Path in its exclusive directedness towards Nirvāna, symbolized by the *Caitya,* but this symbol itself underwent great changes and became every more complex and universal in attitude.

The urge towards the Infinite in the Mahāyāna led to an exaggerated fondness for huge numbers, endless classifications and enumerations, which filled out the gaps between really great visions and profound discoveries. If Europe had not found an ideal outlet for its spiritual expansion in mathematics and astronomy, etc., its longing for the Infinite might have taken a similar poetical and imaginative course.

The habit of multiplying each and everything, until the mind reels with unimaginably vast figures, is like the stammering of a child whose experiences have outrun his power of speech; it is the stammering of the intellect, bound to a world of three-dimensional concepts, vainly trying to describe the sensations and visions of a higher dimension. But the incompleteness or deficiency of expression should not mislead us to underrate the nature and value of the experiences behind it, or to doubt the sincerity of the emotions which prompted it.

On the other hand, we have to admit that a great deal of misunderstanding on our part is due to preconceived ideas and wrong interpretations. People in those times spoke an entirely different language, not only in the philological sense, but spiritually. Numbers, for instance, had for them a predominantly symbolical and poetical meaning, a sentimental value, rather than a mathematical. It therefore needs more than philological skill to enter the spirit of certain types of Mahāyāna literature, and we should therefore rather admit our ignorance, when things appear to us unintelligible, than attribute lack of intelligence or sincerity to the authors of those texts. On account of the much greater effort which was necessary to produce, to spread, and to preserve written documents in those days—when writing and reading were not yet commonly practiced, but reserved for a small elite, and then only for matters of great importance—we can safely say that the literature which survived centuries or even millenniums can claim to be more representative of the best that was produced in those times, than most of what is printed in our time.

But we must take care not to be misled by the similarity of expressions or the equality of word-symbols with those of our modern literature or our present-day way of thinking. The value of each symbol depends on the system of which it is an integral part. If this is already true with regard to symbols with which we believe ourselves to be quite familiar, how much more careful have we to be in judging or interpreting symbols which have grown under quite different cultural conditions and for which there is no parallel in our present civilization, as for instance in the case of *mantras* and *Dhāranīs,* which cannot convey any meaning to the uninitiated, i.e., if separated from the spiritual background or the religious practice and experience out of which they grew. If modern scholars describe such *mantras* as "unmeaning gibberish" with its "silly secrets" and "contemptible mummery and posturing" (*mudrās*), they only show that their mental arrogance is equal to their ignorance.[7]

The universal attitude of the Mahāyāna in pursuing its urge toward the Infinite is also apparent in its emphasis on spatial directions, which are applied not only to spiritual exercises, like the four *brahmaviharas* or "divine mental states," but to all transcendental aspects of Buddhahood and to all conscious forces of the universe. Even colors, forms, sounds, elements, emotions, spiritual faculties, etc., are closely associated with directions and spatial positions and thus raised to the level of universal values.

The colors, especially, have become so closely associated with spatial directions that they have lost all material properties and do not represent nature, as seen by the eye, but visions of a higher reality and the knowledge derived therefrom. In Mahāyāna iconography, colors have therefore primarily not an aesthetic but a symbolic value, indicating the character, the qualities, and the place which each figure occupies in the spiritual and cosmic system of which it is a part. Through this coordination of all aspects of the spiritually known universe, the consciousness of a higher dimension is born, in which the symbol has replaced the concept, and intuition takes the place of calculation.

In the Buddhist conception of the universe, the organic "logic of direction" plays a more important role than the inorganic logic of material, three-dimensional extension (*die Logik des Ausgedehnten*, as Spengler calls it), because the Buddhist recognizes reality as dynamic, and not as a static condition. "As long as the world is statically conceived, it has no reality behind it, it is Māyā; the world must be grasped as it 'moves about,' as it becomes, as it passes from one state of being to another. When this movement is arrested, there is a corpse."[8]

To the Buddhist the world is a process of becoming, not a state of being. Becoming, however, is not unqualified change, but the very essence of life and growth, namely organic development; therefore, only an organic kind of logic can deal with it. The elements of such a type of logic are not derived from the bodies of a three-dimensional world, represented by unchangeable units or concepts, but rather from the interrelationship of various movements or living forces, which can only be expressed by symbols and analogies.

There are as many different kinds of logic as there are dimensions, but it appears as if the former were lagging considerably behind the realization of the latter. Though we are conscious of a three-dimensional world, we still think in terms of a two-dimensional logic, based on the law of identity and non-identity, i.e., having only two alternative directions: "either this *or* that." It was the realization of this deficiency in every-day language and thought that led Nāgārjuna, the great Buddhist philosopher of the second century A.D., to an entirely new approach towards the spiritual problems of human life and to the discovery of new dimensions of consciousness. This led to a negation of all philosophical or conventional concepts and to the use of paradoxes in hinting at experiences which go beyond conceptual thought, until a new language had been found, in which the experiences of meditation and inner vision were reflected, a language "beyond the path and usage of the philosophers, which is devoid of all predicates, such as being and non-being, oneness, and otherness, bothness and non-bothness, existence and non-existence, eternity and non-eternity; a language which has nothing to do with individuality and generality, nor false imagination, nor any illusions arising from the mind itself; but which manifests itself as the Truth of Highest Reality, by which, going up continuously by the stages of purification, one enters at last upon the stage of Tathāgatahood, whereby . . . one will radiate its influence to infinite worlds, like a gem reflecting its variegated colors. . . ." (Lankāvatāra-Sūtra I)[9]

References and Notes

[1] Spengler, *Der Untergang des Abendlandes*, Vol. I, p. 234.
[2] Op. cit., p. 509.
[3] Op. cit., p. 505.
[4] St. Kramrisch, *A Survey of Painting in the Deccan*, p. 6.
[5] Op. cit., p. 7.
[6] Spengler, op. cit., Vol. I, p. 230.
[7] Cf. A. L. Waddell, *Lamaism*, pp. 143-145. Our mathematical and chemical formulas and symbols will probably appear as "unmeaning gibberish" to later civilizations, and our theories about the universe as childish as medieval speculations appear to us.
[8] D. T. Suzuki, *Essays in Zen Buddhism*, Vol. III, p. 290.
[9] D. T. Suzuki's translation, ed. by Dwight Goddard, *A Buddhist Bible*, Dutton, N. Y., p. 279.

3

TIME AND SPACE AND THE PROBLEM OF FREE WILL

A VIEW INTO SPACE is at the same time a view into the past. Space is visible time—visible, however, only in one direction. We are like travelers on the backseat of a fast-moving vehicle, from which can be seen only what has passed by, not what is coming.

However, who knows whether we do not move in a circle, so that a view into the remote past would be equal to a view into the future? Even if the circle would not be closed, but develop into a kind of three-dimensional spiral, there would be a great deal of similarity between past and future. However that may be: we might compare the circle to the rigid law of repetition, governing all merely relative processes, while the deviation from the circle into a three-dimensional spiral (by which the movement enters from the second into the next higher dimension) indicates a certain measure of free will in the higher forms of life.

The discovery that no straight movement can be found in the universe, but that everything, including the light, moves in curves, justifies the above-mentioned idea. "The extended theory of relativity," says Haldane in *Possible Worlds* (p. 4), "seems to lead inevitably to the view that the universe is finite, and that progress in any direction would ultimately lead back to the starting-point."

We can see worlds which are many thousands of lightyears away, and perhaps even more distant worlds may be discovered, until one day we may find out that one of them is our own world—however, not as it is now, but as it was billions of years ago. And this is perhaps why we shall never discover, or rather, recognize it, and why we shall go on penetrating the universe without ever coming to an end. Because space (though it may be finite in the form in which we know it), ever recedes before us and transforms itself under our very eyes into a new infinity, namely, that of time.

Thus, if we contemplate the starry sky, it is not the present universe which we see with our eyes, but a universe of the past—and what is still more remarkable—a universe of which the different parts have not even existed simultaneously (but some a few minutes and others some millions of years ago), though we see them in the same moment.

But do we not live, even in our nearest surroundings, more in the past than in the present? Do we not almost live in a world of phantoms, if we are conscious of the fact that our bodies themselves are actually the visible appearance of our past consciousness, which has built up this material form according to its particular tendencies and state of development? This is perhaps the reason why all our bodily sense-organs are directed toward the past, i.e. toward the consolidated forms and the vibrations emanating from them, but not toward the future or the present in the real sense.

The body by its nature is actually materialized karma, the consciousness of past moments of existence made visible. Karma is nothing else but the acting principle of consciousness which as effect (*vipāka*) also steps into visible appearance.[1] The appearing form is thus essentially "past," and therefore felt as something alien by those who have developed out of and beyond it.

The hybrid position of the body as the product of a long-passed consciousness, and the basis of the present one, expresses itself also in the fact that one part of its functions is conscious and subject to our will, as for example the movements of our limbs, the faculty of speech, etc.—while another part runs its course unconsciously and is not subject to our will (and therefore to our present consciousness), as for example the circulation of the blood, digestion, internal secretions, the growth and disintegration of cells, and so on. Breathing holds an intermediate position, because it can be raised from an unconscious into a conscious function. Thus breathing is able to combine the present with the past, the mental with the corporeal, the conscious with the unconscious. It is the mediator, the only function in which we can lay hold of what has become and what is becoming, through which we can master the past and the future. It is therefore the starting-point of creative meditation.

We live mostly in an indirect, reactive world, and only rarely do we experience actual reality and thus live in the present. Our usual reactions are habitual, due to routine and therefore based upon the past, stored up in form of instinct, memory, conceptual and emotional associations, etc. Though these functions are necessary for the coherence and continuity of our mental and physical life, they form only the substructure of our existence, the passive side of life; they are our individual as well as our common inheritance. As long as this inheritance predominates, we live essentially in the past.

Our consciousness, however, is not bound to one direction, like the body and its senses, but partakes of the present and the future as well—provided we give it an opportunity, by freeing it at least temporarily from the burden of the past.

This happens in moments of contemplation or intuition (in religious contemplation as well as in the contemplation of works of art or the beauty of nature), in states of profound absorption or concentration. In such a state every object, whether mental or material, is turned into a subjective and direct experience, in which no previous associations disturb the freshness or distort the originality of the impression. To live in the present means to see everything with a perfectly pure, unprejudiced and open mind, to experience everything as profoundly as if we had never known it before. It means to retain (or to restore) the freshness and alertness of mind which is the characteristic quality of genius.

Generally we live away from life, either by being occupied with the past, or by anticipating the future. Both these attitudes of the mind mean bondage, karma in its active as well as in its reactive form. To overcome one's *sankhāras*[2] is equal to overcoming and freeing ourselves from the past.

Therefore the Buddhist meditation has no other purpose than to bring the mind back into the present, into the state of fully awakened consciousness, by clearing it from all obstacles that have been created by habit or tradition. I have heard a lama say that the part of a master, adept of the "Short Path," is to superintend a "clearing." He must incite his novice to rid himself of the beliefs, ideas, acquired habits and innate tendencies which are part of his present mind, and have been developed in the course of successive lives whose origin is lost in the night of time. On the other hand, the master must warn his disciples to be on his guard against accepting new beliefs, ideas, and habits as groundless and irrational as those which he shakes off. The discipline on the "Short Path" is to avoid imagining things. When imagination is prescribed, in contemplative meditation, it is to demonstrate, by that conscious creation of perception and sensations, the illusory nature of those perceptions and sensations which we accept as real, though they too rest on imagination; the only difference being that, in their case, the creation is unconsciously effected. The Tibetan reformer, Tsong Khapa, defines meditation as "the means of enabling oneself to reject all imaginative thoughts together with their seed."[3]

From this standpoint the words of Tilopa gain special significance:

> Act so as to know thyself by means of symbols in thine own mind,
> Without imagining, without deliberating, without analyzing,
> Without meditating, without introspecting; *keeping the mind in its natural state.*[4]

As long as we live in the past, we are subject to the law of cause and effect, which leaves no room for the exertion of free will and makes us slaves of necessity. The same holds good for what we call "dwelling in the future," which generally is only a state of reversed memory—a combination of past experiences, projected into the future. When, however, the past or the future are experienced in clairvoyant states, they become present, which is the only form in which we can experience reality (of which the other forms are so to say "perspectively distorted reflexes"). Only while dwelling in the present, i.e. in moments of full awareness and "awakedness," are we free.

Thus we are partaking of both: the realm of law or necessity as well as the realm of freedom. Science—which is only concerned with that which has become, with the consolidated *form,* but not with the *nature* of reality or the actual process of *becoming,* and thus deals with a reactive rather than an actual world—can only conceive of a universe in which law or necessity governs supremely and *exclusively.*

Science, therefore, cannot be a judge in the question of determinism or indeterminism, or free will with respect to living things, i.e. "self-regulating and self-preserving" organisms endowed with consciousness—nor can philosophy be so long as it relies on scientific facts and methods, such as logical deduction, etc., which all belong to the same reactive world, to the same secondary time-dimension. Abstract reasoning will always lead to an extreme and one-sided result, by reducing the problem to a number of solid concepts and ideologically watertight compartments, which are shifted about on an artificial plane (which in reality exists as little as those conceptual units) and allow themselves to be neatly grouped either on this or on the opposite side of the equation, so that the result will always be either positive or negative, or at any rate a definite decision between the two sides.

The tacit assumption that the world which we build up in our thought is the same world which we experience in life (to say nothing about the world "as such") is the main source of error. The world which we experience includes the world of our thought, but not vice-versa. Because we live in several dimensions, of which the intellect (the faculty of thinking and reasoning) is only *one.*

If we intellectually reproduce experiences which belong to other dimensions, we do a similar thing to the action of the painter who represents three-dimensional space on a two-dimensional surface. He can do this by sacrificing certain qualities and by introducing a new order of proportions, which are only valid within the artificial unit of his painting and from one particular viewpoint. The laws of this perspective correspond to the laws of logic. Both of them sacrifice the qualities of a higher dimension; they select and confine themselves to one viewpoint, so that their objects appear from one side only (namely, the side which is related to their preconceived viewpoint), and under different proportions, namely, foreshortened.

But while the artist consciously translates his impressions from one dimension into the other—and not with the intention of imitating or reproducing objective reality, but in order to express a certain experience or attitude towards it—the intellectual thinker generally believes he has reproduced reality in his thoughts, mistaking the foreshortening perspective of his two-dimensional logic for a universal law. The use of logic in thinking is as necessary and justified as the use of perspective in painting—but only as a means of expression and not as a criterion of reality.

Thus it cannot be the business of philosophy to decide whether determinism or indeterminism is the real character of the world, for there is no "either-or"—no two possibilities between which we have to decide or to choose—but only two sides of the same phenomenon. The problem consists only in the definition of the relationship between the two sides.

If the logician cannot combine these two sides of our experience in his picture of the world, in other words, if he finds it incompatible with the laws of logic, then he only proves that his logic is unfit to deal with reality. Because here we have to do with the most direct form of reality, with the most fundamental facts of human experience, which neither philosophy nor religion can dare to deny or to neglect:

1. The fact that we feel free and responsible for our actions, and that this innermost experience of free will is the conditio sine qua non of our very existence as conscious individuals. Without free will we would be reduced to the state of automatons and the faculty of consciousness would not only be superfluous but a positive hindrance.

2. The fact that we live in a world governed by laws which, though they restrict our freedom, give us an opportunity to regulate and to direct and plan our actions, thus bringing our

behavior in harmony with our surroundings.

We cannot change the law of causality, but as soon as we know that certain causes produce certain results, we are able to decide between several courses of action open to us. Once chosen, we are bound to follow the course of events, resulting from our first step.

It may be comparatively seldom that we are confronted with a genuine opportunity to choose, because generally one situation grows of necessity out of another and calls for a definite course of action. But the fact that we exercise our faculties of discrimination, reasoning, and decision cannot be denied, nor can the fact that if different individuals were confronted with the same situation, their decisions would differ from each other.

Here the determinist will say that this proves no free will, because each individual simply acts according to his inborn character, to which he is fettered like the stone to the law of gravitation. This is an objection which is as silly as it is logical, because here we begin playing with words, regardless of their relationship to living experience (as if each individual were a reality in itself or a mathematical magnitude with a fixed value).

Free will means the expression of one's *own* will, that is, the will that corresponds to one's own nature. Thus the expression "free will" already presumes and includes the idea of individuality or individual character. Will itself can only arise in an individual, and if it is free, it expresses the particular character of the individual.

The difference between a law of nature and free will is that the one acts automatically and with universal sameness, while the other is conscious and individual. A will which would act incoherently, and without relationship to our own nature, would be meaningless and could certainly not be called free will, though it were free from any conceivable law. We would rather call it madness.

Thus we can summarize:

1. Free will (or freedom in general) is not arbitrariness.
2. Free will can never be an object of observation, but only a subjective experience. The problem of freedom and necessity is an entirely subjective problem and can never be solved objectively (by science or philosophy).
3. Free will is a relative term, signifying the relationship of

a conscious individual towards its surroundings or towards a certain situation.

4. Therefore, there can be no absolute free will.

5. Free will means the freedom to express one's own will according to one's own nature and insight (degree of development) in contrast to a mechanical reaction, which follows a general law without insight into or understanding of its nature.

6. Free will does not imply that it has no law, or that its own law is in opposition to general laws. It may or may not follow general laws, and in many cases it modifies them and converts them into individual law.

We may compare our individual will to a railway engine, general law to a system of railway lines. The engine can choose the line it wants to travel along, but it cannot change the line.

The two apparently contradictory realms of freedom and necessity (ethos and logos, free will and law) have their meeting-place in the human individual. What appears as necessity from outside may be the most genuine expression of freedom, of free will, if it coincides with the inner law or nature of the individual.

And here arises the main question: Are not perhaps the laws which we objectify and which consequently we regard as imposed upon us against our own will, are not those very laws our spiritual creation and therefore intrinsically the expression of our own innermost will? How can the philosopher assume that he stands outside the world and the individual, and pretend to be an "objective" observer in a matter where inner experience (upon which the very laws he wants to examine are based) is the only source of information? He is like a man in a moving vehicle, who speaks about movements around him, without being aware that he himself is moving.

We may fittingly sum up our situation in A. Eddington's significant words (in *Space, Time, and Gravitation*): "We have found a strange foot-print on the shores of the unknown. We have devised profound theories, one after another, to account for its origin. At last we have succeeded in reconstructing the creature that made the foot-print. And Lo! It is our own!"

With this admission science enters a new phase of its course, in which the physical and the metaphysical are no longer contradictions, and in which the exploration of the universe will lead to the discovery and recognition of new dimensions of the human mind.

References and Notes

[1] Karma, in Buddhism, is a strictly psychological, not a metaphysical term. It has not the meaning of irrevocable fate or destiny, but of "action." The definition of action, according to the Buddha's words in *Anguttara-Nikaya* VI, 63, is, "Cetanaham bhikkhave kammam vadami," ("Volition, O monks, is what I call action"). In other words, only where there is intention, i.e. consciously motivated exertion, can we speak of "karmic" action, and only such action has character-forming consequences, determining our inclinations and thus our future actions and reactions. Character is nothing but the tendency of our will, formed by repeated actions. Every consciously performed deed leaves a subconscious trace (samskara). It is like a path formed by the process of walking, and wherever such a once-trodden path exists, there we find, when a similar situation arises, that we take to this path spontaneously. This is the law of action and reaction which we call karma, the law of movement in the direction of least resistance, i.e. of the frequently trodden and therefore easier path. It is what is commonly known as the "force of habit." Just as a potter forms vessels out of formless clay, so we create through deeds, words and thoughts, out of the still unformed material of our life and our sense-impressions, the vessel of our future consciousness, namely that which gives it form and direction.

[2] These are formative tendencies, caused by former actions, making up our character and determining our fate.

[3] A. David-Neel, *With Mystics and Magicians in Tibet*, (Penguin Ed) p. 245.

[4] Evans-Wentz, *Tibetan Yoga and Secret Doctrine*, Oxford University Press, p. 149 f.

4

THE MYSTERY OF TIME

TIME AND SPACE constitute the two greatest mysteries of the human mind. Deeper even than the mystery of space is that of time—so deep, in fact, that it took humanity thousands of years to become conscious of its implications. Apparently the human mind becomes first aware of space and much later of the reality of time. Even a child is more or less conscious of the reality of space, while the time-sense is practically absent and develops at a much later stage. The same happens in the development of human civilization. The discovery of space, as an element of spiritual importance, precedes a similar discovery of time.

This can be explained by the fact that space-feeling is first and foremost connected with the movement of the body, whereas time-feeling is connected with the movement of the mind. Though space-feeling starts with the body, however, it does not remain at this stage, but gradually changes into a spiritual function, by creating a space conception which is independent from the body, independent of material objects, independent even of any kind of limitation: culminating in the experience of pure space or the infinity of space. Here we no longer speak of "conception," because infinity cannot be conceived, mentally "pictured" or objectivated, it can only be *experienced*. Only when man has penetrated to this experience and has mentally and spiritually digested and assimilated it, can we speak of the discovery of time as a new dimension of consciousness.

In early Buddhism the experience of space was recognized as an important factor of meditation, for instance in the Four Divine States of consciousness (*brahmavihāra*), in which the consciously created feelings of selfless love, compassion, sympathetic joy, and spiritual equanimity are projected one after another into the six directions of space, namely the four points of the compass, the zenith and the nadir. These directions had to be vividly imagined, so as to make space and its penetration by the mind a conscious experience. In a similar way, space became the main subject of contemplation in the higher or more advanced stages of meditative absorption (*jhāna*)[1] until consciousness completely identified itself with the infinity of space,[2] thus resulting in the experience of the infinity of consciousness,[3] in which the meditator becomes one with the subject of his meditation.

In Mahāyāna Buddhism, space played an even more important part in the development of religious art and its symbolism, in which a universe with myriads of worlds and solar systems and infinite forms of life and dimensions of consciousness was conceived—leading to the creation of new systems of philosophy, metaphysical speculation and a vastly refined psychology. The concept of time, however, was merely treated as a secondary, if not negative, property of existence—namely, as that on account of which existence was illusory, a passing show of transient phenomena.

It was only with the advent of the Kalacakra School in the tenth century A.D. that religious seers and thinkers realized the profound mystery which is hidden under the conventional notion of time, namely the existence of another dimension of consciousness, the presence of which we feel darkly and imperfectly on the plane of our mundane experience. Those, however, who crossed the threshold of mundane consciousness in the advanced stages of meditation, entered into this dimension, in which what we feel as time was experienced not merely as a negative property of our fleeting existence, but as the ever present dynamic aspect of the universe and the inherent nature of life and spirit, which is beyond being and non-being, beyond origination and destruction. It is the vital breath of reality—reality, not in the sense of an abstraction, but as actuality on all levels of experience—which is revealed in the gigantic movements of the universe as much as in the emotions of the human heart and the ecstasies of the spirit. It is revealed in the cosmic dance of heavenly bodies as well as in the dance of protons and electrons, in the "harmony of spheres" as well as in the "inner sound" of living things, in the breathing of our body as well as in the movements of our mind and the rhythm of our life.

Reality, in other words, is not stagnant existence of "something"; it is neither "thingness" nor a state of immovability (like that of an imaginary space), but movement of a kind which goes as much beyond our sense-perceptions, as beyond our mathematical, philosophical and metaphysical abstractions. In fact, space (except the "space" that is merely thought of) does not exist in itself, but is created by movement; and if we speak of the curvature of space, it has nothing to do with its prevailing or existing structure (like the grain in wood or the stratification of rocks), but with its antecedent, the movement that created it. The character of this movement is curved, i.e. concentric, or with a tendency to create its own center—a center which may again be moving in a bigger curve or circle, etc.

Thus, the universe becomes a gigantic *maṇḍala* or an intricate system of innumerable maṇḍalas (which, according to the traditional Indian meaning of this word, signifies a system of symbols, based on a circular arrangement or movement, and serves to illustrate the interaction or juxtaposition of spiritual and cosmic forces). If, instead from a spatial point of view, we regard the universe from the standpoint of audible vibration or *śabda*, "inner sound," it becomes a gigantic symphony.

In both cases all movements are interdependent, interrelated, each creating its own center, its own focus of power, without ever losing contact with all the other centers thus formed.

"Curvature" in this connection means a movement which recoils upon itself (and which thus possesses both constancy and change, i.e. rhythm) or at least has the tendency to lead back to its origin or starting-point, according to its inherent law. In reality, however, it can never return to the same point in space, since this movement itself moves within the frame of a greater system of relationships. Such a movement combines the principle of change and nonreversability with the constancy of an unchangeable law, which we may call its rhythm. One might say that this movement contains an element of eternity as well as an element of transiency, which latter we feel as time.

Both time and space are the outcome of movement, and if we speak of the "curvature of space" we should speak likewise of the "curvature of time," because time is not a progression in a straight line—of which the beginning (the past) is lost forever and which pierces into the endless vacuum of an inexorable future—but something that recoils upon itself, something that is subject to the law of ever-recurrent similar situations, and which thus combines change with stability. Each of these situations is enriched by new contents, while at the same time retaining its essential character. Thus we cannot speak of a mechanical repetition of the same events, but only of an organic rebirth of its elements, on account of which even within the flux of events the stability of law is discernable. Upon the recognition of such a law which governs the elements (or the elementary forms of appearance) of all events, is the basis upon which the *I-Ching* or "The Book of Changes," the oldest work of Chinese wisdom, is built.

Perhaps this work would better be called "The Book of the Principles of Transformation" because it demonstrates that change is not arbitrary or accidental but dependent on laws, according to which each thing or state of existence can only change into something already inherent in its own nature, and not into something altogether different. It also demonstrates the equally important laws of periodicity, according to which change follows a cyclic movement (like the heavenly bodies, the seasons, the hours of the day, etc.), representing the eternal in time and converting time quasi into a higher space-dimension, in which things and events exist simultaneously, though imperceptible to the senses. They are in a state of potentiality, as invisible germs or elements of future events and phenomena that have not yet stepped into actual reality.

These elements are, so to say, eternally recurring spiritual or transcendental realities and universal laws which in Indian cosmology and philosophy have been described as the rhythmic origination and dissolution of world-systems. The same principle repeats itself, according to this view, in the periodic appearance of enlightened beings, who—though different in their individual qualities and characters, as well as in their external forms of appearance—represent the same knowledge and conscious realization of the supreme universal law, which is the main meaning of the Sanskrit term *dharma*.

This sameness—or as we may say just as well, this eternal presence of the "Body of the Law" (*dharmakāya*), which is common to all Buddhas, to all Enlightened Ones—is the source and spiritual foundation of all enlightenment and is, therefore, placed in the center of the *Kālacakra-Maṇḍala*, which is the symbolical representation of the universe. *Kāla* means "time" (also "black"), namely the invisible, incommensurable dynamic principle, inherent in all things and represented in Buddhist iconography, as a black, many-headed, many-armed, terrifying figure of simultaneously divine and demoniacal nature. It is "terrible" to the ego-bound individual, whose ego is trampled underfoot, just as are all the gods, created in the ego's likeness, who are shown prostrate under the feet of this terrifying figure. Time is the power that governs all things and all being, a power to which even the highest gods have to submit.[4]

Cakra means "wheel," the focalized or concentric manifestation of the dynamic principle in space. In the ancient tradition of Yoga the *cakra* signifies the spatial unfoldment of spiritual or universal power, as for instance in the *cakras* or psychic centres of the human body or in the case of the *Cakravartin*, the world-ruler who embodies the all-encompassing moral and spiritual powers.

In one of his previous books on Buddhist Tantrism, H. V. Guenther compares the *Kālacakra* symbol to the modern conception of the space-time continuum, pointing out, however, that in Buddhism it is not merely a philosophical or mathematical construction, but is based on the direct perception of inner experience, according to which time and space are inseparable aspects of reality.

Only in our minds we tend to separate the three dimensions of space and the one of time. We have an awareness of space and an awareness of time. But this separation is purely subjective. As a matter of fact, modern physics has shown that the time dimension can no more be detached from the space dimension than length can be detached from breadth and thickness in an accurate representation of a house, a tree, or Mr. X. Space has no objective reality except as an order or arrangement of things we perceive in it, and time has no independent existence from the order of events by which we measure it.[5]

Both space and time are two aspects of the most fundamental quality of life: movement. Here we come to the rock-bottom of direct experience, which the Buddha stressed in his emphasis upon the dynamic character of reality, in contrast to the generally prevailing notions and philosophical abstractions of a static *Ātmavāda,* in which an eternal and unchangeable ego-entity was proclaimed. (The original concept of *ātman* was that of a universal, rhythmic force, the living breath of life—comparable to the Greek "pneuma"—that pervaded the individual as well as the universe.)

We generally speak of time not only as if it were something in itself, something that we could take for granted, but even as if time were only one. We seldom realize that this word covers a dozen different meanings or, more correctly, different categories of relationship. We have to distinguish between mathematical time, sidereal time, solar time, local time, physical time, physiological time, psychological time, and so on. And the latter two are as different in every individual as local time is different from place to place.

An hour in the life of a child is an infinitely longer time-measure than in the life of a grown-up, because the life-rhythm of a child goes at a much faster pace than that of an adult or an aged person. And just as the time-sense changes subjectively and with age, both for physiological as well as for psychological reasons, in a similar way,

> the nature of time varies according to the objects considered by our mind. The time that we observe in nature has no separate existence. It is only *a mode*

of being of concrete objects. We ourselves create mathematical time. It is a mental construct, an abstraction indispensable to the building up of science. We conveniently compare it to a straight line, each successive instant being represented by a point. Since Galileo's days this abstraction has been substituted for the concrete data resulting from the *direct* observation of things. . . . In reducing objects to their primary qualities—that is, to what can be measured and is susceptible of mathematical treatment—Galileo deprived them of their secondary qualities, and of duration. *This arbitrary simplification made possible the development of physics. At the same time it led to an unwarrantably schematic conception of the world.*[6]

Indeed, it led to a science which was based on a "post mortem" of our world, on the static end-results of what was once alive, a world of facts and dead matter.

The concept of time is equivalent to the operation required to estimate duration in the objects of our universe. Duration consists of the superimposition of the different aspects of an identity. It is a kind of *intrinsic movement of things* . . . . A tree grows and does not lose its identity. The human individual retains his personality throughout the flux of the organic and mental processes that make up his life. Each inanimate or living being comprises an *inner motion,* a succession of states, a rhythm which is his very own. Such motion is *inherent time* . . . . In short, time is the specific character of things . . . . It is truly a dimension of ourselves.[7]

To search for time outside of ourselves or separated from the objects of our observation—so to say "time in itself"—is like isolating the directions of space from the observer and to speak of an "absolute east" or a "north as such" or a "west in itself." "Absolute time" is as nonsensical as the denial of time; the former because the very concept of time denotes a relationship either between a subject and an object or between the different parts of an existing or assumed system of correlated things or forces; the latter (i.e. the denial of time) because time is a definite experience, whether we can define it in words or not.

We also cannot define "life," though we do not doubt we

possess it. In fact, the more real an experience is to us, the less it can be defined. Only lifeless objects, things which have been artificially separated from their surroundings or their organic or causal connections, and have thus been isolated and limited by the human intellect, can be defined. An experience of reality (and that is all we can talk of, because "reality as such" is another abstraction) cannot be defined but only circumscribed, i.e., it cannot be approached by the straight line of two-dimensional logic, but only in a concentric way, by moving around it, approaching it not only from one side, but from all sides, without stopping at any particular point. Only in this way can we avoid a one-sided and perspectively foreshortened and distorted view, and arrive at a balanced, unprejudiced perception and knowledge. This concentric approach (which moves closer and closer around its object, in order finally—in the ideal case—to become one with it) is the exact opposite of the Western analytical and dissecting way of observation: it is the integral concentration of inner vision (*dhyāna*).

This integrating vision, and the new conception of the world that is born from it, has been formulated by one of the most creative and significant philosophers of our time, Jean Gebser, in his monumental work, *Foundations and Manifestations of the Aperspective World,* in which he writes:

> The origin, out of which every moment of our life is lived, is of a spiritual and divine character. He who denies this, denies himself; and there are many nowadays who do this. He who does not deny it, in all simplicity and openmindedness, is already a promoter of the aperspective conception, of the integral structure of our consciousness, which has its origin in the process of becoming conscious of the whole, as well as becoming aware of its transparency.[8]

This requires a new kind of logic, which—though known in India for millenniums—has remained unnoticed in the Western world. This logic is not based on the axiom of mutually exclusive opposites ("either-or") and the rejection of a third possibility, but upon a fourfold formula which postulates four possibilities with regard to an object, namely (1) its existence, (2) its non-existence, (3) its existence as well as its non-existence, (4) its neither-existence-nor-non-existence.

We have dealt with this in more detail in a previous essay,[9] and therefore confine ourselves here only to the following short explanation of these four propositions: The first two are related to the realm of concrete objects or fixed entities, which allow us to speak of identity or non-identity. The third proposition refers to the realm of relativity and corresponds to the processes of organic life; while the fourth refers to the realm of transcendental experience, beyond sense-perception and conceptual thought, because its objects are infinite and only accessible to intuition or to the experience of higher dimensions.

In Europe the attempt to create a logic based on three possibilities or axiomatic "truth-values" has been made by Reichenbach, who defines the new type of logic in the following way:

> Ordinary logic has two values; it is based upon the two axioms "truth" and "error." It is, however, possible to find a middle value of truth, which we can call "indeterminability," and we can add this truth-value to the group of statements which in the Bohr-Heisenberg interpretation have been called "meaningless" .... If, however, we have a third truth-value, namely indeterminability, then the *tertium non datur* is no longer valid as an infallible formula; there *is* a "tertium," a middle value, which is represented by the logical condition "indeterminable."[10]

This condition of indeterminability (which figures in the Indian system as No. 3 and 4) can be regarded as a state of integration of apparently contradictory, but in reality, however, of co-existing aspects of the same thing or process; this has been found true in modern nuclear physics, in which the wave-theory and the corpuscular theory are equally valid or applicable to the actual facts, though the two theories are logically exclusive.

Western logic is the exact counterpart of Western perspective which, starting from one single point in space, projects itself in a straight line upon an object, excluding all other simultaneously existing aspects and objectively given data. The attempts of modern art to overcome the one-sidedness of perspective by the transparency and superimposition of several aspects of the same object correspond to Gebser's endeavor to prepare the way for a nonperspective world-view, which frees us from the fetters of a purely dualistic, one-sided logic, and leads us to the experience of a total and unified reality, in which our world becomes more and more transparent to the awakened mind.

Let us, therefore, circle around our problem still further. What does time mean from the standpoint of experience? Most people would answer: duration! But duration we have, even when there is no experience of time, as in deep sleep. The experience of time, therefore, is something more than duration: it is movement. Movement of what? Either of ourselves or of something within or outside ourselves. But now the paradox:

The less we move (inwardly or outwardly), the more we are aware of time. The more we move ourselves, the less we are aware of time. A person who is mentally and bodily inactive feels time as a burden, while one who is active hardly notices the passage of time. Those who move in perfect harmony with the innermost rhythm of their being, the pulsating rhythm of the universe within them, are timeless in the sense that they do not experience time any more. Those who move and live in disharmony with this inner rhythm, have existence without inherent duration, i.e., merely momentary existence without direction or spiritual continuity and, therefore, without meaning.

What we call "eternal" is not an indefinite duration of time (which is a mere thought-construction, unrelated to any experience) but the experience of timelessness.

Time cannot be reversed. Even if we go back the same way, it is not the same, because the sequence of landmarks is changed, and moreover, we see them from the opposite direction—or as in memory, with the added knowledge of previous experience. The experience of time is due to movement plus memory. Memory is comparable to the layers of year-rings in a tree. Each layer is a material addition, an addition of experience-material, which alters the value of any new experience, so that even repetition can never produce identical results.

Life—just like time—is an irreversible process, and those who speak of eternal recurrence of identical events and individuals (as Ouspensky in his book, *A New Model of the Universe*) mistake rhythm or periodicity for mechanical repetition. It is the most shallow view that any thinker can arrive at, and it shows the dilemma into which scientific determinism is bound to lead. It is typical of the intellect that has lost its connection with reality and which replaces life with the phantoms of empty abstraction. This kind of reasoning leads to a purely stagnant and mechanical world-view, ending in a blind alley.

Whether the universe as a whole can change or not is quite irrelevant; important alone is that there is a genuine *creative* advance possible for the individual and that the past that is ever growing in him as a widening horizon of experience and wisdom will continue so to grow until the individual has reached the state in which the universe becomes conscious in him as one living organism, not only as an abstract unity or a state of featureless oneness. This is the highest dimension of consciousness.

What do we understand by "dimension"? The capacity to extend or to move in a certain direction. If we move outward, we can only do so in three dimensions, i.e., we cannot go beyond three-dimensional space. The movement, however, which produces and contains these dimensions is felt as time, as long as the movement is incomplete or as long as the dimensions are in the making, i.e., not conceived as a complete whole. The feeling of time is the feeling of incompleteness. For this reason there is no time in moments of highest awareness, intuitive vision or perfect realization. There is no time for the Enlightened Ones.

This, however, does not mean that for an Enlightened One the past has been extinguished or memory blotted out. On the contrary, the past ceases to be a quality of time and becomes a new order of space, which we may call the Fourth Dimension, in which things and events which we have experienced piecemeal can be seen simultaneously, in their entirety, and in the present. Thus the Buddha in the process of his enlightenment surveyed innumerable previous lives in ever widening vistas, until his vision encompassed the entire universe. Only if we recognize the past as "a true dimension of ourselves," and not only as an abstract property of time, shall we be able to see ourselves in proper perspective to the universe, which is not an alien element that surrounds us mysteriously, but the very body of our past, in whose womb we dream until we awake into the freedom of enlightenment.

References and Notes

[1] The *Pāli*-term "*jhāna*," as used by the early Theravadins, has a more general connotation than the corresponding Sanskrit term "*dhyāna*," which

may be described as a state of "inner vision," beyond discursive thought or logical thought-operations.

[2] *ākāsānancāyatana* (Pāli)

[3] *viññanañcāyatana* (Pāli)

[4] That the "gods" of Buddhist iconography and their symbols and functions do not belong to the realm of metaphysics, but to that of psychology, has been correctly pointed out by C. G. Jung in his Commentary on the *Secret of the Golden Flower*. Speaking of the great Eastern philosophers, he says: "I suspect them of being symbolical psychologists, to whom no greater wrong could be done than to take them literally. If it were really metaphysics that they mean, it would be useless to try to understand them. But if it is psychology, we can not only understand them, but we can profit greatly by them, for then the so-called 'metaphysical' comes within the range of experience. If I accept the fact that a god is absolute and beyond all human experience, he leaves me cold. I do not affect him, nor does he affect me. But if I know that a god is a powerful impulse in my soul, at once I must concern myself with him, for then he can become important . . . like everything belonging to the sphere of reality." (C. G. Jung, *Psyche and Symbol*, Doubleday Anchor Books, 1958, p. 344.)

We may add that the divine figures of Buddhist iconography do not only "come within the range of experience," but have actually their origin in the experiences of meditational practices (*sādhana*), so that any iconography that is not based on a knowledge of these *sādhanas* must remain utterly superficial and has no value for a real understanding of this profound subject, which has nothing to do with primitive idolatry but deals with psychic reality.

[5] H. V. Guenther, *Yuganaddha, the Tantric View of Life*, Chowkhamba Sanskrit Series, Banaras 1952, p. 185.

[6] Alexis Carrel, *Man the Unknown*, p. 156f.

[7] Op. cit., p. 157.

[8] Jean Gebser: *Ursprung and Gegenwart, Fundamente und Manifestationen der aperspectivischen Welt*, Vol. II, p. 382.

[9] "Logic and Symbol in the Multi-Dimensional Conception of the Universe," *Main Currents*, 25,3, Jan.-Feb. 1969, p. 59.

[10] Quoted by Gerbser, op. cit., p. 215.

5

THE PROBLEM OF PAST AND FUTURE

BOTH TIME AND SPACE are the outcome of movement, the characteristic of life, from its highest spiritual manifestations down to the simplest physical phenomena. By intellectually separating time from space, and both of them from the experiencing subject, we arrive at an abstract concept which has neither vitality nor reality. In order to imbue it with a semblance of movement, we divide it into past, present and future, out of which neither the past nor the future seem to possess actual reality. The present, however, according to this division, is merely the dividing line between the past that is no more and a future which is not yet: it is a point without extension, without dimension, and therefore without the possibility of movement. Yet we feel the present as the most real aspect of time, the only point in which movement is possible.

Consequently some modern thinkers try to cut through the Gordian knot by declaring that there is no time and that the only solution to the riddle of life consists in living exclusively in the present, treating the past and the future as non-existent and illusory. In this way they arrive at their concept of spontaneity as the only true principle of life, forgetting that spontaneity is built on practice; in other words, that it is a product of long repeated actions in the past, actions that have been carried out consciously and deliberately over a long period, and which have become so ingrained in one's nature that they need no further decision or effort of will.

The wonderful instincts of animals (which by far outdo our cleverest logical operations) are based on this accumulation of past experience, and the same holds good of the human genius, the man of unerring "spiritual instinct" (which we call "intuition"), or the virtuoso, whose technical perfection is the fruit of years of intensive practice, and whose accomplishments have become part of his subconscious or unconscious nature. In spite of popular belief, a genius does not fall from heaven—except from the heaven of his own making. Even the Buddha, according to Buddhist tradition, had aeons of practice on the Bodhisattva Path behind him, before he became a Buddha, a Fully Enlightened One. In the same way we have to assume that children who display extraordinary faculties and accomplishments, before they had a chance to acquire them through education or training since their birth, can only have acquired them in a pre-natal existence. "The mechanistic theory of heredity," as J. S. Haldane says, "is not only unproven; it is impossible. It involves such absurdities that no intelligent person who has thoroughly realized its meaning and implications can continue to hold it." Science is unable to explain the astonishing feats of child-prodigies who—as, for instance, Mozart or Beethoven—could master complicated musical instruments and the even more complicated and subtle laws of musical composition. Mozart composed minuets at the age of four, while Beethoven had composed three sonatas even before he had reached this age. To explain this through the hereditary factors and combinations of chromosomes is as unconvincing as explaining the human mind as a product of the brain. The brain is as much a product of the mind as the chromosomes are a product of forces about whose nature we know as little as we do of what we call gravitation, light, or consciousness. The more we try to reduce the world into a play of cause and effect instead of seeing the infinite interrelationship of all phenomena, and each individual as a unique expression and focalization of universal forces, the further we get from reality.

However, even if we admit that all the powers and faculties of the universe are within us, unless we have activated them through practice or made them accessible through training they will never become realities that influence our life. They will neither appear nor materialize effectively if we merely rely on the potentialities of our "unconscious mind," as the mediocre products of modern worshippers of the "unconscious" amply demonstrate in all fields of art and thought.

Just because the depth-consciousness (which I think is a better term than the "unconscious") contains an unlimited wealth of forces, qualities, and experiences, it requires a well-ordered, purposeful, and trained mind to make use of this wealth in a meaningful way, i.e. to call up only those forces, contents of consciousness or their respective archetypal symbols which are beneficial to the particular situation and spiritual level of the individual and give meaning to his life. "A more perfect understanding of the dynamic potentialities of the unconscious would entail the demand of a stricter discipline and a more clearly conscious direction," as Lewis Mumford said in his review of C. G. Jung's *Remembrances*.

As a reaction against the overintellectualization of modern life, the chaotic excesses of certain modern artists and writers may be understandable, but as little as we can live by the intellect alone, can we live by the "unconscious" alone. Nothing of cultural or spiritual value has ever been produced in this way.

Those who think that any conscious effort or aspiration is a violation of our spontaneous genius, and who look down upon any technique or method of meditation or the fruits of traditional experience as below their dignity, only deceive themselves and others! We can be spontaneous and yet fully conscious of the forms and forces of tradition. In fact, all culture consists in a deep awareness of the past. Such awareness, however, should not be confused with a clinging to the past or with an arbitrary imitation of its forms of expression; on the contrary, full awareness and perfect understanding free us from the fetters of the past, without thereby losing the fruits of our former experiences. We do not free ourselves from our past by trying to forget or to ignore it, but only through mastering it in the light of higher, i.e. unprejudiced knowledge.

If we allow the past undissolved and undigested to sink into the subconscious, the past becomes the germ of uncontrollable—because unconscious—drives and impulses. Only those things which we have perfectly understood and consciously penetrated can be mastered and can have no more power over us. The methods of healing employed by modern psychotherapy as well as by the most ancient meditation-practices are based on this principle. Even the Buddha attained his Enlightenment only after having become conscious of his complete past. This past, however, included the past of the whole universe. By becoming conscious of it, he freed himself from the power of hidden causes.

Ignorance is bondage, knowledge is liberation. So long as we are ignorant of the causes of the past, we are governed by them, and in so far they determine our future. The course of our future is "predestined" only to the extent of our ignorance.

> Fate is a very real aspect of our lives as long as we remain in ignorance, as real as the other aspect of freedom. What we call fate is the pulling and moulding of our lives from sources of which we are unconscious. Where there is the Light of consciousness all is freedom; wherever *to us* that Light does not penetrate is Fate. To the adept *Siddha* whose consciousness enfolds the whole range of manifested being there is no fate at all.[1]

Genuine meditation is an act of opening ourselves to that Light; it is the art of invoking inspiration at will, by putting ourselves into a state of intuitive receptiveness, in which the gates of the past and the present are open to the mind's eye. But unless the mind's eye is cleared of the dust of prejudice and selfishness, it will not be able to grasp the meaning of its visions, to assess their value or importance and to make use of them. Two people may hear the same symphony: to the musically untrained or uncultured mind it will be a mere noise, to the cultured or musically receptive it will be a revelation, an experience. Even the grandest and most sublime vision conveys nothing to the ignorant, or something that may be thoroughly misleading. (Herein lies the danger for those who use trance-inducing or consciousness-transforming "psychedelic" drugs such as Mescalin, LSD or the like, without having the knowledge or the critical faculty to judge or to evaluate the resulting phenomena and experiences.)

When I spoke about the gates of the past and the present, which are opened in introspective meditation, I did not mention the future. Neither did the Buddha when describing the experiences of his Enlightenment. Why was that so? Because the future is essentially contained in the past and focalized in the present.

Jean Gebser, one of the most creative and stimulating thinkers of modern Europe—whose philosophy is the gigantic attempt to integrate the most advanced knowledge of our time with the spiritual sources of the past—defines evolution as the unfoldment in time and space of something that is already potentially existent in its essential features, though indeterminable in its individual realization. The manner in which we accomplish this individual realization is the task of our life and the essence of our freedom, which latter consists in our choice either to cooperate with the laws of our universal origin and to be free, or to ignore and to oppose them, and thus to become the slaves of our own ignorance.[2] The more we recognize this our origin, the more we are able to cooperate with it and thus with the universal law (*dharma*) of our inherent nature. And likewise: he who perceives the outlines of the past can recognize or foresee the structure of the future. Their similarity is such that most clairvoyants are unable to distinguish between them, as confirmed by research-scholars such as Alexis Carrel, who says with regard to clairvoyants:

> Some of them perceive events which have already happened or which will take place in the future. It should be noted that they apprehend the future in the same way as the past. They are sometimes incapable of distinguishing the one from the other. For example they may speak at two different epochs of the same fact, without suspecting that the first vision relates to the future and the second to the past.[3]

This, and other similar statements, have been taken by some people as proof that the future exists in the same sense as the past, namely as an accomplished fact, hidden only to the limited faculties of perception of our human mind. But certain clairvoyant experiences, of which a striking example was reported by a well-known research-scholar (the mathematician Dunne, as far as I remember), seems to contradict this view. It is the well-authenticated story of a man who, after having bought a ticket for a sea voyage, dreamt that the boat on which he was traveling caught fire and sank. He saw vividly all the details and his own part in the events, such as his efforts to save himself and others from the impending doom. The dream was so overwhelmingly real that he returned the ticket. A short time later he read in the papers that the steamer, on which he had booked his passage, had met with a disaster and that the things had happened exactly as he had dreamt—except with regard to his own person! If the future event had been unalterably fixed or existed in some "timeless dimension," he could not have changed his decision and escaped the impending fate.

What is foreseeable are probably certain general conditions under which the future events take place, and these general conditions have as much stability or constancy as a landscape through which we drive. If we know the speed of our movement and the road or the direction which we want to take, we can safely predict where we shall be at a certain future time and what landmarks we shall have to pass on the way. This then is not because it exists in a future dimension of time, but because we move in a certain direction under already existing conditions, or more correctly, conditions whose rate of change is so much slower than our own movement that we can regard it as a constant and, in this sense, existing factor. Once we move in a certain direction, we are bound to meet certain events. But whether we move or not, and which direction we choose, this lies in our hand—provided we have the knowledge to foresee the results of our actions. This knowledge can come only from the past, from the remembrance of past experiences.

Here the question arises, whether the future is a real quality of time or merely a mental projection of the past into the opposite direction.

We can think of the past without reference to the future.

But we cannot think of the future without reference to the past. If an astronomer can predict future events with accuracy, it is because of his knowledge of the past movements of heavenly bodies, from which he deduces certain universal laws. These laws are, in other words, the sum total of the past in its timeless aspect, in its everpresent potentiality, in the actuality of the present moment.

The past is ever present, but due to the momentariness and limited range of our ordinary individual consciousness (or rather that part of it which we use in our everyday life)—which can dwell only on one point at a time, and which therefore has to be in constant motion in order to cover a wider range of events, facts, or objects—due to this momentariness we experience only that one point as present, on which our mind is focussed, and all other points as past (or, according to our expectation, as future). If we could see all the points simultaneously, the past would appear as another dimension of space.

Rainer Maria Rilke, perhaps the greatest mystic poet of our time, wrote in one of his letters:

> It appears to me more and more as if our ordinary consciousness were inhabiting the top of a pyramid, whose basis within us (and, so to say, below us) broadens out to such an extent that the further we are able to descend into it, the more widely included seem to be those data of earthly and universal existence which are independent of time and space. Since my earliest youth I have felt the probability (and I have also lived accordingly, as far as possible) that in a deeper cross-section of this pyramid of consciousness, the simple fact of being could become an event for us, that pure presence and simultaneous existence of everything, which in the "normal" upper apex of self-consciousness, one is able to experience as a "successive process." To hint at a (human) figure who would be capable of perceiving the past as well as the things that have not yet arisen, as ultimate presence, has been an urge with me when writing my *Malte,* and I am convinced that this view corresponds to a real state, though it may contradict all conventions of our actual life.[4]

The aspect of "being" is nothing other than the total aspect of becoming. There is no question of choosing between these two aspects, as to which is the more real or true. Both are ever united, and those who try to build a philosophy upon only one of them, to the exclusion or negation of the other, lose themselves in verbal play. Even if time, as we understand it, is an imperfect way of seeing things, the movement on which it is based and the consciousness which perceives it are real factors of immediate experience and profound significance.

If time is movement, and movement is not merely mechanical motion but an autonomous expression of individual life, then the future is not something already existing (or existing in an absolute sense), but evolving out of the pattern of individual movements. Even if the sum total of all these movements amounts to something like an eternal "Body of Reality" or whatever we may call the ultimate state of transcendental quietness, harmony and completeness, for which the Plenum-Void of Śūnyatā is perhaps the most adequate expression—the fact remains that each individual pattern has its own meaning and justification, and this consists in an inalienable experience of freedom, without which no individual life would be possible or would have been able to come into existence.

Though in the average sentient being this freedom may consist only in an infinitesimally small part of his conscious activity, it is sufficient to break the rigidity and monotony of mechanical law. Even if from the individual pattern of behavior, the patterns of future events can be foreseen with a high degree of probability, we have to admit that probability is not certainty, not unalterable law, but merely the way of least resistance. The degree of probability becomes higher the more we are concerned with the general aspect of things or events, and lower the more we are concerned with the individual aspect. As Jung has said,

> The more theory lays claim to universal validity, the less capable it is of doing justice to the individual facts. The statistical method shows the facts in the light of the ideal average but does not give us a picture of their empirical reality. While reflecting an indisputable aspect of reality, it can falsify the actual truth in a most misleading way. This is particularly true of theories which are based on statistics. The distinctive thing about real facts, however, is their individuality. These considerations must be borne in

mind whenever there is talk of a theory serving as a guide to self-knowledge. There is and can be no self-knowledge based on theoretical assumptions, for the object of self-knowledge is an individual—a relative exception and an irregular phenomenon. Hence it is not the universal and the regular that characterize the individual, but rather the unique.[5]

This uniqueness is not a contradiction to the basic universality of the individual, but a focalized expression of that universality at a certain moment of time and in a certain spatial relationship to other phenomena of the universe at that moment. On the universal scale everything appears as law, on the individual scale law dissolves into mere patterns of probability. Law is the general frame in which individual movement, individual life, takes place. Just as a picture gets its meaning, i.e. becomes a "picture," because it is related to a frame, so freedom has meaning only within the framework of or with reference to law.

Law, however, is the accumulated, crystallized past, the conscious as well as the unconscious memory, the sum total of past events or movements (or "emotions"), which in the individual condenses itself into form-tendencies which we call "character." But since character is not something different from the individual, but that in which individuality consists, we cannot separate these two concepts and play the one out against the other by saying that because an individual acts according to his character, therefore there is no freedom of action. On the contrary, if an individual were forced to act against his character, he would be unfree. Freedom is neither waywardness nor lawlessness, but the expression of one's inner law. Freedom and law do not exclude each other (as little as the picture excludes the frame or the frame the picture). Though the frame imposes a limitation on the picture, it strengthens it at the same time. In a similar way laws, though imposing limitations upon our freedom, not only strengthen it, but make it possible. Freedom consists in the right application of laws, in making the right use of them, and this depends again on the degree of our knowledge or insight into the nature of things[6], i.e., into our own nature. It is only there that freedom can be found. To express one's own inner law, one's character, in one's actions, is true self-expression, and self-expression is the hallmark of freedom. Freedom, like all spiritual realities, is one of the great paradoxes of life, and like life itself it is beyond proof or logical definition.

The problem of freedom is closely bound up with the problem of the future. If the future were something existing, in the same way as the past, there would be neither freedom nor meaning in the unfoldment of individual life, no responsibility for our actions, no moral or ethical values: life would be reduced to the clockwork of a mechanical process which runs its course to an inevitable end or in an endless circle of blind necessity or predetermined action. No system of thought that believes in ethical values and ultimate freedom or liberation through individual effort and a certain measure of free will and insight, can subscribe to such a view. The Buddha himself rejected this fatalistic outlook of pure determinism in his emphasis on self-reliance and in his condemnation of Makkhali Gosala's doctrine of predestination (*Samaññaphala Sutta* 20).

The Buddha treated the past as an unquestionable fact, the present as the decisive time-element, but he never speculated about the future. Though he often spoke about the past, of previous existences as well as of previous world-cycles and of the Buddhas of the remote past, he never indulged in prophesies. This in itself is significant and shows that the past and the future cannot be treated on the same footing, or as possessing the same degree of reality.

Since time and space are the two inseparable poles of the same reality, we should expect a parallelism of their structure. But do the three dimensions of space correspond to similar three dimensions of time? Obviously not; because if we divide time into past, present and future, then the present is not a dimension at all, but the incommensurable point which separates the past from the future. Nor can we say that the past and the future are opposite dimensions; they are one and the same movement, pursuing the same direction. If the past and the future would constitute movements in quite different or opposite directions, we would be justified in calling them different dimensions.

But time is movement in one direction only, and has therefore only one dimension, as indicated by the phrase, "three dimensions of space and one of time," which latter, therefore, has also been called "the fourth dimension." Of this question (which we shall consider in a subsequent essay), Alexis Carrell had this to say:

On the surface of our planet those dimensions are discerned through particular characteristics. The vertical is identified by the phenomenon of gravity. We are unable to make any distinction between the two horizontal dimensions. As for the fourth dimension, or time, it takes on a strange aspect. While the other three dimensions of things are short and almost motionless, it appears as ceaselessly extending and very long.[7]

No concrete thing has only three spatial dimensions. A rock, a tree, an animal cannot be instantaneous. Indeed we are capable of building up in our minds beings entirely described within three dimensions. But all concrete objects have four. And man extends both in time and in space. To an observer living far more slowly than we do, he would appear as something narrow and elongated, analogous to the incandescent trail of a meteor. Besides he possesses another aspect, impossible to define clearly. For he is not wholly comprised within the physical continuum. Thought is not confined within time and space.[8]

References and Notes

[1] Sri Krishna Prem, *The Yoga of the Kathopanishad* (London: John Watkins, 1955), p. 66.

[2] "To speak of a renunciation of free will is not only unnecessary but wrong. We do not live without the freedom of decision, because our whole life consists primarily in our remaining faithful to the decisions which we have once made in the invisible and in full freedom. What is felt as renunciation represents itself merely as a transposition from the visible into the invisible. As a decision arrived at in the past it became valid for our present life; and that constellation in which this happened is at the same time our innermost core which rests in our deepest being and is thus our constant companion." (Jean Gebser, *Der unsichtbare Ursprung* [The Invisible Origin], Olten and Freiburg, Walter-Verlag, 1970, p. 35.) Gebser's monumental work, *Ursprung und Gegenwart* (Origin and Presence) appeared in two volumes at Deutsche Verlagsanstalt, Stuttgart, in 1953 and 1966, and unfortunately has not been published in English translation.

[3] Alexis Carrell, *Man the Unknown*, p. 156.

[4] *Briefe von Muzot*, p. 291.

[5] C. G. Jung, *The Undiscovered Self*, Mentor Books, p. 17.

[6] Even our freedom to handle and utilize material things depends on the stability of mechanical or physical laws.

[7] Alexis Carrell, op. cit., p. 165.

[8] *Ibid.*, p. 156.

6

THE TWO ASPECTS OF REALITY

SINCE IN AN OUTWARD DIRECTION we cannot go beyond the three dimensions of what we call space from the standpoint of our usual consciousness, the only other direction in which we can move is inward, namely, in the reverse direction of extension, i.e. in a direction which is completely different from that of physical time and three-dimensional space: the direction toward the center and the origin of everything. If we—to use a simile—regard the horizontal as the direction of our space-time development or individual unfoldment, then the vertical represents the direction of our inner, concentrative absorption into the universal center of our essential being and therewith the process of our becoming conscious of the timeless presence of all possibilities of existence in the organic, all-embracing structure of the living universe. But while the horizontal, for all that we know—i.e. according to the laws of all spatial movement—has the tendency to move in an unimaginably big circle (which, therefore, appears to us like a straight line) or in a spiral, in which certain phases repeat themselves rhythmically, though without being identical, the vertical represents the central axis of this revolving movement, namely the timeless, ever-present origin, inherent in all living processes. It is what poetically has been expressed as the "eternity of the moment," which can be experienced in a state of perfect inwardness or absorption, in which we turn toward the center of our own being, as realized in states of meditation and creative inspiration.

In a former work[1] I have depicted both these directions in a diagram, in which the movement parallel to or following the periphery represents the space-time development of the individual, while the movement which runs at right angles or perpendicular to this in the direction toward the center indicates the ever increasing states of absorption or inwardness. The further this inwardness proceeds, i.e. the nearer it moves toward the center, the more universal becomes our experience. In reaching the center, the completeness and universality of consciousness is being realized.

Consciousness thus proceeds from the more limited to the more comprehensive, from lesser to greater intensity, from lower to higher dimensions, and each higher dimension includes the lower ones by coordinating its elements in a wider and more intricate structure of relationships. The criterion of a consciousness or recognition of a higher dimension, therefore, consists in the coordinated and simultaneous awareness of several directions of movement or extension within a higher unit, without annihilating the features which constituted the character of the integrated lower dimensions. This may be illustrated by the simple fact that the two-dimensional square is not annihilated in the three-dimensional cube.[2]

Thus the reality of a lower dimension is not devaluated or eliminated by the higher one, but only relativized. This is not only true with regard to spatial dimensions, but even more so in regard to time-dimensions, or what we experience as different forms or principles of time. "Only the recognition of all those time-forms which constitute man, liberates him from the exclusive validity of the mental time-form, creates distance and enables him to integrate those other time-forms. The courage to recognize the actuality of pre-rational magic time-lessness and of the irrational mythic time-principle, besides the mental time-concept, makes the leap into the a-rational time-freedom possible. This is not a freedom from earlier time-forms which are inherent in every human being's constitution; it is first of all a freedom *towards* them. From this kind of freedom which as such can only be achieved by a consciousness that is capable of placing itself independently 'above' the earlier time-forms, only from such a freedom can a conscious approach to the origin succeed."[3]

"Origin," however, does not mean a beginning in time, but the ever-present origin (*sahaja*), in which sense the much misunderstood terms *sahaja-kāya* and *Adibuddha* have been used in the terminology of the *Kalacakra* School of medieval Buddhist philosophy (about tenth century A.D.). *Sahaja-kāya* means literally the "inborn," "innate" body, that is, the natural universal body, the embodiment of universal order (which is also expressed in the term *dharma-kāya*), underlying every individual consciousness, but realized only by the Enlightened Ones who are fully awakened to their inner reality and are, therefore, called *Buddhas*. *Adibuddha,* which literally means "first, foremost or original Buddha," has similarly nothing to do with a sequence in time—and can, therefore, not be regarded as a kind of God-Creator from which the universe has sprung (as many scholars have surmised), but represents the ever-present dynamic principle of enlightenment (*bodhicitta*: the urge for the realization of enlightenment) at the center of every form of consciousness, from which time (*kala*) and space (symbolized as *cakra*) emerge.

In other words: we do not live in time, but time lives within us; because time is the innermost rhythm of our conscious existence, which appears outside of ourselves as space and materializes in the form of our body and its organs. From this point of view we may say that the body is the crystallization of our consciousness, namely, the sum total of former volitions, aspirations and actions of our conscious mind (what is called *karma* or consciously motivated "action" in Buddhism).

It is remarkable that Gebser—though coming from a different cultural background and starting from entirely different premises—arrives at similar conclusions and finally even at a world-view in which Eastern and Western thought become equal partners—*equal,* because each of them has attained to the same fundamental insight in his *own* way. Gebser expresses this in the following words: "The body (in so far as we conceive it also in terms of space) is nothing but solidified, coagulated, thickened, materialized time, which requires space for its unfoldment, formation and materialization, because space represents a field of tension, and due to its latent energies it is the medium or carrier of the active time-energies, in which both these dynamic principles, the latent one of space and the acting one of time, condition each other."[4]

We also could say: space is the *possibility* of movement, time the *actuality* or the realization of movement; or, space is externalized, objectivated time, time projected outward. Time, on the other hand, is the internalized, subjectivated space—the remembrance and inner transformation of spatial movement into the feeling of duration or continuity. Time and space are related to each other like the inside and the outside of the same thing. Reality comprises both and simultaneously goes beyond both of them. Those who experience this reality live in a dimension beyond the space-time continuum and experience the universe as a timeless body. This is the ultimate teaching of the *Kalacakra* philosophy.

Here we may be reminded of Fa-tsang's interpretation of the message of the *Āvatamsaka-Sutra,* according to his monograph, called "The Meditation by which Imagination Becomes Extinguished and One Returns to the Source":

> There is one Mind which is ultimate reality, by nature pure, perfect and bright. It functions in two ways. Sustained by it, the existence of a world of particulars [extended in space] is possible; and from it originates all activity [extended in time], free and illuminating, making for the virtues of perfection *pāramitā.* In these two functions which we may call existential and moral, three universal characters are distinguishable. Existentially viewed, every particular object, technically called *anuraja,* "particle of dust" [the smallest possible unit or atom, as we would call it nowadays] contains in it the whole *Dharmadhātu* [ultimate reality]. Secondly, from the creational point of view, each particle creates all kinds of virtues [or "qualities," in a more general sense]; therefore, by means of one object the secrets of the whole universe are fathomed. Thirdly, in each particle the reason of *śunyātā* [the incommensurable element of metaphysical reality, in contrast to its phenomenal or formal elements] is perceivable.[5] (Explanations in brackets are mine.)

Śūnyāta is that incommensurable element of metaphysical reality which, in contrast to its phenomenal or formal elements, can only be circumscribed as *"emptiness* from all conceptual designations," similar to "space" which includes and contains all things and movements and is at the same time contained in them. *Śūnyāta* is, so to say, the spiritual space whose *emptiness* (this is the literal equivalent of *śunyāta*) makes possible the wealth of forms and activities and the freedom which exists prior to any law ("at the first step we are free, at the second we are slaves"), the purity and liberty of action of the Origin. It is, in order to put it into Gebser's words, that "which is 'before' time and space, that thanks to different structures of consciousness has become more and more realizable through timelessness, time-awareness, time and space," and that "in the conscious achronicity becomes experienceable. The unoriginated becomes time-free, emptiness becomes fullness, in the transparency the 'diaphainon,' the spiritual becomes perceptible: Origin and Presence. We preserve the whole, and the whole preserves us."[6]

Śūnyatā is the emptiness of all conceptual designation, because it is the essence of the *whole*, which lies hidden in the center of each individual, in the innermost depth of our consciousness, which Fa-tsang calls "the Source." Time and space, therefore, extend between this timeless and spaceless center and the infinity (or ultimate distance) which we experience in the expansion of space and the accumulation of time-remembrance, constituting the infinity in time-extension. Thus time does not move from the future (as if it were existing there already) into the past—as it would appear if time had independent reality, instead of being a property of things or the intrinsic nature of living beings—but it is, as Bergson puts it, "the continuous progress of the past," from the center of all being, as we might say, "which gnaws into the future and which swells as it advances.—The piling up of the past upon the past goes on without relaxation. In reality, the past is preserved by itself, automatically. In its entirety, probably, it follows us at every instant.—Doubtless we think with only a small part of our past, but it is with our entire past, including the original bent of our soul, that we desire, will and act."[7]

Here again we see that the future does not play any role in the actual process of time, and why the entire past has to be raised into the light of consciousness, before the control of desire, will and action can be achieved and perfect enlightment can be attained. Enlightenment means to bridge the two poles of time—past and present—as well as the two poles of space: the near and the far. The "here" of space and the "now" of time correspond to each other, like the infinite distance in space and the infinite past in time. In other words, both time and space swing between the poles of ultimate nearness and ultimate distance.

The relationship between time and space is a double polarity, and the more we can see this, the more we shall realize that, as we said before, the three dimensions of space do not correspond to the threefold division of time. Nobody has made this clearer than Ludwig Klages, from whose significant work *Der kosmogonische Eros* I translate the following passage:

> Space and time, belonging together as two poles, have this in common, that each of them is stretched out be-

tween the poles of nearness and distance. As certainly as nearness is only one, irrespective of where I am, and as, on the other hand, [the concept of] spatial distance is only one, irrespective of whether we look towards the east or the west, towards the north or the south, in the same way there can be only one distance in time, in relationship to one and the same temporal nearness (presence). If there were two, namely, besides the distance of the past, another distance of the future, then the character of the distance of a future point of relationship would in some way be contrary to the character of the distance of a past point of relationship. But since the opposite is true, the duality of time-distance is a pure invention, and one of them must be an illusion! For the following reasons we must regard the future as such. If I think of the past, I remember a reality that existed; if, however, I think of the future, I think of something unreal, i.e. of something that exists only in the act of thinking. If all thinking beings would suddenly disappear, the past that really existed would remain exactly as it was before, while the name 'future' would simply lose its meaning, if there were no beings with the thought of a future! The future is not related to the past like one distance of time to another opposite distance of time, but as a mere concept is related to reality: *the future is not a quality of real time.* The past and the present, and not the past and the future, are the poles of time, and therefore temporal distance is the same as distance in the past. Only in images, i.e. in images of the past, can time be realized and made visible. Reality is eternal, and real time is the *pulsating* of eternity. The illusion 'future' created the spectre of death, or annihilation of existence, and the passionate desire for immortality.[8]

What we call "future" is only a possibility, inherent in the direction of our movement. To give a concrete example: if we are moving in a certain direction, or let us say, on a road with a bridge at some distance ahead of us, then this bridge (as well as any other feature of this road) becomes a part of our future, *provided* we persist in following the chosen road or direction. On the other hand, once we have crossed the bridge, this fact becomes an irreversable, undeniable and ineradicable part of our past. The past possesses reality not only as a fact, as something that has undeniably happened or existed, but even more so as something that acts upon future happenings, whose course is determined to an overwhelming extent by the actions and conditions of the past. The future, however, being only a potentiality, cannot act upon the present (except as an expectation, based on previous experience and conclusions drawn from it) and much less upon the past. It is in this sense that we cannot ascribe reality to the future. The *real time,* however, is more than all our conceptual ideas about it, but, as Klages metaphorically and profoundly expresses it, is "the *pulsating* of eternity."

Thus it depends on the nature of time which we create through the inner rhythm of our life and the depth of our consciousness, whether we are mortal or immortal. Those who live in the illusory time of their peripheral consciousness, of their intellect, and in the space-time continuum of an assumed external world, identify themselves with what is mortal. Those who live in harmony with the *pulse of eternity,* identify themselves with what is immortal. They know that the whole of eternity is within themselves. In this connection, the words of another modern writer will gain special significance: "It may be we shall find our immortality not in some miraculous proof of survival after death, but in some changed apprehension of the nature of time."[9]

Consciousness is the primary and space-time a secondary quality of reality. The movements and conformations within the all-embracing depth-consciousness (*ālaya-vijñāna*)—which modern psychology has rediscovered, but at the same time degraded into the concept of the unconscious*—appear as the

---

* "It is sufficiently revealing to what extent the psychological literature of our days identifies the merely unconscious with the 'repressed' and the forgotten, thus depreciating the purely antithetical concept itself. 'Unconscious'—if one wants to use this misleading concept at all—is in any case only one dimension less than what is being revealed through the next dimensional level. This, however, does not signify a generic opposition between the unconscious and consciousness, but merely a different kind of consciousness."[10]

"Present-day psychological terminology which postulates an 'unconscious' in contrast to consciousness, becomes thereby guilty of a falsification of fundamental psycho-somatic facts. This terminology and the subsequent wrongly structurized phenomena are a typical example of the faulty conclusions which arise from a radically applied dualism."[11]

"It has long ceased to be a secret that the venerable root-concept of modern psychology 'the Unconscious' is a rather uncritical and obscure concept."[12]

notions of time and spatial extention to the individual mind, who separates the various phases of movement and momentarily appearing forms, thus limiting his vision and breaking up reality into transitory phenomena. These phenomena, though not real in the ultimate sense, are not to be dismissed as mere hallucination, because they do not appear without causes, and these causes are the expression of an inherent order, the immanent law of reality. In other words, these phenomena have a relative reality, and only for those who take them as ultimate truth do they turn into a misleading illusion (*samsāra*).

For those who are caught up in their own individual past, because they cling to isolated aspects without seeing the whole picture of the interdependent origination of all phenomena, the future will appear as fixed and unalterable as the past, and indeed, by clinging blindly to those aspects, they themselves produce such a future. In this way an endless cycle of cause and effect, birth and death is created, from which there is only *one* way that leads out of this vicious circle: the "letting-go," the giving up of all entanglements through craving or possessiveness, which again and again entraps us in the ephemeral, in the chain-reactions of cause and effect, and which prevents us from seeing and realizing the all-embracing wholeness and universality of our true nature.

Liberation from those entanglements is possible only "if we are ready to accept that the *whole* of our human existence, i.e. all levels of our consciousness, which form and support our present as well as our coming consciousness, should be integrated into a new reality. This requires the full depth of our past, which we must experience over again in a decisive sense. He who denies or condemns his past, deprives himself of his future. This is true for each single human being as much as for humanity."[13]

For the wise, who have penetrated the realm of ultimate causes, down to the ever-present origin, who have raised into the light of full awareness what to others appears as the dark realm of the past—of them is true what Asvajit said of the Buddha, when asked to sum up the quintessence of the Buddha's teaching:

> *Ye dharma hetuprabhavā, hetum tesām Tathāgato hyavadat, Tesām ca yo nirodha, evamvādī mahāśramanah.*

"The causes of all cause-originated things have been revealed by the *Tathāgata* (the Buddha), and also their cessation. This is the teaching of the Great Ascetic."

The liberation from the power of those causes lies in the recognition of their true nature. As long as they are seen under the aspect of time (i.e. incompleteness) or, more correctly, under the aspect of temporal and spatial isolation, and not in their dynamic and ever-present relationship, we fail to understand the profound significance of the law of Dependent Origination (*pratityasamutpāda*), proclaimed by the Buddha, which is far more than the proclamation of a merely mechanical law of causality, as superficial observers are apt to think.

Even Ānanda, the Buddha's closest disciple, seems to have been in danger of this misconception when he proudly proclaimed how self-evident and easily understandable the *Pratityasamutpāda* appeared to him; whereupon the Buddha rebuked and warned him: "Do not speak thus, Ānanda; do not speak thus! Deep is the Law of Dependent and Simultaneous Origination and profound in its appearance. It is because people do not perceive and realize this *Dharma,* that they are overwhelmed by suffering and unable to free themselves from the rounds of rebirth and death."[14]

The idea of causality appears simple to those who are accustomed to think in terms of abstract logic and mundane commonsense. This kind of causality presupposes a temporal and unchangeable course of events, a sequence which is fixed and foreseeable. The *Pratityasamutpāda,* however, does not depend on any temporal sequence (though it may unfold in time), but may just as well be understood as the simultaneous cooperation of all its factors, each link representing the sum total of all the others. Or, if we want to express this from the standpoint of time: each form of appearance is based on an infinite past and thus on an infinity of causes, conditions and relationships, which does not exclude anything that has been or ever will come into existence. This is the basis of Rilke's pyramid of individual consciousness (mentioned previously).

But when the past is realized in its all-encompassing completeness, it loses its time-quality and is converted into something which we can only call a higher dimension of space, for the simple reason that all that apparently has happened in time is seen or sensed simultaneously, and therefore experienced as timeless presence (in contradistinction to the mere concept of the "present," as something in-between the past and the future). If this were not so, the causes of an infinite past would be forever beyond our control, could never be reached or modified, and still less *neutralized*. They would go on forever with unfailing necessity. But by raising them again into the present, the "one-after-another" is transformed into "the-one-within-the-other," a relationship so beautifully and profoundly described in the *Avatamsaka Sutra* in the vision of *Maitreya's Tower* (representing the universe), in which all things reflect and penetrate each other as well as the experiencing subject, without losing their respective individuality. Thus the universe and the experiencer of the universe are mirrored in every phenomenon, and therefore, nothing can be said to "originate" or to be "destroyed" in a final or absolute sense. What is destroyed is only our dependence on any single phenomenon or motive.

The perfect mutual interpenetration of forms, processes, things, beings, etc., and the presence of the experiencing subject in all of them—in other words, the simultaneity of differentiation and oneness, of individuality and universality, of form and emptiness—is the main thesis of the great Buddhist philosopher Nāgārjuna, who lived in the second century of our era. His philosophy of the "Middle Way" consists in a new orientation of thought, freed from the rigidity of the concept of "substance" or that of a static universe, in which things and beings were thought of as more or less independent units, so that concepts like "identity" and "non-identity" could be applied to them and form the basis of discursive thought. Where, however, everything is in flux, such concepts—and a logic derived from them—cannot be adequate and, therefore, the relationship of form to emptiness and vice-versa cannot be conceived as a mutually exclusive nature or as absolute opposites, but only as two aspects of the same reality, co-existing in continuous co-operation. Because "form" (*rūpa*) must not be confused with "thing-ness" or materiality, since each form is the expression of a creative actor or process in a beginningless and endless movement, whose precondition, according to Nāgārjuna, is precisely that mysterious "emptiness" (or "plenumvoid," as it has been aptly called) expressed in the term *Śūnyāta*.

In this experience of timeless reality beyond the realm of opposites, the relative is not annihilated in favor of the absolute nor is the manifoldness of life sacrificed to an abstract unity, but the individual and the universal penetrate and condition each other so completely that the one cannot be separated from the other. They are as inseparable as time and space, and like these they represent two aspects of the same reality: time is the dynamic aspect of individual (and therefore incomplete) action and experience; space is the sum total of all activity in its ever-complete and therefore timeless aspect.

The incomplete, however, is as necessary and important an element as that of completeness. It is that which supplies the impetus, the desire for completeness, for perfection. This impetus is the very essence and the *conditio sine qua non* of life. Therefore Novalis says in one of his "Fragments": "Only that which is incomplete can be understood and can lead us on. What is complete can only be enjoyed." And at another place: "All illusion is as necessary to truth, as the body to the soul." (Is not this also the function of *māya*?) If we modify this thought with regard to the concept of time, we might formulate it thus: Transiency is as necessary to immortality (or to the experience of eternity), as the body is to the soul, or as matter is to mind. And in saying so, we might note that these are not irreconcilable or totally exclusive opposites, but rather the extreme points in the amplitude of the swinging of a pendulum, i.e. parts of the same movement. By becoming conscious of the inner direction and relationship of our transient life, we discover the eternity in time, immortality in transiency—and thus we transform the fleeting shapes of phenomena into timeless symbols of reality.

Liberation is not escapism, but consists in the conscious transformation of the elements that constitute our world and our existence. This is the great secret of the Tantras and of the mystics of all times. Among modern mystics nobody has expressed this more beautifully than Rilke, though few may have recognized the profound truth of his words, when he said:

> Transiency hurls itself everywhere into a deep state of being. And therefore all forms of this our world are not only to be used in a time-bound (time-limited) sense, but should be included into those phenomena of superior significance in which we partake (or, of which we are part). However, it is not in the Christian sense, but in the purely earthly, profoundly earthly, joyfully earthly consciousness, that we should in-

troduce what we have seen and touched *here,* into the widest circumference. Not into a 'beyond' whose shadow darkens the earth, but into the whole, into the universe. Nature, the things of our daily contact and use, all these are preliminaries and transciencies: however, they are, as long as we are here, our possession, our friendship, participants of our pain and pleasure, in the same way as they were the trusted friends of our ancestors. Therefore we should not only refrain from vilifying and deprecating all that which belongs to this our world, but on the contrary, on account of its very preliminary nature which it shares with us, these phenomena and things should be understood and transformed by us in the innermost sense.—Transformed?—Yes, because it is our task to impress upon ourselves this preliminary, transient earth in so deep, so painful, so passionate a manner, that its essential nature is 'invisibly' resurrected within us.[15]

This resurrection takes place in every act of retrospective insight and spiritual awakening, as we have seen in the process of the Buddha's enlightenment. It is an act of resurrection, in which the ultimate transformation takes place and in which all causes come to rest in the light of perfect understanding and in the realization of *śūnyātā*, in which all things become transparent and all that has been experienced, whether in joy or in suffering, enters into a state of transfiguration. Then "all the worlds of the universe hurl themselves into the invisible as into their next deeper reality,"[16] a reality that is ever-present within us, beyond time and space.

References and Notes

[1] *The Psychological Attitude of Early Buddhist Philosophy* (London, Rider & Co., 1961).
[2] More about this is to be found in my *Foundations of Tibetan Mysticism* (London, Rider & Co., 1959), pp. 217 221: "Māya as the creative principle and the dimensions of consciousness."
[3] Jean Gebser, *Ursprung und Gegenwart,* Fundamente und Manifestationen der aperspektivischen Welt, Vol. II, p. 12 (Stuttgart, Deutsche Verlags-Anstalt, 1949-53).
[4] Ibid., Vol. I, p. 52.
[5] D. T. Suzuki, *Essays in Zen Buddhism,* III, p. 72f.
[6] Jean Gebser, op. cit., Vol. I, p. 405.
[7] Henri Bergson, *Creative Evolution,* Arthur Mitchell, trans., pp. 4-5.

[8] Ludwig Klages, *Von kosmogonischen Eros* (Munich, Georg Muller, 1922).
[9] From an unpublished book-manuscript by Elise Aylen, entitled *The Sea of Glass*.
[10] Gebser, op. cit., Vol. I, p. 329.
[11] Ibid., p. 327.
[12] Medard Boss, *Indienfahrt eines Psychiaters*.
[13] Gebser, op. cit., Vol. I, p. 8.
[14] *Mahanidana Sutta, Digha-Nikaya* of the Pali Canon.
[15] Rainer Maria Rilke, *Briefe aus Muzot* (Leipzig, Insel-Verlag, 1937).
[16] Ibid.

INDEX

ABIDHARMA, meditation process defined, 132
ABSOLUTE, in Western philosophy, 35; nonrelationship, 36; superfluous, 159; meaning to Indians, 195
AHIMSA, sacredness of life, 198
ĀKĀŚA, defined, 237
AKṢOBHYA, in mandala, 82, 84
ĀNANDA, Buddha's favorite disciple, 106-7
AMITĀBHA, in mandala, 76, 82; takes color of, 79-80; wisdom of, 79; meditative absorption, 84; in meditation, 93
AMOGHASIDDHI, volition and action, 84
ANĀTMAN, not "soullessness", 7; perspective of, 9; nonsubstantiality, 11; egolessness, 116
ART, and meditation, 151; intuitive, 152; and religion, 153; and beauty, 154-5; contemplative, 154; as yoga, 155; inner meaning, 155; Tibetan religious, 155; abstract, 160; color and sound, 165
ĀTMAN, original concept, 261; level of consciousness, 195; not on plane of relative, 199
ĀTMAVĀDA, misunderstood, 8
AUROBINDO, SRI, 73; 216-7
AVALOKITEŚVARA, form of, 77; communication of, 90; mantra of, 91
AVIDYĀ, religous term, 38

BAECK, LEO, 100
BĪJAX, primary mantra sound, 88, 97
BARDO THÖDOL, initiation in, 189; teaching of, 192
BECOMING, poem, 172
BEING, poem, 173
BINYON, LAURENCE, 220
BODHI, Budda mind, 20; inner knowledge, 79
BODHISATTVA, vow, 21; Avalokiteśvara, 25, 39; mañjusri, 39; luminous bodies of, 75; infinite number of, 141; Christ as, 144
BOHRIN, 232
BRAHMA, principle of, 171
BRAHMAN, absolute, 33; creative aspect, 34
BREATHING, 114-5, 119, 125, 128
BUDDHA, teachings, 3-6, 22; anātman idea, 7, 9; enlightenment, 12, 270-1; Buddha-mind, 20; Buddha nature, 30; Middle Way, 37; Buddhahood, 48, 87; compassion, 52; of Infinite Light, 53, 59; Dhyani, 54, 57, 59, 60, 63, 66, 75, 76, 85, 87, 97; Vairochana, 59; liberation, 62; Lotus throne, 102; Maitrī of, 144; living, 192; Tathāgata, 286
BUDDHISM (BUDDHIST), tradition, 2; spiritual impulse, 3; schools of, 23; thought and culture, 4; concept of *dhammas*, 5; specific character, 6; early scriptures, 12; Sādhaka, 142; in Ceylon, 193

INDEX

CAKRA, main centers, 54; of psychic energy, 71; crown, 72, 93; anāhata, 78; heart, 92-3; throat, 93, 97; dharma, 186
CARREL, ALEXIS, 271, 276
CH'AN, followers of, 24, 48; refined psychology of, 24; dhyana school of China, 13, 16; symbol of, 18; monastery, 18; mental attitude, 19; masters of, 20; story, 27; idea of, 28; fruitful attitude, 29; Sixth Patriarch, 51; meditative practices, 64; see also ZEN
CHRISTIANITY, 193
CONSCIOUSNESS, universal, 51, 223, 235; three kinds of transformed actions, 53; body of, 113; space, 241, 278

DEPENDENT ORIGINATION, 9-10, 183, 286
DHAMMA, Buddhist concept of, 5; Pali for dharma, 5
DHAMMAPADA, keystone of Buddhist ethics, 52
DHARMA, religious attitude, 23; insight into, 29; dharma-kaya, 53; moral law, 79; wheel of, 89; moral world order, 198; in Sanskrit, 260
DHARMAKAYA, universal body, 53, 75, 78, 87, 91-4, 279
DHYĀNA, meditative realization, 13; school of, 13, 16; dhyānamudrā, 53
DIAMOND BODY, mind created, 51
DIAMOND SUTRA, 18, 20
DISSOLVING, poem, 174

EIGHTFOLD PATH, 32
EINSTEIN, A., 208
ENLIGHTENMENT, tree of, 11, 56; Buddha's, 12, 58, 65; leap across boundary, 21; search for, 21; seven factors of, 134; state of, 200; bridge past and present, 282
ENLIGHTENED ONE (s), 39, 43, 55, 75, 92, 102, 107, 140-1, 143, 148, 151, 228, 260, 266

FOUR NOBLE TRUTHS, 6
FREEDOM, and law, 275

FREE WILL, conscious, 255
FREUD, and the Unconscious, 30

GEBSER, JEAN, 263, 267, 271, 280
GLASENAPP, HELMUTH VON, 5
GOD, as creator, 141; fairy tale about, 206, scapegoat, 209; distinguishing essence of, 211
GOETHE, 158, 213
GUENTHER, H.V., 260

HALDANE, J.S., 34, 249, 268
HEISENBERG, W., 31, 230, 232
HĪNAYĀNA, contemporary, 5; small vehicle, 42; schools, 134
HRĪH, seed syllable, 76, 89
HUI NENG, see SIXTH PATRIARCH
HUM, see OM
HUMPHREYS, CHRISTMAS, poem by, 207

I-CHING, oldest book of Chinese wisdom, 100; Book of Changes, 259
ILLUMINATION, of Buddha, 8
ILLUSION, 34, 36
IMAGINATION, creative, 42, 75
IMMORTALITY, 221
INDIVIDUALIZATION, 33, 40, 191

JAINISM, nontheistic, 23; ahimsa in, 198
JUNG, C.G., and the unconscious, 30, 236, 274

KALPANA, conceptual thought, 11
KARMA, action, 79; action and reaction, 198; body materialized, 249
KARUNĀ, compassionate involvement, 84
KEYSERLING, COUNT HERMAN, 195
KLAGES, LUDWIG, 282-4
KOAN, 157-8
KRISHNA, 167, 169

LANKAVATĀRA SŪTRA, 11, 194, 248
LAO-TSE, 47
LAW, wheel of, 209
LOGIC, multidimensional, 231-2; Eastern, 231; Western, 231; Indian, 232; laws of, 253

INDEX

MAHARSHI, RAMANA, 195
MAHĀSIDDHAS, Masters of Mystic Path, 13
MAHĀYĀNA, early teachings, 4; dharma theory in, 5; meditation schools, 16; enlightment, 21; literature, 64, 239; visualization, 134; tradition, 140; infinity, 239; space in, 257
MANDALA, mystic circle of, 31; symphonic, 51; Buddha of, 59; stūpa in Sanchi, 62; center, 73, 89; of Amitābha, 80; sections, 89; universal temple, 95; lotus, 102; poem, 119, 178
MANTRA (MANTRIC), mantric word, 53; vision and sound in, 67; bīja, the seed, 67, 74; mantric power, 75, 78; four movements of, 82; symbol words, 90-1; for primordial sound, 94; prayer and, 146
MAYA, to awakened and unawakened, 34; outcome of creative consciousness, 36; static, 247
MEDITATION, and Buddha doctrine of liberation, 16; spontaneous, 109; posture, 122; Burmese school, 129; preparations for, 131; stages of, 133; and art, 151; highest, 152; cosmic, 171; Tantric, 171, 203, 207, 227; poems of, 172-9; space experience, 243
MIDDLE WAY, 37, 101, 287
MILAREPA, prayer of, 77
MIND, mind-body functions, 127; three essentials, 129
MORGAN, CHARLES, 211
MUDRĀ, gesture, 54; dana, 58; dhyanā, 59; abhaya, 59; dharmacakra, 60; āñjali, 92; padma, 92; namaskāra, 92
MULTIDIMENSIONAL SYMBOL, 134
MYSTERIES, of body, 75; of speech, 75; of mind, 84, 92

NIRMĀNAKĀYA, vessel of, 75; action, 78; realization, 86; spiritual unfoldment, 92; spiritual transformation, 94
NIRVANA, 43, 65, 143, 187; parinirvana, 58

NONSUBSTANTIALITY, doctrine of, 8
NOVALIS, 102, 157, 288

OM, 76
OUSPENSKY, 234

PADMASAMBHAVA, exponent of Vajrayāna, 93
PĀLI, canon, 4, 6, 9, 11; scriptures, 5; texts, 10
PARADOX, 16; new language of, 157
PARAMĀRTHA SATYĀ, 10
PATANJALI, principles of yoga, 135
PERFECTION, 225
PLOTINUS, 233
POWER, 81
PRAJÑA, wisdom, 22, 77, 84
PRAJÑA PĀRAMITĀ SŪTRA, 11
PRANA, 73, 115, 119, 121
PRAYER, form of meditation, 131, 137; in Buddhism, 140, 142, 145
PSYCHIC CENTERS, three, 74; Chinese concept, 96
PSYCHIC ENERGY, 71

RATNASAMBHAVA, 84
REASONING, faculty of, 33
RILKE, R.M., 206, 273, 286, 288
RINZAI, fourfold contemplation, 64

SĀDHAKA, and mantras, 95; realization of, 95; Tibetan, 212
SĀDHANA, new kind of, 13; meditative practice 30; Tantric, 42, 90; deep satisfaction, 69; progressive, 78; prolonged practice of, 79; continuity of, 84; inherent plan of, 94; possibilities of, 118; texts, 213
SAMADHI, perfect unification, 133; peak experience, 135; poem, 178; way to, 226
SAMGHOGAKĀYA, creative vision, 78; Body of Bliss, 92; inspirational delight, 94
SĀMKHYA, nontheistic, 23
SAMSĀRA, treadmill, 43; turned into Nirvana, 65; unenlightened world, 184; symbol of, 185; transformed, 187; cycles of births and deaths, 198; illusion, 285

INDEX

ŚĀNTIDEVA, 145
SARVĀSTIVĀDA (SARVĀSTIVĀDINS), dharma theory in, 5; beliefs of, 238
SATORI, profound insight, 157
SAVARI, story of, 25
SHIVA, transformer, 170; dissolving, 171
SIDDHAS, accomplished one, 24; stories of, 24
SIXTH PATRIARCH, 16, 17, 21, 51
SKANDHAS, 43, 64; *rupa*, 46; *vedanā*, 46; *samjna*, 46, 53; *vijnāna*, 46; five, 60
SPENGLER, 243, 247
ST. FRANCIS OF ASSISSI, prayer of, 143
SŪNYAM, non-absolute, 10
ŚŪNYATĀ, experienced in enlightenment, 11; Great Emptiness, 14: not in absolute sense, 37; two aspects of, 51; explosion of, 94; Buddhist term, 104; plenum-void, 105, 167, 274, 287; understand, 106;, no-*thing*ness, 133; as resonance, 155; in Mahāyāna, 210; spiritual space, 281
SUZUKI, D.T., 106, 198

TANTRAS (TANTRIC), 28, 37, 40, 48, 64; *sādhaka*, 42; secret of, 288
TAOISM, 93
TATHĀGATA, 14
THERAVĀDA, THERAVĀDINS, school of Buddhism, 4, 50; Pali scriptures of, 5; standpoint of, 238
TIBETAN BOOK OF THE DEAD, 192
TILOPA, words of, 251
TRANSFORMATION, law of, 35, 182; ultimate, 289
TSONG KHAPA, 251

TULKU, 192
TURNING INWARDS, poem, 175

UNCONSCIOUS, 138
UNIFICATION, poem, 176
UPANISHADS, 72, 195
UPEKṢĀ, 144

VAJRAKĀYA, integration of bodies, 92-4
VIJÑĀNA, *mano-*, 86; *alaya-*, 86
VIJÑĀNAVĀDINS, special merit of, 11; consciousness of, 12
VAJRAYĀNA, built on early teachings, 4; mandalas of, 62; three great mysteries of, 75; adamantine being, 87; deepest aspects of, 100; visualization, 134
VĪRYA, joyful attitude, 30
VISHNU, 169; Being, the principle of, 169; principles of, 171

WEI-LANG, see SIXTH PATRIARCH
WISDOM, 22, 39; Great Mirror, 47, 51, 52, 58, 64, 72, 84; Equality, 47, 52, 62, 64; Distinguishing, 47, 53, 59, 64, 69, 77, 84; Accomplishes All work, 47, 53, 59, 62, 68, 74; Dharma-Realm, 48, 85; Four, 59, 64, 65, Vairocana, 62; Essential Oneness, 74

YOGA, 23, 54
YOGĀCĀRA, YOGĀCĀRINS, mainstream of, 13; early, 48

ZEN, 13-14; 24, 27-9, 42, 48, 52, 64, 130, 155, 214

Milton Keynes UK
Ingram Content Group UK Ltd.
UKHW020024200124
436311UK00010B/63